BUSINESS AND GENERAL REFERENCE BOOK SERIES FROM IDG

Entertaining For Dummies

P9-CJR-820

Cheat Sheet

Ten Reasons to Entertain at Home

- ✔ It's cheaper than going to a restaurant.
- ✔ You can decide who will sit next to you.
- ✔ You can make new friends.
- ✔ The conversation can be more intimate.
- ✔ You get to taste-test everything.
- ✔ You are guaranteed the biggest piece of dessert.
- ✔ You don't have to wear shoes.
- ✔ You don't have to drive home.
- ✔ Gifts from guests.
- ✔ Leftovers.

Tasks You Can Do a Day Ahead

- ✔ Arrange the flowers.
- ✔ Set up the bar.
- ✔ Refrigerate white wine and other beverages; check your ice supply.
- ✔ Set the table.
- ✔ Make a seating plan and place cards.
- ✔ Set out serving utensils and dishes.
- ✔ Buy perishables.
- ✔ Prepare and refrigerate vegetables and the salad.
- ✔ Set up the coffee machine and cups.
- ✔ Fill salt and pepper shakers.
- ✔ Cook everything that can possibly be cooked in advance and reheated.

How to Make Entertaining Easy on Yourself

- ✔ Serve two courses rather than three.
- ✔ Serve the same meal every time you entertain.
- ✔ Serve food that's easy to prepare and make ahead.
- ✔ Select foods that you can serve at room temperature.

- ✔ Buy dinner already prepared.
- ✔ Let your children help set the table, pass food, clear the table, and help clean dishes.
- ✔ Choose dishes attractive enough to go directly from the oven to the table.
- ✔ Clean up as you go.

...For Dummies: Bestselling Book Series for Beginners

Entertaining For Dummies®

Cheat Sheet

How to Make Your Party Shine

- Invite a diverse group of guests.
- Seat dynamic, vivacious, gregarious people at the heads of tables.
- Greet each guest as if he or she is the one person in the world you most wanted to see.
- Turn down the lights and burn candles.
- Decorate with masses of one element (flowers, fruit, candles, cookies, and so on).
- Play music.
- Serve exotic cocktails.
- Serve the very freshest food.
- Offer more than one dessert.
- Make or buy something for guests to take home as a party favor.

How to Really Mess Things Up

- Start with a negative attitude.
- Don't think through anything.
- Keep the overhead lights on.
- Attempt to prepare all the fanciest recipes you can find.
- Over-decorate with too many highly fragrant flowers.
- Make guests wait for a drink.
- Order an enormous centerpiece guests can't see over or through.
- Stay in the kitchen all night.
- Serve dinner an hour late.
- Monopolize one person.
- Let guests help with the dishes.

How to Evaluate Your Party

1. **Did you have a good time?**

   Or were you too nervous or frazzled to care? See Chapter 3 to get organized.

2. **Did you feel excited, refreshed, and recharged the day after?**

   Or were you so exhausted that you never want to entertain again? Better planning is the answer. See Chapter 3.

3. **Did your guests enjoy each other?**

   Or were they yawning, yelling, or yearning to escape? Avoid this problem with a dynamic guest list. See Chapter 2.

4. **Did your party create a buzz around town, in your neighborhood, or among your guests?**

   Or did it fall as flat as a pancake? After you've read *Entertaining For Dummies*, it's doubtful you will ever have this problem.

5. **Did anyone call or write to say thank you?**

   Or are you left to wonder if your party was really that bad? If nobody bothered to say they had a good time, see Appendix A to figure out what to fix.

6. **Did the leftovers taste delicious?**

   Or did the dog refuse to eat them? Make your menus worth recycling for another meal. See Chapters 7 and 8.

7. **Were you totally yourself?**

   Or did you put on airs and try to impress people? See Chapters 1 and 17 to understand why this is a mistake you don't want to make.

...For Dummies: Bestselling Book Series for Beginners

Endorsements for Entertaining For Dummies™

"If you cannot entertain after reading this book, it is possible that you are hopeless and shall be condemned to wandering the earth alone forever."

— Pat Conroy, Best-selling novelist

"The chapter on business entertaining is a must-read for everyone - self-employed, mail clerk, or chief executive officer. This book is a clear, concise road map to the art of successful and fun entertaining. If you play to win, this book is an invaluable resource."

— Bob Woodrum, Managing director, Korn-Ferry International

"Entertaining is one of the most powerful ways to sell ideas, and *Entertaining For Dummies* provides suggestions to make entertaining easy, fun and effective. Grab it, read it, and study it, and you will reap dividends you never dreamed possible."

— Ida Crawford Stewart, Former Vice President and Personal Assistant To Estee Lauder

"What an innovative and informative approach Suzanne Williamson together with Linda Smith have presented to an activity that people fear almost as much as public speaking. This book is brilliantly written and wonderfully presented. Not a stone left unturned."

— Marion O'Neill, Ph.D., Clinical Diplomat

"This book will give every reader the confidence to give a spectacular party, and the courage to invite even the authors to it. The sound advice is more than common sense; it reads like a gentle and friendly nudge to get busy and start planning that bash you've been wanting to throw but really didn't think you could pull off."

— Lynne Hummell, Special Sections Editor, *The Island Packet*

"*Entertaining For Dummies* covers every conceivable hosting situation, from Boy Scout wiener roast to dinner for the world's most important boss. Whether tiny events or huge events, with the authors' complete to 'do's' and 'don'ts' and five basic lists, you'll be inspired to entertain often, well, and with style."

— Charlotte Hale, Author/Speaker

"The authors serve up good, sound advice, a pragmatic philosophy, and a bundle of truly original and borrowable ideas."

— Nancy Hewitt, Former Senior Editor of *American Home*

"With enthusiasm and wit, Suzanne and Linda have been able to bring the joy and passion of life's experiences to the reader."

— Claire Kalish, Designer of Residential Interiors, and Illustrator and Co-Owner of Table Fables

Praise for Suzanne Williamson

"Suzanne Williamson is that rare creature on this planet: wholly original, and absolutely *sui geneous*. You do not meet her likes twice. If you have seen her on stage, you won't forget her. She combines (seamlessly) personal beauty of a uniquely distinctive style, warmth, outrageousness, humor, and incorrigible seductiveness. What she says is always to the point, useful, thoughtfully observed. Women in audiences, young and old, will love her; men, young and old, will be wowed by her."

— Reid Buckley, The Buckley School of Public Speaking

"Our eleventh annual Food and Wine Classic was a great success! The participants were very complimentary, and your elegant "Entertaining Made Easy" seminar contributed greatly to our program."

— Bernd Lembcke, The Cloister, Food and Beverage Director

"Your presentation was humorous, informative and very down-to-earth! Everyone can appreciate the stress involved when it comes to entertaining at home. Now they are relieved to know they can avoid most of the 'Pre-Party Panic' by following your simple plan."

— Cathy Ashby, Office Manager, The Associated Contractors of East Tennessee, Inc.

" Your program was fantastic! In addition to being enlightening and informative, your humor and sense of fun put our group totally at ease."

— The Westin Resort Marketing Department

"Suzanne Williamson Pollak has a passion for food — cooking it as well as consuming it. She channels her creative energies from the kitchen to the classroom with 'Entertaining at Home,' zesty seminars designed to aid hosts and hostesses in preparing the perfect dinner party."

— *Island Scene*

"A sure-fire way to make a convention a success."

— Brian Munigan, National Director of Sales, Hyatt Hotels, Washington, DC

"You were more than merely fascinating. Your seminar was great and very informative. . . . The reaction was very favorable."

— Lee Bledsue, The Ritz-Carlton, Atlanta

 ™

BUSINESS AND GENERAL REFERENCE BOOK SERIES FROM IDG

References for the Rest of Us!™

Do you find that traditional reference books are overloaded with technical details and advice you'll never use? Do you postpone important life decisions because you just don't want to deal with them? Then our *...For Dummies*™ business and general reference book series is for you.

...For Dummies business and general reference books are written for those frustrated and hard-working souls who know they aren't dumb, but find that the myriad of personal and business issues and the accompanying horror stories make them feel helpless. *...For Dummies* books use a lighthearted approach, a down-to-earth style, and even cartoons and humorous icons to diffuse fears and build confidence. Lighthearted but not lightweight, these books are perfect survival guides to solve your everyday personal and business problems.

> *"More than a publishing phenomenon, 'Dummies' is a sign of the times."*
> — The New York Times

> *"...you won't go wrong buying them."*
> — Walter Mossberg, Wall Street Journal, on IDG's ...For Dummies™ books

> *"A world of detailed and authoritative information is packed into them..."*
> — U.S. News and World Report

Already, millions of satisfied readers agree. They have made *...For Dummies* the #1 introductory level computer book series and a best-selling business book series. They have written asking for more. So, if you're looking for the best and easiest way to learn about business and other general reference topics, look to *...For Dummies* to give you a helping hand.

ENTERTAINING
FOR
DUMMIES™

ENTERTAINING FOR DUMMIES™

by Suzanne Williamson with Linda Smith

Foreword by Pat Conroy

IDG BOOKS WORLDWIDE™

IDG Books Worldwide, Inc.
An International Data Group Company

Foster City, CA ◆ Chicago, IL ◆ Indianapolis, IN ◆ Southlake, TX

Entertaining For Dummies™

Published by
IDG Books Worldwide, Inc.
An International Data Group Company
919 E. Hillsdale Blvd.
Suite 400
Foster City, CA 94404
www.idgbooks.com (IDG Books Worldwide Web site)
www.dummies.com (Dummies Press Web site)

Library of Congress Catalog Card No.: 97-80184

ISBN: 0-7645-5027-6

Printed in the United States of America

10 9 8 7 6 5 4 3 2 1

1B/RV/QZ/ZX/IN

Distributed in the United States by IDG Books Worldwide, Inc.

Distributed by Macmillan Canada for Canada; by Transworld Publishers Limited in the United Kingdom; by IDG Norge Books for Norway; by IDG Sweden Books for Sweden; by Woodslane Pty. Ltd. for Australia; by Woodslane Enterprises Ltd. for New Zealand; by Longman Singapore Publishers Ltd. for Singapore, Malaysia, Thailand, and Indonesia; by Simron Pty. Ltd. for South Africa; by Toppan Company Ltd. for Japan; by Distribuidora Cuspide for Argentina; by Livraria Cultura for Brazil; by Ediciencia S.A. for Ecuador; by Addison-Wesley Publishing Company for Korea; by Ediciones ZETA S.C.R. Ltda. for Peru; by WS Computer Publishing Corporation, Inc., for the Philippines; by Unalis Corporation for Taiwan; by Contemporanea de Ediciones for Venezuela; by Computer Book & Magazine Store for Puerto Rico; by Express Computer Distributors for the Caribbean and West Indies. Authorized Sales Agent: Anthony Rudkin Associates for the Middle East and North Africa.

For general information on IDG Books Worldwide's books in the U.S., please call our Consumer Customer Service department at 800-762-2974. For reseller information, including discounts and premium sales, please call our Reseller Customer Service department at 800-434-3422.

For information on where to purchase IDG Books Worldwide's books outside the U.S., please contact our International Sales department at 415-655-3200 or fax 415-655-3295.

For information on foreign language translations, please contact our Foreign & Subsidiary Rights department at 415-655-3021 or fax 415-655-3281.

For sales inquiries and special prices for bulk quantities, please contact our Sales department at 415-655-3200 or write to the address above.

For information on using IDG Books Worldwide's books in the classroom or for ordering examination copies, please contact our Educational Sales department at 800-434-2086 or fax 817-251-8174.

For press review copies, author interviews, or other publicity information, please contact our Public Relations department at 415-655-3000 or fax 415-655-3299.

For authorization to photocopy items for corporate, personal, or educational use, please contact Copyright Clearance Center, 222 Rosewood Drive, Danvers, MA 01923, or fax 508-750-4470.

About the Authors

 **Suzanne Williamson** is a wife and mother of four teenage children. She was born in Beirut, Lebanon, and lived in Libya, Somalia, Nigeria, Ghana, and Liberia before moving to the United States at the age of eighteen. Her parents gave parties all over Africa — parties that included every kind of guest: diplomats, deadbeats, aristocrats, archeologists, novelists, and big game hunters.

Giving dinner parties became a creative outlet for Suzanne and a way to get some adult conversation when her children were small. Now, she entertains because bringing people together and feeding them are her favorite things to do.

For the past decade, Suzanne has been speaking about entertaining. Her audiences have totaled over 10,000 people from all over the world. Her speaking topics range from "How to Give an Unforgettable Dinner Party and Actually Enjoy Yourself at the Same Time" to "Etiquette and Social Graces for Business." Some of her clients have included the Food and Wine Institute, Ford Motor Company, General Electric, and Templeton Fund Worldwide.

She is currently co-authoring a cookbook with the best-selling novelist, Pat Conroy.

Linda Smith dreamed of being a writer from the age of nine when she got her first rejection slip from *Reader's Digest*. She got sidetracked in college, majoring in elementary education. She graduated *magna cum laude* from Georgia Southern University and went on to teach first and sixth grade reading and English. She worked as a model teacher at the Marvin Pittman Laboratory school, in Statesboro, Georgia, training student teachers in her classroom.

After marrying, and while taking a sabbatical from teaching, Linda began writing a weekly newsletter to her tennis team. Because the newsletter was so well received and so eagerly anticipated each week, she took it as an omen to aim higher. In 1993, she began pursuing a freelance writing career, beginning with local and regional publications and working her way into the national market. She met Suzanne Williamson on the tennis court, where the seeds of a book on entertaining were planted.

When she's not tied to her computer, Linda enjoys tennis, bicycling, in-line skating, and aerobics classes. She says that her fitness routine helps keep her creativity flowing while combating stress.

She is currently co-authoring a book on how to give parties for children.

ABOUT IDG BOOKS WORLDWIDE

Welcome to the world of IDG Books Worldwide.

IDG Books Worldwide, Inc., is a subsidiary of International Data Group, the world's largest publisher of computer-related information and the leading global provider of information services on information technology. IDG was founded more than 25 years ago and now employs more than 8,500 people worldwide. IDG publishes more than 275 computer publications in over 75 countries (see listing below). More than 60 million people read one or more IDG publications each month.

Launched in 1990, IDG Books Worldwide is today the #1 publisher of best-selling computer books in the United States. We are proud to have received eight awards from the Computer Press Association in recognition of editorial excellence and three from *Computer Currents'* First Annual Readers' Choice Awards. Our best-selling *...For Dummies*® series has more than 30 million copies in print with translations in 30 languages. IDG Books Worldwide, through a joint venture with IDG's Hi-Tech Beijing, became the first U.S. publisher to publish a computer book in the People's Republic of China. In record time, IDG Books Worldwide has become the first choice for millions of readers around the world who want to learn how to better manage their businesses.

Our mission is simple: Every one of our books is designed to bring extra value and skill-building instructions to the reader. Our books are written by experts who understand and care about our readers. The knowledge base of our editorial staff comes from years of experience in publishing, education, and journalism — experience we use to produce books for the '90s. In short, we care about books, so we attract the best people. We devote special attention to details such as audience, interior design, use of icons, and illustrations. And because we use an efficient process of authoring, editing, and desktop publishing our books electronically, we can spend more time ensuring superior content and spend less time on the technicalities of making books.

You can count on our commitment to deliver high-quality books at competitive prices on topics you want to read about. At IDG Books Worldwide, we continue in the IDG tradition of delivering quality for more than 25 years. You'll find no better book on a subject than one from IDG Books Worldwide.

John Kilcullen
CEO
IDG Books Worldwide, Inc.

Steven Berkowitz
President and Publisher
IDG Books Worldwide, Inc.

Eighth Annual
Computer Press
Awards ≥1992

Ninth Annual
Computer Press
Awards ≥1993

Tenth Annual
Computer Press
Awards ≥1994

Eleventh Annual
Computer Press
Awards ≥1995

IDG Books Worldwide, Inc., is a subsidiary of International Data Group, the world's largest publisher of computer-related information and the leading global provider of information services on information technology. International Data Group publishes over 275 computer publications in over 75 countries. Sixty million people read one or more International Data Group publications each month. International Data Group's publications include: **ARGENTINA:** Buyer's Guide, Computerworld Argentina, PC World Argentina; **AUSTRALIA:** Australian Macworld, Australian PC World, Australian Reseller News, Computerworld, IT Casebook, Network World, Publish, Webmaster; **AUSTRIA:** Computerwelt Osterreich, Networks Austria, PC Tip Austria; **BANGLADESH:** PC World Bangladesh; **BELARUS:** PC World Belarus; **BELGIUM:** Data News; **BRAZIL:** Annuário de Informática, Computerworld, Connections, Macworld, PC Player, PC World, Publish, Reseller News, Supergamepower; **BULGARIA:** Computerworld Bulgaria, Network World Bulgaria, PC & MacWorld Bulgaria; **CANADA:** CIO Canada, Client/Server World, ComputerWorld Canada, InfoWorld Canada, NetworkWorld Canada, WebWorld; **CHILE:** Computerworld Chile, PC World Chile; **COLOMBIA:** Computerworld Colombia, PC World Colombia; **COSTA RICA:** PC World Centro America; **THE CZECH AND SLOVAK REPUBLICS:** Computerworld Czechoslovakia, Macworld Czech Republic, PC World Czechoslovakia; **DENMARK:** Communications World Danmark, Computerworld Danmark, Macworld Danmark, PC World Danmark, Techworld Denmark; **DOMINICAN REPUBLIC:** PC World Republica Dominicana; **ECUADOR:** PC World Ecuador; **EGYPT:** Computerworld Middle East, PC World Middle East; **EL SALVADOR:** PC World Centro America; **FINLAND:** MikroPC, Tietoverkko, Tietoviikko; **FRANCE:** Distributique, Hebdo, Info PC, Le Monde Informatique, Macworld, Reseaux & Telecoms, WebMaster France; **GERMANY:** Computer Partner, Computerwoche, Computerwoche Extra, Computerwoche FOCUS, Global Online, Macwelt, PC Welt; **GREECE:** Amiga Computing, GamePro Greece, Multimedia World; **GUATEMALA:** PC World Centro America; **HONDURAS:** PC World Centro America; **HONG KONG:** Computerworld Hong Kong, PC World Hong Kong, Publish in Asia; **HUNGARY:** ABCD CD-ROM, Computerworld Szamitastechnika, Internetto online Magazine, PC World Hungary, PC-X Magazin Hungary; **ICELAND:** Tolvuheimur PC World Island; **INDIA:** Information Communications World, Information Systems Computerworld, PC World India, Publish in Asia; **INDONESIA:** InfoKomputer PC World, Komputek Computerworld, Publish in Asia; **IRELAND:** ComputerScope, PC Live!; **ISRAEL:** Macworld Israel, People & Computers/Computerworld; **ITALY:** Computerworld Italia, Macworld Italia, Networking Italia, PC World Italia; **JAPAN:** DTP World, Macworld Japan, Nikkei Personal Computing, OS/2 World Japan, SunWorld Japan, Windows NT World, Windows World Japan; **KENYA:** PC World East African; **KOREA:** Hi-Tech Information, Macworld Korea, PC World Korea; **MACEDONIA:** Computerworld Macedonia; **MALAYSIA:** Computerworld Malaysia, PC World Malaysia, Publish in Asia; **MALTA:** PC World Malta; **MEXICO:** Computerworld Mexico, PC World Mexico; **MYANMAR:** PC World Myanmar; **NETHERLANDS:** Computer! Totaal, LAN Internetworking Magazine, LAN World Buyers Guide, Macworld Netherlands, Net, WebWereld; **NEW ZEALAND:** Absolute Beginners Guide and Plain & Simple Series, Computer Buyer, Computer Industry Directory, Computerworld New Zealand, MTB, Network World, PC World New Zealand; **NICARAGUA:** PC World Centro America; **NORWAY:** Computerworld Norge, CW Rapport, Datamagasinet, Financial Rapport, Kursguide Norge, Macworld Norge, Multimediaworld Norge, PC World Ekspress Norge, PC World Nettverk, PC World Norge, PC World ProduktGuide Norge; **PAKISTAN:** Computerworld Pakistan; **PANAMA:** PC World Panama; **PEOPLE'S REPUBLIC OF CHINA:** China Computer Users, China Computerworld, China InfoWorld, China Telecom World Weekly, Computer & Communication, Electronic Design China, Electronics Today, Electronics Weekly, Game Software, PC World China, Popular Computer Week, Software Weekly, Software World, Telecom World; **PERU:** Computerworld Peru, PC World Profesional Peru, PC World SoHo Peru; **PHILIPPINES:** Click!, Computerworld Philippines, PC World Philippines, Publish in Asia; **POLAND:** Computerworld Poland, Computerworld Special Report Poland, Cyber, Macworld Poland, Networld Poland, PC World Komputer; **PORTUGAL:** Cerebro/PC World, Computerworld/Correio Informático, Dealer World Portugal, Mac*In/PC*In Portugal, Multimedia World; **PUERTO RICO:** PC World Puerto Rico; **ROMANIA:** Computerworld Romania, PC World Romania, Telecom Romania; **RUSSIA:** Computerworld Russia, Mir PK, Publish, Seti; **SINGAPORE:** Computerworld Singapore, PC World Singapore, Publish in Asia; **SLOVENIA:** Monitor; **SOUTH AFRICA:** Computing SA, Network World SA, Software World SA; **SPAIN:** Communicaciones World España, Computerworld España, Dealer World España, Macworld España, PC World España; **SRI LANKA:** Infolink PC World; **SWEDEN:** CAP&Design, Computer Sweden, Corporate Computing Sweden, Internetworld Sweden, it.branschen, Macworld Sweden, MaxiData Sweden, MikroDatorn, Nätverk & Kommunikation, PC World Sweden, PCaktiv, Windows World Sweden; **SWITZERLAND:** Computerworld Schweiz, Macworld Schweiz, PCtip; **TAIWAN:** Computerworld Taiwan, Macworld Taiwan, NEW ViSiON/Publish, PC World Taiwan, Windows World Taiwan; **THAILAND:** Publish in Asia, Thai Computerworld; **TURKEY:** Computerworld Turkiye, Macworld Turkiye, Network World Turkiye, PC World Turkiye; **UKRAINE:** Computerworld Kiev, Multimedia World Ukraine, PC World Ukraine; **UNITED KINGDOM:** Acorn User UK, Amiga Action UK, Amiga Computing UK, Apple Talk UK, Computing, Macworld, Parents and Computers UK, PC Advisor, PC Home, PSX Pro, The WEB; **UNITED STATES:** Cable in the Classroom, CIO Magazine, Computerworld, DOS World, Federal Computer Week, GamePro Magazine, InfoWorld, I-Way, Macworld, Network World, PC Games, PC World, Publish, Video Event, THE WEB Magazine, and WebMaster; online webzines: JavaWorld, NetscapeWorld, and SunWorld Online; **URUGUAY:** InfoWorld Uruguay; **VENEZUELA:** Computerworld Venezuela, PC World Venezuela; and **VIETNAM:** PC World Vietnam.   3/24/97

Authors' Acknowledgments

From Suzanne:

Greatest thanks to my husband, Peter, and to my children: Pete, Caroline, Charles, and Christopher.

Special thanks to Pat Conroy.

Thanks, also, to my partner, Linda. She translated my notes, organized my thoughts, and helped me overcome all my doubts. Ours has been a wonderful partnership.

And for their unending patience, ideas, and expertise, thanks to Todd Williamson, Cynthia Carter, Happy van Beuren, and Bob Woodrum. Also, thanks to Susan Bass, Reid Buckley, Mary Coleman, Ruthie Edwards, William Guggenhiem, Claire Kalish, Rosalee Maloney, Anisa McDonald, Crystal Moorhouse, Inga Owen, Kathleen Pandola, Cherie Perigo, Francie Puntereri, Mike Reilly, Joni Rosser, Christine Stembridge, Diana Stevens, Enrico Tomas, and Nancy Winch.

In loving memory of my father, Charles Williamson, and his elegant presence at parties.

From Linda:

All my love and greatest gratitude to my husband, Zack, for making it possible for me to pursue my dream of being a writer.

Thanks to my partner, Suzanne, for always putting our friendship first.

Thanks to Lynne Hummell and Nancy Stephens for the many freelance assignments. And finally, to my dear friends and fellow writers, Nancy Hewitt and Charlotte Hale: Thanks for your wise advice, generous compliments, and enduring faith.

In loving memory of my mother, June Weaver, and my grandmother, Mary Whitworth Couch, whose persistence and positive attitude live on through me.

From both:

Thanks to Sarah Kennedy and to all the staff at IDG Books for making our vision a reality. Special thanks to project editors Colleen Rainsberger and Kelly Oliver who prodded us to "add the flowers to the plant"; to Patricia Yuu Pan, Christy Beck, and Diane Smith, whose ideas and keen copyediting whipped the text into shape; and to all those who worked behind the scenes to bring this book to fruition.

And to our agent, Carolyn Krupp: Thanks for making it all happen.

Publisher's Acknowledgments

We're proud of this book; please send us your comments about it by using the IDG Books Worldwide Registration Card at the back of the book or by e-mailing us at feedback/ dummies@idgbooks.com. Some of the people who helped bring this book to market include the following:

Acquisitions, Development, and Editorial

Project Editors: Colleen Rainsberger, Kelly Oliver

Executive Editor: Sarah Kennedy

Copy Editors: Patricia Yuu Pan, Christine Meloy Beck, Diane Smith

Technical Reviewer: Angela Hixson

General Reviewers: Jason Galloway, Justin Huston

Editorial Manager: Leah P. Cameron

Editorial Assistants: Michael Sullivan, Donna Love

Production

Project Coordinator: E. Shawn Aylsworth

Layout and Graphics: Cameron Booker, Elizabeth Cardenas-Nelson, Linda M. Boyer, Angela F. Hunckler, Brent Savage

Special Art: Elizabeth Kurtzman

Proofreaders: Ethel Winslow, Christine Berman, Kelli Botta, Michelle Croninger, Joel K. Draper, Nancy Price, Janet Withers

Indexer: Sherry Massey

Special Help

Nickole J. Harris, Acquisitions Coordinator; Ann K. Miller, Editorial Coordinator; Tina Simms, Copy Editor

General and Administrative

IDG Books Worldwide, Inc.: John Kilcullen, CEO; Steven Berkowitz, President and Publisher

IDG Books Technology Publishing: Brenda McLaughlin, Senior Vice President and Group Publisher

Dummies Technology Press and Dummies Editorial: Diane Graves Steele, Vice President and Associate Publisher; Kristin A. Cocks, Editorial Director; Mary Bednarek, Acquisitions and Product Development Director

Dummies Trade Press: Kathleen A. Welton, Vice President and Publisher

IDG Books Production for Dummies Press: Beth Jenkins, Production Director; Cindy L. Phipps, Manager of Project Coordination, Production Proofreading, and Indexing; Kathie S. Schutte, Supervisor of Page Layout; Shelley Lea, Supervisor of Graphics and Design; Debbie J. Gates, Production Systems Specialist; Robert Springer, Supervisor of Proofreading; Debbie Stailey, Special Projects Coordinator; Tony Augsburger, Supervisor of Reprints and Bluelines; Leslie Popplewell, Media Archive Coordinator

Dummies Packaging and Book Design: Patti Sandez, Packaging Specialist; Lance Kayser, Packaging Assistant; Kavish + Kavish, Cover Design

◆

The publisher would like to give special thanks to Patrick J. McGovern, without whom this book would not have been possible.

◆

Contents at a Glance

Cartoons at a Glance

By Rich Tennant

page 7

page 133

page 75

page 185

page 319

page 281

Fax: 508-546-7747 • **E-mail:** the5wave@tiac.net

Table of Contents

Foreword

*E*ntertaining is one of the most loaded and puzzling words in the English language. It carries a payload and a firepower that I find dizzying and extreme, and it causes sheer panic in me if the word rises up when I have invited guests for dinner. I have always been able to feed my guests, but it is too much of a burden on myself to enter into that uncertain territory where I also must entertain them. "Entertaining" has always been something that English royalty did because they were to the manor born or people who lived on Central Park West did because they were lucky enough to live on Central Park West. It is a word that makes me itchy, clumsy, and unsettled. I would rather do anything with anyone, anytime, than entertain them. That is a responsibility I have affably dodged my entire life.

No more. In this marvelous and informative book, Suzanne Williamson and Linda Smith have demystified the art of entertaining for me and anyone else who gets the shakes when the idea of planning or attending a party comes up. Bootleg copies of this book will make their way into social gatherings all over the country once the word is out. This book tells you how to act, what to do, what to say, how to answer, how to enter, and how to leave every conceivable social situation that is likely to happen to a person during the last years of this century. It is a thrillingly exhaustive study of how to entertain your fellow human beings. If everyone acted the way these women suggest that they do, there would be no crime, war, policemen, soldiers or gossip columnists.

I have been to Suzanne Williamson's home. From personal experience, I can tell you that Suzanne practices what she preaches and that a dinner at her home is a taste of paradise on earth. Entertaining is an art form to her, and these two women have done the rest of us a great favor by sharing their graceful expertise. If you cannot entertain after reading this book, it is possible that you are hopeless and shall be condemned to wandering the earth alone forever. This wonderful book removes the fear of entertaining and makes it easy — a snap of the fingers.

—Pat Conroy

Introduction

. . . .

*S*ome people define entertaining as one of life's little necessities. In this book, we define entertaining as an art that can change your life. Obviously, hospitality can help you develop stronger personal and business relationships. But entertaining can be so much more.

You can use the process of entertaining as a tool to enhance many areas of your life and to fulfill many needs. Instead of treating entertaining as a linear progression or a chore to be rid of as quickly as possible, shift your point of view. You invite guests, buy food, cook, clean, and recover. Focus on each step and enjoy it. Turn these routines into small pleasures, and use them as a means to nurture yourself.

Do you need to lead a more balanced life? Connect with others? Open up your creativity? Take a risk? Fall in love? Practice a little seduction? Add more joy to your life? You don't have to make a conscious decision. When entertaining becomes a part of your life, opportunities occur naturally. Here's what can happen:

- ✔ **Entertaining can inspire you to get your act together.** If your house looks like the Addams Family lives there, plan a party. The get-together may be just the push you need to get your household back in order — move the furniture around, clean the rugs, haul newspaper piles to the recycling center, wipe the fingerprints off the windows, and have the kids wash behind their ears.

- ✔ **Entertaining can improve your family life.** Many of today's families don't eat meals together. How can you expect to communicate if each family member lives in his or her own world? Use dinners at home as a way to gather your family and reconnect. Focusing on the family unit may be the most important kind of entertaining you do. (See Chapter 13 for more on making everyday events special.)

- ✔ **Entertaining can be the key to a successful career.** Business entertaining sets you apart from everyone else. You can increase your productivity by establishing personal relationships with your coworkers, your boss, and your customers. (See Chapter 17 for details on how to enhance your career while outside the office.)

✔ **Entertaining can be a creative outlet.** If you spend your days doing the same old things, entertaining can add a little spice to your life. Whether you are up to your nose in smelly diapers or overwhelmed by deadlines, having a party is a way out. If everything else is choking the life out of you, entertaining can be a breath of fresh air. Planning a party can slow you down and connect you to what is really important: family and friends.

✔ **Entertaining can allow you to control your own social life.** No more waiting for the phone to ring, no more blind dates, and no more forced friendship and dull conversation. You decide with whom you want to spend your time. When you show others how special they are by inviting them into your home, that personal connection can create a lasting bond that comes back to you tenfold.

✔ **Entertaining can keep you young.** As you get older, continuing to entertain is important. You can get a laugh, an idea, or a new slant on something from anyone you invite.

✔ **Entertaining can boost your confidence and improve your self-esteem.** By entertaining, you can become a master of personal relations, organization, time management, strategic planning, and much more. You may not think that you have these abilities, but you can develop them by entertaining. After you become more experienced, these skills spill over naturally into every other area of your life, boosting your marketability in the business world and your overall confidence and self-esteem.

About This Book

This book is a complete guide to entertaining, designed to help everyone from the beginner to the most advanced host. It's jam-packed with suggestions for developing your guest list, creating the atmosphere you want, making menus, minding your manners, coping with disasters, and more.

This is not *War and Peace,* and we don't expect you to sit down and read this book from cover to cover. You don't have to master everything about entertaining at once. However, if you are new to entertaining, we do suggest that you begin at the beginning. In Part I, you discover the basic principles of entertaining, which are the same in every situation. After you understand the basics, you can comfortably and confidently give any variety of party. After you read Part I, you can skip around the rest of the book for more ideas.

Foolish Assumptions

We assume that you want to find out about entertaining, or you would not have forked over your hard-earned money for this book. But even so, we imagine what you are thinking: "Here comes another one of those books with rules about which fork is for what and complicated recipes that take two days to prepare — one for finding all the exotic ingredients and another for deciphering the instructions." Surprise! This is not a rule book nor a cookbook. As far as we're concerned, you can forget the rules, and you don't even have to know how to cook.

If you are looking for a list of everything you need for entertaining, forget that, too. We are not assuming that you have any specialized equipment, furniture, space, or skills. Whether you live in a mobile home or the White House, you already have everything you need for entertaining. Whether you are a student, a newlywed, a stay-at-home mom, or a chief executive, you have the time. Whether you cook like a professional chef or don't know how to boil water, you have the skill. This book is designed to help you figure out what makes sense for you and to help you plan a party that suits your personality and lifestyle.

How This Book Is Organized

This book is divided into five major parts. Each part contains chapters that further divide the subject into logical and manageable chunks of information.

Part I: Party Planning 101

In Part I, you find the real nuts and bolts of entertaining — the parts you cannot ignore regardless of the size or type of party you have in mind. You get a whirlwind tour of just what you need to host a successful party, and then you figure out how to get organized. What would a party be without the guests? We offer tips on how to create a guest list, and then show you how to invite them by making an offer they can't refuse. Explore the space around you — we show you how to make the most of it. In this part, you discover many secrets for creating the atmosphere that's just right for your party.

Part II: Eating and Drinking

Part II is the meat and potatoes — and a whole lot more. If you love to cook, enjoy the many useful suggestions for developing menus. Even if you hate to cook or don't know how, we have solutions for you as well. You find ways to augment and balance your menu, and you even get help deciding what drinks to offer (alcoholic and nonalcoholic).

Part III: Minor Details, Major Impressions

In Part III, you delve into the incidentals. You find traditional and fun ways to set and decorate your table. You explore a range of entertainment options and take a look at tips on what you need. We also show you how a gracious host or hostess acts — and reacts — at the table, in conversation, and in case of embarrassment or emergency.

Part IV: Occasional Opportunities

Part IV adds purpose to your party. You can enhance your life by celebrating everyday accomplishments and entertaining just for the fun of it. Holidays and other obligations require entertaining acumen, and we show you how. If you're thinking of having a really big party, for whatever reason, don't be afraid — we're here to help! You find special ways to give parties for children and teens. And you discover how entertaining can help you meet your business goals.

Part V: The Part of Tens

No ...For Dummies book is complete without testing your ability to count to ten. We, the authors of this book, never claimed to be mathematical geniuses, but we tried. Part V offers ten times five (50) menu ideas. You also find solutions to the ten most common cooking disasters. We offer up ten ideas for parties that may be worth trying once in your lifetime. Last, you get a quick review on the ten most frequently asked questions about entertaining.

Part VI: Appendixes

Part VI shows you that no party is complete until you have relived it in your mind. You figure out how to evaluate your party so that you know what to repeat or delete for your next party. We prod your party-planning instincts by offering more reasons to entertain. You also find a listing of sources for all your entertaining needs.

Icons Used in This Book

 This symbol marks important information that greatly increases your odds for success.

 Although we try not to put any restrictions on your imagination, experience has taught us a few things that don't work. You can ignore this symbol and learn the hard way, or you can trust us and heed the warning.

 Some themes seem to come up over and over again. It's not that we don't have anything new to say. It's that we think some important issues bear repeating. When you see this symbol, prepare to be brainwashed.

 This information emphasizes the right attitude for a successful party. Anyone can host an unforgettable gathering. Success begins with a "can do" attitude.

 You don't want your party to be boring or bland. We show you ways to kick it up a notch.

 These are the extra details that can elevate your party from ordinary to awesome.

 Make it easy on yourself. Entertaining doesn't have to be complicated.

 Entertaining is not a mechanical process. Entertaining is about people, and the key to success begins in your heart. This symbol is a reminder to stay focused on what's really important.

Where to Go from Here

Anyone can take guests to a restaurant and pay the bill, and that's one way of entertaining. However, the act of inviting guests into your home and offering them food and drink is a gift. It's a very personal compliment — a simple and important way of showing people that you care about them and want to spend time with them.

You may feel unfulfilled if you read this book and never plan a party. Go ahead and take the plunge. Invite a few friends over for dinner, hors d'oeuvres, or simply a cup of tea and cookies. Soon you may begin to think of entertaining as a joy, not a job — an opportunity, not an obligation. Confidence is just around the corner.

Part I
Party Planning 101

The 5th Wave   By Rich Tennant

OVER PLANNING A PARTY

"At 1700 hours position yourselves along the perimeter of the living room. As they enter we'll hit them with the nuts and bread sticks. At 1750 hours Dolores will move to their right flank and advance with the drinks, driving them from the kitchen. As they weaken from dancing we'll cut off their supplies and force them into the driveway."

In this part . . .

*I*n this part, we break down your party plan into simple, manageable parts. We help you get organized, put together a winning guest list, and make an offer your friends can't refuse.

But suppose that you live in a tiny apartment with a table for four, and fifteen people are coming for dinner? We reveal spaces in your home you never dreamed of using for entertaining. We also give you the secret formula for creating just the right atmosphere for your party. So what are you waiting for?

Chapter 1

Getting Started: You Have What It Takes

- -

- -

A good party is never an accident. Making your party unforgettable means having a plan that includes everything. In this chapter, we give you a quick summary of what you need to host a successful party. *Hint:* Hosting a successful party has nothing to do with where you live or how you set a table; it has everything to do with relaxing and enjoying other people.

If you are new to entertaining, the first step — deciding to host a party — is the hardest. Start now by making up your mind. Here, we give you a gentle shove out of the nest. In the rest of the book, we teach you to fly. So open your eyes and spread your wings.

Party Parts

Whether you plan to have a backyard barbecue or a black-tie gala, the skeleton for the party is the same: a setting, some guests, food, drinks, and the atmosphere (decorations, entertainment, and so on). Successful entertaining, however, is more than just the sum of these parts. How you put these parts together, which ones you choose to emphasize, and how you incorporate your own personality makes each party unique.

No matter what kind of party you are planning, success boils down to these three things:

  ↙ A positive attitude

  ↙ A fun mix of guests

  ↙ A sensible plan

In the chapters that follow, we explore each of the parts of a party individually so that you can make the most of each one. In this chapter, we show you how to put those parts together — starting with your attitude.

Developing the right attitude

The right attitude for entertaining begins with understanding what you are really trying to do. You are trying to give yourself and your guests a little enjoyment — nothing more, nothing less. It's not important if your party is elegant, expensive, or extravagant. What's important is reaching out to be with people.

Stuff you *do not* need:

  ↙ A resplendent dining room

  ↙ Hepplewhite chairs

  ↙ Sparkling crystal

  ↙ Heirloom silver

  ↙ State-of-the-art appliances

  ↙ Gourmet cooking skills

  ↙ Perfectly behaved children

  ↙ Blooming orchids

  ↙ An enormous CD collection

  ↙ A swimming pool

  ↙ A huge backyard

  ↙ A cappuccino machine

  ↙ A mirrored bar

  ↙ A fat wallet

What you *must* have:

  ↙ Intuition

  ↙ Flexibility

  ↙ Common sense

  ↙ A positive attitude

  ↙ A fun mix of guests

  ↙ A sensible plan

Your own style is the key to successful entertaining. If you want to be a great host, forget about putting on airs and trying to be something you're not. The greatest parties are not necessarily about making an impression, but they are always about putting people at ease and having fun. The single characteristic that makes you an outstanding host is being yourself.

Remember to listen to yourself. Pay attention to your own feelings and intuitions, and then go with your style. If you are a triple-strand-pearl, all-the-right-forks-and-spoons kind of woman or a three-piece-custom-made-suit kind of man, don't be afraid to have an elegant dinner party and ask your guests to dress up. (An outdoor pig pickin' is obviously not you.) On the other hand, if you are a let-your-hair-down, go-barefoot kind of person, go ahead and give a relaxed, casual party where guests will feel free to put their feet up. Either way, your party will be totally cool when it's totally you.

You may never discover the cure for cancer or win a Pulitzer prize, but here is what you can do: Give your family, friends, and acquaintances the gift of food, drink, and conversation. Perhaps they will experience that feeling, rare in life, of cozy enchantment — a sense of having a few short hours of contentment, relaxation, and deep happiness. Years later, it can be comforting and astonishing to both the host and the guests to realize that something as simple as a party can leave such a deep impression.

Power of the people

Now that you have the right attitude, you are probably dying to start inviting people. And that's what entertaining is really all about. No matter how positive your attitude, no matter how perfect the setting, the atmosphere, or the food, your party isn't worth having if you don't have the right mixture of guests.

Before you plan your party, think about the people you want to invite. Note that we did not say *must invite* or *should invite*. If you invite people who leave you lukewarm, your party may never heat up.

A good place to start is by considering what you want to accomplish with your guest list. Maybe you want to do something nice for someone, get together with close friends, make some new friends, establish a better relationship with a business associate, or, best of all, mix everyone together. We don't know who your friends are, so this one has to be up to you. If you're not sure whom to invite, turn to Chapter 2 for some guidelines.

Coming up with a plan

Parties don't begin when your guests walk in the door; they begin in your mind and imagination. The instant you decide to have a party, start visualizing it. Picturing the party doesn't have to be complicated — it can take two minutes or ten. We are talking about a general picture, not some vivid obsession that keeps you awake all night.

Ten excuses for not entertaining — banished!

Parties are supposed to be fun, not torture. The following are solutions to the ten most common reasons why some people would rather go for a root canal than give a party. After you read this, you can cancel your dental appointment and start making a guest list.

1. **"My house isn't nice enough."** Unless you are on the tour of homes, no one is coming over to judge your house. If you feel that they are, don't invite them. If space is the problem, see Chapter 5 to discover nooks and crannies you didn't even know existed.

2. **"I don't have time."** Make yourself a priority, and find time for the things you want to do.

   Working too hard? Entertain on Saturday night. Spend an hour on Saturday preparing. Recover on Sunday.

   If you have children, try portioning out work in 15-minute segments over a few days. If your children are old enough to reach the sink, set the table, or take out the trash, delegate some duties to them.

3. **"I'm too nervous."** Then you need to relax. That's what meditation, marathons, and massages are for. Throwing a party can be nerve-wracking, especially if you don't entertain very often. The key is being organized so that you can use the day of the party to relax. See Chapter 3 for tricks and tips on getting organized.

4. **"My wallet is too thin."** You can find many ways to fit entertaining into your budget. You don't have to serve a five-course dinner. Have a tea party or a dessert party. Check out Chapter 8 for more shoestring solutions.

5. **"What if no one shows up but my cat?"** *or* **"What if people don't like my party?"** See Chapter 4 for tips on giving invitations that will have guests dying to come to your party. Find out how to get responses ahead of time so that you know whom and how

many guests to expect. An invitation that comes from the heart is enough to make most people love your party and you.

6. **"I don't know people well enough to ask them,"** translated as **"I'm afraid they'll say no."** What better way to get to know them? Invite anyone. It never hurts to ask. If they don't want to come, they can just say no. Let *them* come up with the excuses.

7. **"I don't have the skills."** Rome wasn't built in a day. Try out one skill at a time. This book helps you do it. Start small and practice on your family and friends. Soon you'll be ready to expand your guest list.

8. **"I'm too shy."** Entertaining is a good way to overcome your own bashfulness or use it to ease the discomfort of others. Breathe deeply; buy a new outfit; invite your best friend to help you get through it. Not everyone is meant to be the life of the party.

9. **"I'm overwhelmed; it's too hard."** Make it easy on yourself. Even if you hate to cook, you can serve delicious food that doesn't require you to turn on the heat. (See Chapter 7.) And if you organize your time, there's no reason to be in a tizzy. (See Chapter 3 for up-to-the-minute solutions.)

10. **"I just don't have the self-confidence."** Neither does anybody else. They're faking it. The way to develop more confidence is by doing the thing that you think you can't. Get your feet wet. Have a party. And never underestimate the value of faking it. If you act confident, soon you'll find that you *are* confident.

One way to start visualizing a successful party is to think of things that you enjoy. Most likely, these are the same things that can make your guests happy, too:

- ✓ Do you like meeting new and interesting people? So do your guests.

- ✓ Does a cool drink comfort you? What you offer your guests within the first five minutes of their arrival can help make them comfortable.

- ✓ Does soft lighting make you feel relaxed? Your guests may appreciate a break from harsh office lights and blinding sunlight.

- ✓ Does a picnic outside sound like heaven when you've been cooped up indoors all day? Looking forward to a change of scenery gets guests excited.

- ✓ Does good food whet your appetite for a good time? Just knowing that they don't have to cook or clean up makes guests grateful for your offerings.

Chapter 3 offers more ideas to help you further develop your mental picture.

Many hosts get hung up on the food, no matter what kind of party they are having. Although there's no denying that good food makes people happy, good food is not what makes or breaks the party. In fact, we devote only three chapters to eating and drinking. If you don't want to cook, you can find ways around it. (See Chapters 7 and 8 for suggestions; also, see Appendix C for mail-order options.) If you enjoy cooking and food is a big deal to you, the possibilities are endless. Whatever you decide to serve, remember, it's the people who make the party, not the food.

Secrets to Success

Successful entertaining is not about going by anybody else's rules. You don't have to own specific things or invite a specific set of people. We live in an age when sterling, stainless, and plastic all have their places in our kitchen drawers, just as the plumber, the dentist, and the yoga instructor all have their places at our tables. You are no longer restricted by the one correct wine to serve with fish, a single way to set a table, a specified length of time to sit at the table, a time limit for a cocktail party, or using a gingham-lined basket for a picnic. You are free to do what feels right to you.

The real secret to a successful party lies in doing whatever it takes to make your guests feel comfortable. You want them to leave your party feeling totally relaxed and/or revived, as if they've been on a mini vacation.

Before you can make your guests feel comfortable, you must be at ease yourself. If you are running around like a chicken with its head cut off, your guests can't relax. So have your plan in place and get yourself organized so you can concentrate on people other than yourself.

When guests arrive, be observant. If you sense that a guest is uncomfortable, ask that person to help you. If you are wearing a coat and tie and a guest shows up in shirt sleeves, remove your coat and tie so that he doesn't feel out of place. Let common sense be your guide.

Besides making guests comfortable, one of the best ways to ensure the success of your party is to plan a little something to shock or surprise them. Turn your back on the predictable. Present something out of the ordinary — something alluring, alarming, or amusing — anything to give your guests a jolt, get them out of their immediate lives and into another world for a few hours. We're not talking about something obvious or gimmicky, but something that suits your personality and makes you comfortable. Your surprise can be who you invite, what you wear, where you have your party, or what you serve.

Here are some ways to add an element of surprise:

- Light the room with candles — no electricity. The light can be very alluring.

- Invite guests who don't know each other. The guests may feel a little alarmed that they don't know anyone else, but it can add excitement to the party.

- Lead guests into the kitchen to participate in the cooking — a guaranteed amusement for everyone!

You are not trying to shock guests in an obnoxious way. You want them to leave your party thinking, "I had a wonderful time," "I feel like a new person," or "Maybe I should think about having a party myself." Guests will feel this way when you provide an evening of unexpected pleasure.

A historical dinner with a big surprise

Napoleon's friend was giving a dinner party in honor of the czar. For the occasion, he procured an enormous salmon weighing over 100 pounds. Before dinner, the salmon was placed on a beautifully garnished platter and carried around by the servants to be viewed by the guests.

Just when the guests had all admired the salmon, one of the servants tripped. The guests watched in horror as the salmon slid from the platter and landed on the floor. They were disappointed and embarrassed for the sake of the host until they heard him say, "Serve the other one." To the guests' astonishment, the second salmon was even more impressive than the first, weighing over 150 pounds. Little did they know, this intentional accident was staged strictly to shock, surprise, and delight them.

Although we don't necessarily recommend that you pull a stunt like dropping food on the floor, you can see what a clever host Napoleon's friend was. He is long departed, but his dinner party made history.

Chapter 2

Guess Who's Coming to Dinner

In This Chapter

▶ Making the guest list

▶ Deciding how many people to invite

▶ Planning the seating arrangement

*M*ost people plan their parties backward. They start by fretting over the food, the flowers, the tablecloth, or some other minor detail. All these elements have their place, but one stands out unequivocally as the most vital to the life of the party.

That one indispensable element isn't the size of the house or its beauty. It isn't the fine china, the lovely centerpiece, the fancy hors d'oeuvres, or whether the food is hot when it arrives on the table. It's the *people* who make the party. Making the guest list is your first priority.

In this chapter, you discover different approaches to making your guest list, including how many people to invite and how to achieve a good balance of personalities. You also get tips on planning the seating arrangements to help you make the most of the mix.

Making the guest list and plotting the seating arrangement can be giddy, liberating fun. When you spice up your party with a terrific guest list, people look forward to coming to your house. Your guests will remember raging conversations and intriguing personalities long after they've forgotten the food.

Making a List, Checking It Twice

Most people invite particular guests for one of the following reasons:

✔ They always invite the same people

✔ They need to pay back invitations

✔ They want something from one of the guests

Although there is nothing wrong with using entertaining to pay back invitations or get on the good side of someone, making a guest list can encompass so much more.

If you normally use the preceding methods to determine your guest list, try a new approach. Instead of going outside and inviting people for an ulterior motive, turn inward. Ask yourself these questions:

- ✔ Who matters to me?
- ✔ Who makes me happy?
- ✔ Who is supportive of me?
- ✔ Who is fun to be around?
- ✔ Who intrigues me?
- ✔ Who do I want to know better?

Gather these people around you, and your party is refreshing and exciting. People are not just feeding on your food, but feasting on each other's personalities, charm, and energy.

Mixing and matching

The key to making an exciting guest list is effectively mixing personalities. Mix sassy, irreverent people with highly serious ones. Combine a handful of everyday boring types with dazzling, creative people.

Creating a guest list doesn't have to be complicated; like everything else you need to know, you probably learned it in kindergarten. Remember the nursery rhyme, "Rich man, poor man, beggar man, thief . . . ?" The modern translation as it applies to entertaining is: Invite people of different professions, nationalities, and personalities — quiet or outgoing, artsy or conservative — any combination of characters that adds diversity (see Figure 2-1).

Every person you invite doesn't have to be someone you know well. Anyone you know from casual conversations or anyone you do business with is a possible guest: your favorite teller at the bank, your hairstylist, the letter carrier, the butcher, or your aerobics instructor. You may be surprised to find out that someone is an accomplished musician, a gourmet cook, an artist, or an expert on some subject that can be interesting to other guests. Get to know another side of people you see everyday by inviting them to appear out of their usual context.

Figure 2-1:
The lifeline of your party is a mixed bag of guests.

Unless you plan to have an office party, avoid inviting all your coworkers. The conversation is bound to be stale and predictable. (See Chapter 17 for tips on entertaining the office crowd.) The same holds true if you invite all your golfing buddies, all your best friends, or all of any particular group. Too many peas from the same pod makes for a dull evening.

For a small dinner party, mix personalities that complement each other and don't clash. Invite only one person you don't know well. For larger parties, such as cocktail parties, dances, or outdoor barbecues, clashing personalities usually aren't a problem, and you can invite many people whom you don't know well. Regardless of the size of your party, never invite exes (as in marriage or dating) without giving fair warning to both parties.

Some methods to the madness

Keeping in mind that you want to achieve a good mix of guests, remember that there is no right or wrong way to go about making a guest list. In fact, you can approach the task in many ways.

Regardless of which method you use to create your guest list, make sure that you include at least one person who makes your liver quiver with excitement. Inviting that person can give you the energy and desire to do the work.

The following are three fun and easy ways to make your guest list:

- ✓ **A painless way:** If the idea of inviting too varied a cast of characters leaves you feeling anxious or exhausted, then don't do it. Go ahead and invite your closest friends. But don't be afraid to include one or two new friends — people who have just moved to town or someone you just met. These are the guests who can elevate your party from a humdrum, been there, done that evening to something new and different. And after you are comfortable inviting one or two new people to your parties, you can begin to expand your guest lists to include different people each time.

- ✓ **An eclectic way:** Think of all the areas of your life and pick your favorite person from each. Invite a coworker along with someone you don't know well but find intriguing. Ask your child's teacher, the guy down the street who teaches yoga, and the carpenter who just fixed your floor. Bringing together a mix of friends and strangers is always interesting, and it usually works.

- ✓ **A wild way:** Invite all the eccentric people you know. Think of the people you know who are doing fun or fascinating things in their lives. Mix them all up at one party and see what happens.

No matter which approach you choose, consider adding one or more of the following types for that extra zing:

- ✓ **A scandalous acquaintance.** Someone who is widely rumored about can certainly add buzz to your party.

- ✓ **An intellectual.** Someone who can elevate conversations or has something to say that everyone wants to hear. (Avoid the intellectual who doesn't know when to stop talking, or the pseudointellectual who bores everyone's pants off.)

- ✓ **A VIP.** Define your own idea of what constitutes VIP status. A VIP isn't necessarily someone with money or social status. A VIP can be someone who possesses great character, a certain charm, or a unique talent. A VIP can be a great storyteller, your town's mayor, the editor of a local newspaper, a sports owner or hero, or your preacher.

- ✓ **A good listener.** Don't confuse quiet with boring. Not everybody can be a talker. Somebody has to listen. A good listener may be your most valuable guest because he or she makes everyone else feel important.

- ✓ **A "seedy character."** Invite one person who is a little odd or off-balance with the rest of your guest list. Choose someone off-beat or a little risqué — someone people would never expect to see at your house. After your other guests get over the initial shock and surprise, they may be delighted by your unusual guest.

What to do about bores and duds

Who are your boring friends, and why should you bother to invite that acute yawn-provoker? If at least one guest is a genuine bore, anyone who gets stuck with her, even for five minutes, can walk away feeling like the life of the party.

What you want to avoid is inviting more than one dull person:

- ✔ The person who is perfectly lovely but has nothing to say

- ✔ The person who is just a decorative object

- ✔ The person who cannot initiate a conversation

- ✔ The person who just sits and sucks the oxygen out of the air

People who are unwilling to give of themselves have absolutely nothing to contribute. If your party is large, you may get away with inviting two duds, but a roomful of them spells death to any size gathering.

After the guests arrive and you find that you have accidentally invited too many bores, all you can do is carry the conversation and hope that the party ends quickly.

A sincere, personal invitation is a wonderful gift. When you give away pleasure, it is bound to come back to you tenfold. So throw caution to the wind! Open your heart; be bold and invite many different guests. The party doesn't have to be perfect or fancy. The thought is what truly counts, and the invitation is long remembered.

What's in a Number?

Many factors affect the number of guests you can accommodate. You must first consider what kind of party you are giving and how much space you have. (See Chapter 5 for solutions to your space problems.) Be realistic about your energy level, too. Inviting many guests is much more draining than inviting only a few.

No exact formula exists for inviting the right or wrong number of guests to any party. However, some numbers just seem to work better than others. Keep in mind that the numbers suggested here are general guidelines. Use them to help you figure out what you can handle and what works best for you.

If entertaining is a new venture for you, start small. Two or three guests can make a perfect party. When you become comfortable with a few guests, you can begin giving larger parties.

No matter what kind or what size party you give, never invite an extra person purely for the sake of creating an even number. Odd numbers of people often generate more intriguing conversations than a group of pairs. Unless the extra person has a dynamite personality, a special charm, or something to add to your party, you are better off without him.

Dinner parties

For a sit-down dinner party, seven is an ideal number. (That's six guests plus you, or five plus you and your spouse or date.) This doesn't mean that you need to cancel your plans if you have only six or panic if the total is eight. You can have a wonderful dinner party with five, six, eight, or more people around a table.

But we didn't just pick the number seven out of the air. The following are a few good reasons why seven can be a magic number at a dinner party:

✔ Seven people around one table can have one conversation. With eight or more, guests tend to talk only to the people directly to their left and right.

✔ Odd numbers are more interesting. Three couples can be a little boring. That one extra person can stir up some excitement and may prevent the group from automatically settling into pairs.

✔ Inviting an extra person is a great way to open your heart to someone who is new in town, someone who needs a little extra tender loving care, or someone who may not receive many invitations.

✔ Even if you live in an efficiency apartment, you can probably find space for a 42-inch round table and serve a sit-down dinner for seven.

If you are planning a large party, you can use the same strategy for a party of any size by seating seven people per table. (See the section "Having Some Fun with Seating Arrangements" for tips on getting the right people together.) Place the tables in the same room so that guests can share the noise and laughter of the party.

Large parties

A large party can be defined as too many people to fit around your dining room table or too many people to fit in your house. To determine how many guests to invite to a large party, ask yourself:

✔ Will the guests be sitting, standing, or both? If you are not serving a sit-down meal, you probably have space for more guests.

✔ What ages are the guests? Younger guests won't mind as much if they are crowded together or have to stand. If your guests are older, be sure that you have enough places for them to sit and space to move around without being bumped from every direction.

✔ Do the guests all know each other? If so, make it a crowd. If not, allow for a little more personal space.

To decide where to have your large party, see Chapter 5 for tips on using space. For more help planning a big party, see Chapter 15.

For large parties, the usual turnout is 80 percent. If you want to have 50 guests attending your party, invite 60 to allow for the 20 percent who won't come.

Cocktail parties

There is no ideal number of guests to invite to a cocktail party. A small cocktail party can be charming with as few as eight guests. A large cocktail party can be exhilerating with as many as 25, 50, or 75 guests. You can have a cocktail party to suit any size crowd.

The average length of a cocktail party is 2–2^1/$_2$ hours. Don't invite more guests than you can talk to during the course of the evening; 50 to 75 guests is a good limit. Unless you are an experienced politician, don't expect to get around to talking to 100 guests.

Make sure that you provide enough room for guests to find you and find the bar. Chapter 5 helps you measure your space and figure out how many people will fit. People do not want their bones crushed, and they want you to know they are there. (Exception: For a college party, pack them in like sardines — the more the merrier.)

Buffets

For a buffet, be sure that you provide enough space for guests to sit comfortably. This does not necessarily mean that they all have to sit at a table or in a plush chair with arms. Guests can be comfortable sitting on pillows on the floor or perched on foot stools, banisters, or stairs. If the affair is casual, people can put their plates on their laps, but they should not have to stand and juggle their plates in their hands.

Having Some Fun with Seating Arrangements

At most casual get-togethers with family or friends, you don't need a seating plan. But sometimes you may want one. For example, if you want your confused teenager to get some unsolicited advice from his great uncle, seat them together at the family holiday dinner. Or, if two of your friends came to blows on the golf course, you may want to separate them at your birthday luncheon.

On occasions other than the most casual with the very best of friends, you may not want your guests sitting willy-nilly. When you plan your guest list, start thinking about how to make the most of the mix. If guests are to be seated, doing a little advance matchmaking can really pay off. You can use the seating arrangement to set up potential conversations and make the party more interesting for every guest.

At most sit-down dinners or luncheons, the host decides and tells people where to sit. When planning your seating arrangement, factor in why you invited each guest. Otherwise, guests tend to sit with their spouse, their best friend, or whomever they were talking with during cocktails. The party doesn't have a chance of rising above ho-hum.

For a small party, you may plan to point guests to their seats. For a larger party, put out place cards in advance, just to be on the safe side (in case guests start seating themselves) and to give yourself one less task to do.

If a guest has the gall to change his place card, it is best to do nothing except strike him from any future guest list.

Smart seating strategies

Don't let slapdash seating sink your soirée. When the responses are in and you know who's coming, take time to think about guests' individual interests, and who might enjoy the company of whom.

When you decide how and where to seat your guests, consider these tips:

- ✔ Seat guests at round tables, if possible. A circle is more conducive to conversation than square or rectangular shapes. A round table also eliminates the need to choose who to seat at the head of the table.

- ✔ Seat male and female guests alternately, if possible. But don't worry if you have an uneven number of men and women.

✔ Seat people together who have a common interest (hometown, job, hobby, or grandchildren).

✔ No matter how many tables you have, seat a male guest of honor to the right of the hostess and a female guest of honor to the right of the host.

✔ Seat only one dominant, energetic person per table. One table cannot handle two Dennis Rodmans. They'll clash, and your party atmosphere will collapse, fizzle, or erupt. Stars like to be stars.

✔ Seat a very large person or any person who might have special needs (wheelchair, crutches, and so on) at the corner or end of the table. This arrangement is more comfortable for that person and avoids possibly dividing the conversation because other guests can't see each other.

✔ Spread shy people and good listeners among tables.

✔ Seat a guest who has never been to your house before in a place of honor — to the right of the host or hostess — as a thoughtful gesture.

✔ Don't seat husbands and wives together unless they are newlyweds. They have plenty of opportunities to talk to each other at home. By separating them, each is free to share stories the other has heard a thousand times. You end up with two individuals contributing to conversations instead of a couple collaborating on the same topics.

✔ Seat a handsome bachelor next to a woman who has been married 40 years. It will be fun for both of them.

CPR for your party

You can use the people at your party to avoid many problems. In fact, a little forethought about seating can save a dying party. To prevent guests from getting restless or to revive a party that's pooping out, use one of the following strategies to infuse energy and breathe new life into it. No need to make a big production of putting your changes into action. With some planning, you can make the change look like a spur-of-the-moment decision or just a bit of frivolous fun.

✔ **The old switcheroo:** Just before dessert, choose one person from each table to move to a different table. (If more than seven guests are at each table, you can switch two people from each table.) Choose a person who is confident, intelligent, and good at starting conversations. Getting a new person at the table is a way to change a stale subject or give it a fresh perspective. Let the people you plan to switch know ahead of time that you may be asking them to move. Give them a subtle reminder when you are ready for them to switch, instead of shouting so that all the guests can hear.

Don't ask too many people to move — not only do you appear bossy, but the table may never regain its momentum. You must also be careful not to get carried away with this scheme. Don't move people around like musical chairs. One switch per party is enough.

- ✔ **Youth serum:** If your teenagers are semibehaved (bright and polite) and not total animals, ask them to join in for dessert. This part of the meal is usually when the party needs a lift. Most adults are interested in what young people have to say. Teenagers often have different views on topics such as politics, education, and current events. Conversation may turn toward the controversial, but most likely will be stimulating.

- ✔ **Sweet retreat:** Serving a dessert buffet is another clever way to change the arrangement and get people moving. Guests feel revived when they get up and stretch. Don't direct people anymore. Let them sit where they want. Some people may seek out a new conversation whereas others may want to return to their seats. The freedom to choose allows guests to relax and get comfortable.

Chapter 3

Secrets to the "Big O": Organization

• •

In This Chapter

▶ Visualizing your party

▶ Managing your time

▶ Making and using lists

▶ Living through the day of the party

▶ Organizing a spur-of-the-moment get-together

• •

*O*rganization, or the lack of it, is many people's nightmare and some people's dirty little secret. Oh sure, we all know someone who is highly efficient and who makes it look easy. But for most of us, just managing our everyday responsibilities is a challenge.

If your whole life is in a state of chaos — you've lost your keys for the umpteenth time, you can't find your appointment book, and the phone is ringing and buried under a stack of unopened mail — you may be thinking, "Who has time to entertain?" Before you throw up your hands and declare yourself doomed to a life of disarray, relax.

Like most instruction manuals, this chapter makes planning a party look more complicated than it really is. (Planning a party is much easier than explaining how to plan one.) In this chapter, you get it all together.

Getting the Big Picture

When planning a party, the very first step is to create the big picture in your mind. But for many people, the first question is where to begin. The instant you decide to have a party, start visualizing what you want to happen and all the fun you will have.

Getting the big picture doesn't have to be complicated — it can take ten seconds or ten minutes — but it is the most vital step to your organization. Think about the steps you need to accomplish before, during, and after the party, not for intimidation but for enlightenment. You don't have to do the steps now, but you can get some idea of each step and how you will accomplish it.

The big picture should include

- When and where to have your party
- Who and how many guests you plan to invite
- What kind of atmosphere you want to create
- What food and drinks to serve
- What you must buy
- What you need to do before the party
- What you will do the day of the party
- How you will get the food out on time
- How you will clean up and recover

You don't need to write anything down yet, except possibly your guest list. Making your guest list first often helps you picture your party and plan the details. If you skipped over Chapter 2, now would be a good time to look there for a few tips on coming up with a great group of guests.

As you create the big picture in your mind, remember not to get bogged down in any one area. Too much time spent on one step leaves you too exhausted to do the others. If you are stuck on one item — say you're not sure about the menu — skip over it temporarily and go back to it when the rest of the plan is clear.

When you think of the whole picture, questions may arise. Is this the right week to entertain? Will I have time to do everything on the list? Do I have too many other things going on? Will I have enough time/energy to clean up, or should I get someone to help me?

Asking yourself questions is good. If you can answer them, you're well on your way to an organized foundation. After you have the whole plan in focus, you can begin to break it down into small, manageable parts or steps. Without a clear idea, the process becomes fuzzy and can cause you to waste time on unnecessary chores.

After you have a mental picture of your party, do a quick reality check. The key is to know how much time you have and what your comfort level is at this point. Be realistic about your time as well as your abilities and budget.

There is no such thing as a "perfect party." Regardless of your abilities, two rules apply universally:

1. Everything takes longer than you think it will.

2. Something always goes wrong.

Realize these two truths and expect them — don't worry about them.

Following are a few ways to ways to gauge your overall plan against the reality of your time and ability:

- ✔ **Entertaining experience.** If you're a beginner, obviously, you don't want to plan a party for 25 guests. A better option may be to invite a few friends for drinks. Start with two or three guests, and when you feel comfortable with this number, try inviting a few more people. Practice on small groups before you venture into larger parties.

- ✔ **Cooking experience.** If you've never cooked anything more complicated than scrambled eggs and toast, think twice before attempting beef Wellington and a flaming dessert for company. Keep your menu simple and use familiar recipes. Experiment with new foods and techniques on yourself, your family, or very close friends before trying them on your party guests.

- ✔ **Time.** If you're short on time, keep your party small and/or keep your plan simple. Be sure that your big picture is not something that involves complicated cooking or elaborate decorating. (See Chapters 7, 8, and 18 for many timesaving menu ideas.)

- ✔ **Energy.** Consider your energy level as well. A party for 12 is far more draining than a party for four to six. Even if you're an expert host and have plenty of spare time, if you don't have a great desire to spend your time planning a party, recognize that fact and plan accordingly. If you're an accomplished host and enjoy entertaining elaborately, go ahead and knock yourself out. Just make sure you allow yourself enough time to execute your plan without becoming flustered.

Only *you* know your limitations, so be brutally honest with yourself when looking at the big picture.

It's about time

Now that you have a general idea of what you would like to accomplish, take a look at your schedule. How much time do you have and how much are you willing to devote to your party? Do you have 15 minutes a day? Do you have an hour on Saturday or Sunday?

Whether you have two weeks or twenty minutes, you can entertain with confidence. The secret is in the timing. Break down the plan so that you can concentrate on one task at a time — take control of the party rather than letting the party control you. By allowing ample time to prepare, you can enjoy the process of following through with your plan.

Are you planning a cozy dinner for four or a great big bash? Different size parties require different timetables. If you are having a large party, you may need several days, several weeks, or several months to prepare. How much time you need depends on how elaborate your big picture is and how much help you have. If you're doing all the cooking yourself and are planning a fancy menu, you may need more time than the host who is having the party catered, ordering takeout, or planning a potluck. Other factors that can affect your time schedule include who you invite as well as what kind of invitation you choose (formal/informal) and how you plan to relay it (in person, by phone, or by mail). See Chapter 4 for details on planning the invitations.

How you organize your time can also depend on what day of the week you choose to entertain. The best day and time for your party depends largely upon your lifestyle and other obligations:

- ✔ Saturday may be your best bet if you work long hours during the week. You can spend Friday evening doing preliminary chores and taking some time to unwind from your work week. You have at least part of the day on Saturday to make the final preparations and Sunday to recover. To prepare for a large party without taking a day off from work, keep your plan simple and start far enough ahead so that you can make a few preparations each night.

- ✔ Friday night may be more convenient if you don't work outside your home and if you have school age children. You can get things done while the kids are at school, and they won't have time to wreck the house before your party.

- ✔ Three-day weekends are a good opportunity for a Sunday afternoon picnic or a Sunday evening dinner, with a cushion of time on both sides for preparation and recovery.

If your obligations dictate a less-than-convenient day and time, take that fact into account when scheduling your preparations. Adjust the big picture to meet what is a realistic schedule for you or plan far enough in advance to get a head start. For example, if you want to have an important client over for dinner on Thursday night, plan a menu you can make ahead. Don't wait until Thursday when you get home from work to start cooking — you won't be good company, and you won't make a good business impression.

Scheduling the preparations

Making out your schedule does not require a great deal of time, even for a big party. Tea for two can be planned in your head and may take as little as ten seconds. To plan a larger party, you may need paper, pencil, and 20 minutes. Continue breaking down the big picture into small, manageable tasks: making a guest list, choosing food and drinks, planning decorations, and so on.

After you have a date in mind and a possible guest list — see Chapter 2 if you haven't thought about whom to invite — remember to include at least one special person you're dying to entertain. Just knowing that person is coming will motivate you to get your act together.

Next, you may need to schedule some time for preparing invitations. If you plan on using the telephone, start dialing before you chicken out and postpone your party. If you are planning on mailing the invitations, allow yourself the time to buy, write, address, and mail them. (Chapter 4 gives you some tips on how much time you need to prepare various types of written invitations for different kinds of parties.)

After planning the invitations, decide what to feed your guests. (For help with menu planning, refer to Part II. For more menu ideas, see Chapter 18.) After you make these basic decisions, you can begin breaking the plan down into lists.

Make lists of everything you need to do. If the lists seem overwhelming, adjust the plan to fit your schedule. If the date of the party is already set, the following small adjustments can make a big difference in reducing your time deficit:

- ✔ Reduce the number of guests.
- ✔ Simplify the menu.
- ✔ Plan to buy some foods already prepared.
- ✔ Ask for help. (See "Enlisting help," later in this chapter.)
- ✔ Hire help.
- ✔ Change the date to allow more time to prepare.

Three Useful Lists to Make

Making lists is one of the best ways to get and stay organized. The three lists that follow come in handy for any and every kind of party. The items on each list will vary according to the type and the size of the party.

If you're an accomplished host or if your party is small, you may not need to make any lists. As you become more experienced, many of these steps will come naturally. But for large parties or complicated menus, even party professionals rely on detailed lists.

Following are a few reasons why making lists is a good idea:

- ✔ Nothing is left to chance.
- ✔ You can mentally assess everything you're going to be doing.
- ✔ Committing chores to paper is the first step toward getting them done.
- ✔ A written list can be passed to someone else — a child, spouse, roommate, or friend — who offers to help.

List No. 1: Shopping list — Everything you need to buy

Write down your menu and all the ingredients you need to buy. Check your pantry for items you may already have. Also, check your drinks. (See Chapter 9 for information on stocking your bar.) You may want to separate this list into columns. One side can be your grocery list, and the other side can be miscellaneous items that you must purchase elsewhere. In addition to the ingredients for your menu and bar, your list may include such items as candles, napkins, a mop, and so on.

When you make your final stop for fresh food items on your grocery list, allow some flexibility in your menu. For example, if the asparagus you had planned to serve looks like dead tree branches, buy the gorgeous green broccoli instead.

List No. 2: Task list — Everything you need to do before the day of the party

The task list helps you keep track of what you need to do before the day of the party. For a dinner party or buffet, the list may include some or all of the following: shopping, food preparation, house cleaning, polishing silverware, ordering flowers, decorating, setting the table, and so on. For an outdoor party, you may need to list tasks such as mowing the lawn or cleaning the grill.

If you invite friends at the spur of the moment, you can keep your task list in your head. For example, asking a few neighbors over to watch a ball game, your task list could be as simple as calling your favorite take-out restaurant, clearing off the sofa, and turning on the TV. For a more formal party or a large crowd, spread your task list out over a longer period of time. Break down each task into segments that can be done quickly or even while you're doing something else. For example, buy the food for your party while you do your regular grocery shopping. Stop by the wine store while you're out running everyday errands. Mix a cake to freeze for the party, and while it bakes, prepare dinner for yourself or your family.

List No. 3: The day of the party list — Everything you have to do the day of the party

Much of your preparation can be done before the day of the party, but some tasks cannot be completed in advance. Divide the day of the party into time segments and make a list including things you need to do in the morning, things to be done later in the day, and only one or two last-minute things to do just before the guests arrive.

No matter what kind of party you are having, this list includes all final preparations. For a dinner or buffet, you can include defrosting food, chopping vegetables, setting up the coffee machine, frosting a cake, setting the table, arranging flowers, and so on. For outdoor entertaining, include tasks such as sweeping the patio, setting out candles or torches, firing up the grill, and so on. For a big party in a space other than your home, the day of the party list may even include travel, decorating, adjusting lights, and a last meeting with caterers, servers, or entertainers.

Don't forget to include some time to shower, dress, and relax. A few years ago, a friend of ours was giving her first seated dinner party. She loved cooking, so she had planned to serve a complicated menu with many courses. She was so engrossed in preparing the food, she forgot to get ready. When the first guest rang the doorbell, she was wearing a bathrobe with her hair wrapped in a towel.

Surviving the Day of the Party

Many hosts are stressed out on the day of the party about making all the final preparations. If you have to work the day of the party, ask yourself the following questions:

Dressing for your party

Getting dressed for your party can get you in the mood for entertaining — it can change your attitude from sick and tired to attractive and fascinating.

The way you dress also makes a difference in everyone's enjoyment of your party. Looking relaxed and feeling comfortable puts you and your guests at ease. The key is to look as attractive as possible without looking like you spent all day on yourself. Give the distinct impression that you concentrated on other things besides your appearance.

Use the process of getting dressed to get in the right frame of mind for your party. Sometimes all it takes to change your mood is a long, hot bath or a cool shower. Find time for a little self-indulgence. If you need to dress by candlelight, buy new clothes, or get a haircut, do whatever it takes to feel terrific.

You don't need to dress to attract attention to yourself; instead, dress to make yourself feel different inside, to give yourself a new outlook, to shed negative images, and to emerge as a new you. One of our favorite hostesses always goes barefoot at her parties — cold or hot, fancy or not — going barefoot makes her comfortable and suits her style.

Different clothes also create different moods. If you wear T-shirts and overalls at work, getting dressed up for your party can be fun and mood changing. However, if you wear a coat and tie or a dress and heels every day, you may prefer to throw on some jeans when you're just having fun. Remember to tell guests what to wear, too. If you tell them the party is casual and suggest they come in shorts, don't greet them at the door wearing your most elegant silk pants. (See Chapter 12 for some suggestions for making guests comfortable if they show up under-dressed for a more formal party.)

At your party, you will be standing up and sitting down, so your whole body will be showing. You want to look good from head to toe. But make sure that your attire allows you to move about comfortably — avoid outfits with so many buttons that it takes you 20 minutes to get in and out of the restroom or clothes so tight you can't sit down and breathe at the same time. If you are going to be cooking, wear something suitable — no dangling sleeves or long hair skimming over the food.

✔ What can I get done before I go to work? (Decorate, defrost some of the food you have prepared in advance, set up the bar and the coffee, set tables, and so on.)

✔ What can I accomplish on the way home from work? (Pick up bread and dessert from the bakery.)

✔ What is left to do when I get home from work? (Shower, arrange flowers, finish chopping vegetables, re-heat food, arrange hors d' oeuvres on platters, and so on.)

Another major concern for many hosts is getting the food out to the guests on time. If juggling the food is a major hang-up for you, relax. Following are a few ways to reduce your stress:

✔ Choose foods that can be served at room temperature. (Many foods can be safely taken out of the oven or refrigerator and left standing for an hour or two before your party.) Set out platters of food prepared earlier in the day — a relaxed way to entertain that removes the hassle of worrying about timing.

✔ To serve piping-hot food, keep two things in mind: oven temperatures and stove tops. Let some items cook on top of the stove while everything else is baking at the same temperature inside the oven. For example, a soup can be simmering on top while chicken, potatoes, and tomatoes all roast at 400 degrees. For a hot dessert, cobblers, pies, soufflés, and so on, can go in the oven when the chicken comes out.

✔ Include cold foods such as cold soups, salads, cheesecake, and so on, that can be taken out of the refrigerator just before serving.

✔ If you're still having difficulty getting food out to your guests, you may be trying to do too many things at once. Try mixing up the temperatures. For example, at a cocktail party or buffet, serve a combination of cold, warm, and hot foods. For a dinner, alternate temperatures by serving a cold first course (made in advance), a hot main course, and a room-temperature dessert (made in advance). By varying the temperatures, you not only save yourself a great deal of frustration, but you electrify your menu as well.

Making and using a timetable

To avoid timing problems, expand your "day of the party" list to include a timetable. A timetable includes all the cooking and serving tasks to be done after the guests arrive.

Creating and referring to a timetable will help you keep everything running smoothly and on time. It can also help ensure that you won't have to serve food incredibly late, which can ruin any party. (Guests get tired wondering when they will eat, sometimes drink too much alcohol, and run out of conversations in the interim.)

Making a timetable also helps you have time to spend with your guests. The whole point of inviting guests is to enjoy their company. You defeat the purpose of the party if you are so preoccupied with serving the food that you never get out of the kitchen.

The case of the missing hostess

A woman we know took great pride in being an organized housekeeper. She was always rushing around, cleaning her house and "getting ready" just in case she had visitors. One night, she invited a few of her neighbors to dinner. The neighbors all knew the hostess was very meticulous, and they looked forward to a relaxing evening in her orderly, well-organized home.

To the guests' great surprise, the evening was anything but relaxing. Although the house was clean and the food was delicious, the hostess spent the entire evening in the kitchen, preparing the food and cleaning up afterward. She never once sat down to talk to her guests. It was like she wasn't there.

For any type of party, (cocktails, dinner, outdoor, or tea) the best way to make your timetable is to work backward. Figure out what time you want people to eat. If you have asked two friends over for drinks and you plan to serve hors d'oeuvres that take 15 minutes to heat, allow enough time to preheat the oven, take the hors d'oeuvres out of the refrigerator or package, heat them, and put them on a serving platter. The same applies if you are having a cookout. If you want serve barbecued ribs hot off the grill at noon, don't wait until guests arrive to turn on the heat.

By putting everything in writing, you know what to do and when to do it, even if you get distracted or confused. For example, if the ice cream is supposed to be churning while guests are eating, your list may save you the embarrassment of forgetting to start the churn. (By the time you discover your mistake, guests may not want to wait another hour for dessert.)

Keep your timetable in the kitchen and use it like a cheat sheet. Think of it as a tool that allows you to relax and enjoy your guests. By relying on your written time schedule to keep you on task, you can concentrate on conversations and having fun. If you have planned your time well, things will seem to "just happen." Nobody needs to know what went on backstage.

Enlisting help

When planning and executing party plans, other people can be a real boon to your organizational goals. Use children, spouses, and friends to help you accomplish part of your lists. The important point is to clearly explain how they are to help you or show them exactly what you want them to do.

Enlisting their help can be an opportunity to show small children how to set a table and older children how to pass food, clear the table, wash and dry dishes, and so on. Spouses can have fun together planning a party and sharing the work. Don't be afraid to ask a friend to pick something up on his way to your house, help stir a sauce, or pour a cocktail. People love helping. It puts them at ease and helps you with your organization.

Cleanup and recovery

When planning a party, the last thing you want to think about is cleaning up afterward. But if you think of the cleanup as a part of the overall plan and include it in your organization, the mess won't come as a surprise to you when the party is over. To avoid feeling overwhelmed by the job, clean up as much as you can as you go along.

Plan time to clean up the kitchen before the guests arrive. Before dinner, fill the sink or a large plastic tub with warm, soapy water. As dishes are cleared, rinse them and place them in the sink or tub. Deal with washing later.

Unless it is Thanksgiving, your guests are your best friends (or your mother), or you have just had major knee surgery, don't let guests do your dishes. Dish washing totally spoils the atmosphere. Let guests help you clear if they offer, but don't let them clean your kitchen.

The last part of your party is recovery. Allow yourself time to put your feet up, give yourself credit, and acknowledge your hard work. Recognize what you did: You organized your time, set realistic goals, and accomplished what you set out to do.

While you're recovering and giving yourself a well-deserved pat on the back, take a moment to reflect on what worked and what didn't. Did your guests go well together? Was your menu too ambitious, or did it work well? Did you give yourself enough time from beginning to end? All this information can help you organize your next party. (See Appendix A for a more complete party evaluation.)

Organizing a Spur-of-the-Moment Party

Don't let any of these well-laid plans and organizational tips intimidate you or keep you from throwing last-minute parties. Spur-of-the-moment get-togethers are often the most fun. Ninety-nine out of one hundred of these parties are successful; because expectations are not high (neither yours nor your guests'), great enjoyment comes as a pleasant surprise.

Keep your pantry, freezer, and bar stocked with a few items for drop-in company and last-minute entertaining. Some items you can keep on hand include candles, tablecloths/napkins, champagne, wine, chocolates, nuts, and so on. Use your imagination to make the most of what you have for spur-of-the-moment gatherings:

Spontaneous fun

Spontaneous parties are often more fun than parties that are too planned or structured. Throwing a last-minute party has many advantages for the host. Following are a few worth noting:

- You don't have to deal with big party plans or long lists.

- You can go with the flow and roll with the punches.

- You don't have time to sweat the small stuff.

- You have to be yourself (no time to fake it), so guests see the real you.

If you're highly structured or a perfectionist by nature, some of these advantages may sound like disadvantages. If you're shy or lack confidence in yourself, they may scare you to death. Try it just once. Maybe you just want to invite friends over for a drink before going out or ask them to come for dessert after a movie. Throwing a spur-of-the-moment party is a great way to loosen up, relax, come out of your shell, discover your hidden abilities, and gain confidence.

- Throw together some pasta and a simple sauce. Serve it with fruit or whatever you have on hand.

- Check your refrigerator for leftovers. Chopped-up meat and vegetables make terrific fillings for crepes, frittatas, omelets, or even bases for soufflés.

- If your cupboards are bare, use the telephone. Order takeout and just figure out a place to put it all.

- See Chapters 7 and 8 for more quick and easy ideas for your last-minute entertaining.

The trick to last-minute entertaining is to organize the time you have and the space around you. Organizing in a short amount of time means you may have to do two or three things at once — hide the clutter under the furniture, dash through the middle of the floor with the vacuum, and unload the dishwasher. You can order take-out food or raid your own pantry or freezer. (Even if you invite someone for drinks, they will be expecting a peanut, an olive, or some morsel of food.)

For instant atmosphere, turn off the telephone ringer, dim the overhead lights, and light a few candles.

When faced with drop-in company or a need to throw together an instant party, take a few minutes to catch your breath. Make up your mind that this last-minute endeavor is fun. Even the best-laid plans are useless if you're so stressed out that you make your guests nervous wrecks.

Chapter 4

Invitations

• •

In This Chapter

▶ Writing or calling, that is the question

▶ Extending invitations by telephone

▶ Sending invitations by mail

▶ Creating unique and unusual invitations

▶ Getting responses

• •

An invitation is a gift. It is a sincere compliment, telling a person that he is wanted, he is respected, and he is special. Extending an invitation shows that you are willing to spend your time and energy entertaining someone.

You can issue invitations verbally or send them in the mail. However you go about it, all invitations must include the basics of when and where. An effective invitation also arouses curiosity, stirs interest, or creates excitement. In this chapter, you figure out how to give invitations in such a way that people say yes and look forward to coming to your party.

Of course, the whole point of the invitation (besides getting people to show up) is to get them to respond in advance so that you can nail down your guest list and know who and how many people to plan for. In this chapter, we show you how to get the responses you want and need.

Deciding Whether to Write or Call

The most appropriate tactic, writing or calling, depends largely on your personality and the type of party you are planning. If the party is formal or very large, send written invitations. Otherwise, the method you choose is entirely up to you.

Verbal invitations are great

✔ For spur-of-the-moment gatherings

✔ For casual parties or semiformal events

✔ When the guest list is subject to change

✔ When you want to create immediate excitement

Written invitations are preferable

✔ For parties planned far in advance

✔ For formal affairs

✔ When you have a definite guest list

✔ When you want to establish a tone or theme

Regardless of whether you write or call, be sure to include all the pertinent information in your invitation. Guests need to know who is inviting them to what sort of event, the date, the time, and the place.

Guests also need to know exactly for whom the invitation is intended. This may seem obvious, but it can create confusion. To prevent misunderstandings, address the invitation to the party whom you are inviting. If you are inviting a husband and wife, address it to "Mr. and Mrs." If the children are invited, too, add "and family." If you're having a ladies-only luncheon, then say so in the invitation so that someone doesn't show up with her spouse in tow. In other words, do everything you can to make it crystal clear whose presence is requested.

Give an unmarried person the option of bringing a guest, unless you are inviting him to fill a specific place in your guest list. Otherwise, he may assume that it's okay and bring a date anyway. (See Chapter 12 for tips on how to handle the unexpected extra guest.) Or he may wonder if it's okay and hesitate to ask. Extending the courtesy to bring a guest is especially important if you know that he is seeing someone regularly.

Invitations by Phone

The telephone may be your most valuable tool if you want an easy, relaxed, and friendly way to issue invitations.

Advantages of telephone invitations:

✔ There's no danger of an uninvited friend seeing the invitation on another friend's refrigerator door.

> ✔ Immediate responses allow flexibility so that you can change and adjust your guest list as needed.
>
> ✔ Verbal invitations are spontaneous, fluid, and fun.
>
> ✔ Verbal invitations are wonderful for advance PR.

You can use the enthusiasm in your voice to get people excited about your party. Start guests thinking about what a wonderful time they will have, all the fascinating people they will meet, and the delicious food they will eat. They will be thrilled to accept your invitation, and they won't forget to show up.

When you call your potential guest, say, "I'm having a few people over for a casual dinner on Friday night. I would love for you to come." What you say next depends on your personality. You may want to continue with one of the following:

"I can't wait to see you!"

"I can't wait for you to meet so and so!"

"I can't wait to cook such-and-such for you!"

You are not trying to force someone to say yes to your invitation or make her feel obligated. You are trying to convey your own excitement so that she will want to come to your party. Your sincere enthusiasm will inspire her to break previous engagements, drive long distances, or do anything not to miss your party. Besides getting a "yes" response, you plant a seed. If a guest expects your party to be exciting, it will be.

Using one guest to entice another

Another smart telephone strategy is to entice guests with other guests. Think of a few people you are dying to entertain. Call them first to verify that they can come. They can be the structure of your party. Get their responses first. Then use your core list to pique the interest of other guests by mentioning who is coming and that you want them to meet this person or vice versa.

"Hello, Bill? I'm having Sharon Stone over on Friday night at 8:00. I've told her all about you, and she's dying to meet you." (A strategic white lie.) "Can you come?"

Chances are, Bill will clear his calendar for an invitation like that. But even if you don't invite movie stars to your party, you can use the same tactic to entice your guests with one another.

For example, suppose that you want to invite a friend who is a fabulous storyteller, a local pet store owner, a magazine editor, and the guy from your office who does amateur comedy gigs on the side.

After these people commit to come, you can use the following lines to entice other guests:

> "My neighbor, Martha Goose, tells some incredible tales. She's from the same area where you grew up. I know you will just love her."

> "My friend Sherlock is coming. I've been telling him all about the mysterious disappearance of your rich uncle."

> "Maxwell is the editor of *Insanity Flair*. I was telling him what a clever way you have with words. I think you two will enjoy each other."

> "You won't believe who's coming. You know the guy who does comedy down at the Dew Drop Inn on Saturday nights? Yeah, that's the one. He works in my office, and he's even funnier in real life."

When guests are intrigued by other guests, most likely, they will accept your invitation, even if they have to rearrange their social calendar, cancel their vacation plans, and take a taxi to get there.

When to call

Don't call with your invitation so far in advance that you put the guest in an awkward position. If you call two months ahead, unless the person is going out of the country, there is no gracious way for him to decline if he doesn't want to come.

You can also seem a bit desperate by phoning people months ahead of time. For a party that far in the future, a written invitation is more appropriate.

Type of party	When to call
Well-planned large party	2–3 weeks in advance
Luncheon or small dinner	7–14 days ahead
Last-minute get-together	The afternoon of the party

For a large dinner party or buffet, calling 2–3 weeks in advance allows you to find out immediately who cannot come and gives you time to invite someone else.

If another guest comes to mind later — you realize that there is someone you should have invited or wish you had — there is nothing wrong with telephoning to ask if he can join your party at the last minute, but be careful how you phrase the invitation.

Obviously, you don't want to say,"I really wanted Mr. Suave A. Debonair at my party. I mailed him an invitation weeks ago, but he just canceled. So I thought I might as well ask you. Can you come at 8:00 tonight?"

Say this instead: "I know this is at the spur of the moment, but I'm having a few friends over for dinner tonight. Several people want to meet you. Dinner is at 8:00. It would mean the world to me if you could join us."

Invitations by Mail

When the party is formal or if you just want to have a little fun, you can't go wrong with written invitations. Whether the occasion is tea for two, your child's birthday party, or a ballroom gala, a written invitation is appropriate for every event. But just like telephone invitations, a mailed invitation needs to spark an interest in your party.

An invitation that arrives by mail is like the entrance hall of your party. The invitation is the first thing people see and the first impression they have of your party.

Written invitations have definite advantages:

- ✔ They set the tone.
- ✔ They tell guests something extra, such as what to wear.
- ✔ They serve as a physical reminder of the date and time so that no one will show up on the wrong night.

Although rules of etiquette are more relaxed in today's modern society, a written invitation is still correct and expected for some types of parties. Always send written invitations for the following types of parties:

- ✔ A formal party (dinner, luncheon, tea)
- ✔ A dinner to honor someone
- ✔ A business party
- ✔ A big party planned well in advance
- ✔ A shower (bridal, baby, housewarming)
- ✔ A ceremony (christening, commencement, bar mitzvah, wedding)

All written invitations must include the same basic information:

- ✔ Hosts' names
- ✔ Type of event

✔ Date

✔ Time

✔ Location

✔ Reply telephone number

Optional information you may want to include:

✔ Rain date

✔ Special parking arrangements

✔ Map

Clearly state who is invited. If you think that there may be any question, you can add a note to clarify: "Children welcome" or "Feel free to bring a date."

Allow yourself time to get the invitations ready and in the mail. Your time schedule can be a major determining factor in the type of invitation you choose to send. You want your guests to receive the invitation far enough in advance to respond appropriately. Use the following table in conjunction with your time schedule to figure out how soon you need to get started.

Type of party	When to mail
Formal dinner	4 weeks ahead
Informal dinner	2–3 weeks ahead
Luncheon or tea	2–3 weeks ahead
Cocktail party	3 weeks ahead
Big bash	4 weeks ahead
Wedding	8 weeks ahead

Choosing the right invitation

Written invitations come in many styles, simple to elaborate, handmade to store-bought. Choose the one that best fits the type of party you are having, the guests you are inviting, the time you have to write out the invitation, and your budget. Expect to pay more for engraved invitations than preprinted or plain cards.

✔ **Formal engraved.** The most appropriate style for formal events such as weddings, graduations, black-tie galas, and so on. However, there is no reason not to use engraved invitations for a less formal affair if it strikes your fancy. Figures 4-1 and 4-2 show examples of this type of invitation. For formal invitations, choose heavyweight white or ecru paper with black ink. Allow four weeks for engraving.

✔ **Prepared by a calligrapher.** If your party plans are somewhat formal and you want to relay a feeling of elegance, hire a calligrapher to write the invitations. Most card shops or stores that sell invitations can refer you to a calligrapher. If not, call the local high school and ask who does the script on their diplomas. If you plan to use a calligrapher, get started early. Calligraphers' schedules vary, and the amount of time needed to complete your invitations depends on how many you need, how much writing is involved, and whether you want the envelopes addressed in calligraphy as well.

✔ **Specially printed.** Appropriate for most any type of party from semi-formal to casual. Print companies can help you choose appropriate designs or, best of all, design your own. Compose an original message or ask for suggestions. Allow 2–4 weeks for printing.

✔ **Fill-in invitations from the card shop.** A compromise between custom printing and handwritten. As shown in Figure 4-3, this is an easy way to announce birthday parties, holiday get-togethers, open houses, picnics, potlucks, and showers. Many fill-in invitations are designed for specific events. They come in styles ranging from elegant to funky.

✔ **Handwritten on blank cards or on your stationery.** Most appropriate for small parties, formal or informal when you want to make it personal. A handwritten invitation is ideal, even if it's only one or two lines long. Figure 4-4 shows an example.

Mr. and Mrs. High Society
request the pleasure of your company
at a dinner
in the honor of
Queen Bee
on Wednesday, May first
at seven o'clock

4172 Easy Street
Hollywood

RSVP

Jackets

000-555-0000

Figure 4-1:
An up-to-snuff formal invitation.

Joe and Susie Homemaker
invite you to
a dinner
in honor of Plain Jane
Wednesday, June 7
8 P.M.
4172 Social Circle
Savannah
Casual
RSVP
000-555-1234 Home
000-555-1111 Work
000-555-2222 Mobile

Figure 4-2:
A less
formal
invitation.

You are invited

For   *A picnic lunch*

On   *June 21st, Noon - 3:00*

At   *Yellowstone Park (map enclosed)*

Yogi Bear

000-555-6789

Figure 4-3:
A fill-in
invitation.

Your invitations do not have to be fancy or perfect. A simple line drawing or some stickers on a notecard, piece of stationery, or ordinary paper is fine. Your guests will be complimented that you went to the trouble and will start looking forward to your party.

✔ **Computer-designed on your PC or at your local card shop.** Great for casual parties and especially for friends who appreciate modern technology and your new computer-publishing skills. If you don't own a computer or don't know how to operate one, many greeting card stores offer computer-generated card services where you can create your own customized invitations quickly and inexpensively.

Stop by for tea at 4:00. 163 Woodland Drive

June Cleaver

_000-555-0000_

Figure 4-4:
A hand-
written
invitation.

Always handwrite the address. Avoid database generated attempts at personalization and stick-on address labels. Guests may inadvertently mistake your invitation for a sales gimmick and route it to File 13.

✔ **E-mail:** Use this method for casual parties and only if you are certain the recipient checks his electronic mail regularly. This is a fun way to issue invitations for your computer club picnic or a "happy hour" invitation to some close business friends.

Be careful how you use computer technology. Some people perceive it as "cold" and less personal than old-fashioned mail. Also, some companies strictly forbid using company equipment for personal use. Be sure to know your company's policy.

Creating Unique and Unusual Invitations

If you really want to create a stir, generate excitement, and get people interested in your party, think about sending invitations that are a bit out of the ordinary. You can create an invitation that is as unique and individual as you want your party to be. Use the invitation to hint at the atmosphere or begin a theme.

When you have a way with words

You can create unusual invitations just by saying something different. If you have a way with words, think of a clever way to spice up your invitations. Make up limericks, compose a poem, or just write something wild and wacky:

Creative writing examples appear in Figures 4-5 and 4-6.

Perhaps you are not so poetic or creative. Think about writing individualized notes to each potential guest (see Figure 4-7). Pretend you are having a casual conversation. Nothing is so sincere or so appreciated as your own words. People know you took the time to make it personai.

When you want to make a bold statement

If you have time and money to spare, and if you really want to make a statement and boldly proclaim that

✔ This party will be different

✔ This party is not to be missed

✔ Go ahead and get excited now

. . . then you want to start with an outrageous invitation.

Use an express delivery service or the U.S. mail to send something more intriguing than the usual card. Decide on the atmosphere you want to create, and think of an object you can mail that represents the theme.

Here are a few examples of creative packaging for your invitations.

✔ **Wine bottle:** Roll up the invitation and put it in an empty wine bottle — perfect for a dinner featuring vintage wines.

✔ **Smooth-shelled coconuts:** Write the invitation on one side of the shell, the address on the other, and have the post office stamp them — great for a tropical party, even more exciting in the dead of winter.

✔ **Lace pillow:** Attach a handwritten invitation. The potential guest receives an invitation and a gift — thoughtful for Valentine's Day.

✔ **Rubber flip-flop:** Write the invitation with a permanent marker on the inside of the shoe (a child's size is just right). Mail it in a brown envelope. Attach a postcard with a beach scene on the outside of the envelope — fun for a casual beach theme.

We could share literally thousands of ideas for invitations. (You can find a few more suggestions in Chapter 20.) But remember, the most original and effective invitations come right out of your own imagination.

Allow up to five days for guests to receive invitations.

You are invited
to dress nicely, behave charmingly,
drink heartily, and dance badly
in celebration of...

Figure 4-5: An invitation that's sure to entice your guests.

You are invited to
a perfectly smashing,
knock-down drag-out,
absolutely fabulous,
no holds barred
brawl of a PARTY...

Figure 4-6: An invitation that says, "This party guaranteed to be a blast!"

Dear Robin,

I'm asking a few friends over to the Batcave on March 2, at 7:30 to celebrate Catwoman's 35th birthday. I hope you can come. Please call me at home 555-0000 or at work, 555-1234, or e-mail me at bman@xxx.com.

Sincerely,
Batman

Figure 4-7: Guests will be surprised and touched to receive an invitation in your own words.

Getting around the post office

For the practical: Going to the post office or mailing center is the best way to ensure that the invitation has the right postage and will reach the recipient. Almost nothing is impossible. These offices are there to help you with your mailing dilemmas.

For the impractical: If the mere thought of going to the post office breaks you out in hives, or if time is more precious than money, just stick way too many stamps on the item and drop it in the closest mail receptacle. The post office delivers almost anything, even coconuts.

Note: Postal regulations do not allow you to mail anything over one pound in outside mail receptacles unless the item has a traceable metered stamp. If your invitation weighs more than a pound, go to the post office to mail it.

Getting Responses

Once upon a time, before voice mail and e-mail, people used the U.S. mail. Hosts sent written invitations and prospective guests wrote notes in reply. Don't expect that to happen today.

Most modern invitations include a reply line at the bottom with a telephone number to which guests can respond.

Avoid using a reply line that says "Regrets only." That term technically means "call if you can't come." But people cannot always be relied upon to take the time to call. Suppose that you invited 25 people and no one called. You may end up with 2 guests or 20. Don't take the chance.

A better option is to use RSVP, which technically means "the favor of a reply is requested." Although most civilized people know that they are expected to let you know if they can or cannot come, unfortunately, many people forget to respond.

Because we live in a world of instant communication, you can improve your chances of getting a response if you include more than one number where the person can reach you. Next time you write RSVP on your invitations, include more than one of the following: your home, work, or mobile phone numbers; your address, your fax number, your e-mail address— anything that makes responding convenient for people.

Expect to receive replies to the invitations within two days to one week. As the party time draws near, you need to finalize your guest list. A perfectly acceptable and necessary step is to call those who have not responded and ask if they are coming.

Whether you issued your invitations by phone or by mail, when you have the guest list nailed down, you may want to send a written reminder. This message can be a printed card or handwritten on a postcard (see, respectively, Figures 4-8 and 4-9). If you sent written invitations, the reminder can be a second copy of the invitation with the reply line crossed out and a note saying, "To remind." Reminder cards arrive one week before the event, and they do not require a reply.

This is to remind you that
Mr. and Mrs. Prim and Proper
expect you for *dinner*
on *Saturday, the seventeenth of September*
at *eight o'clock* P.M.
◆

1 Right Way Lane
Pleasantville, Iowa

Figure 4-8:
A printed reminder card.

Dear Elizabeth,
Dinner is on Saturday, September 17th, at 8:00 P.M.
at our house, 1 Right Way Lane.
Can't wait to see you!
Sincerely,
Richard and Hyacinth

Figure 4-9:
A hand-written reminder card.

Chapter 5

Choosing and Using Space

· ·

In This Chapter

▶ Finding the right space for your party

▶ Making the most of small spaces

▶ Managing large spaces

▶ Using alternative spaces

▶ Renting space

▶ Moving people around in your space

· ·

*T*he atmosphere for a party begins with the setting. This doesn't mean that you should refinance your home and rent the Taj Mahal. It means that you should open up your mind and imagination when you choose and use the spaces available to you.

Whether you live in a hovel or a hotel, you have the space for entertaining. In fact, when it comes to space, more isn't necessarily better. Too much space can be just as great a challenge as not enough. Keep in mind that it isn't how much space you have, but how you use the space you have that determines the success of your party.

Space used with imagination and with a plan can help with atmosphere, conversation, and the overall rhythm and flow of your party. In this chapter, we show you how.

Choosing a Space for Your Party

The key to finding the right space for your party is to match the size of the room (or rooms) with the size of your guest list. Inviting a realistic number of people is the first step to solving all your space problems.

The setting you choose for the number of guests you invite may also depend on the kind of party you decide to give. Different types of parties require different amounts of space. For example, if you are giving a large cocktail party for 25 guests (mostly standing), you need less space than for a casual buffet for the same number of guests (seating themselves randomly). You need even more space for a formal buffet or a sit-down dinner.

A 400-square-foot space with furniture can comfortably hold about 30 people standing. You don't need to waste time measuring to the inch, but estimate your space so that you don't end up having to build an addition to the house to handle your party. Set up tables and chairs in advance, if possible.

Big ideas for small spaces

If you live in a two-room apartment, you may not think that you have space for entertaining. You do. Even if you eat your meals off the kitchen counter and the sofa doubles as your bed, you can still entertain in your home. The challenge is to make the most of the space you have.

Think of any obscure places that can be converted to party space with a little creative rearranging. For example, make the closet into a bar by stashing its usual contents under the bed, behind the shower curtain, or in the trunk of your car. Or clear out the center of the closet and drape beautiful sheets over the coats and brooms to turn the closet into a cocoon. Use a colored light bulb to make the space look more like a bar and less like a closet. Set up a small mirrored table on which to display the bottles and glasses. The mirror makes the space look larger and adds sparkle.

No dining table? No problem.

- ✔ Serve all finger food from your countertop.
- ✔ Set up folding trays for guests to use as minitables.
- ✔ Have guests use their laps to hold plates.
- ✔ Turn a sidetable into a dining table with a sheet of plywood and a tablecloth on top.
- ✔ Seat guests on pillows on the floor around your coffee table and dine Asian style.
- ✔ Purchase a card table that you can stash away when you are not entertaining.
- ✔ Rent or borrow a table.

If your problem is not the lack of a dining table, but rather the lack of a sideboard or other place to set up the food, serve from the kitchen countertop and/or stovetop. To create more work space, lay a cutting board across your sink or across two open drawers.

Choosing a table

If you decide to rent a table, do some advance figuring. Rearrange the furniture if you must. Then measure your clear space and think round, not square. In most cases, round tables are not only more space-efficient but are also more conducive to conversation.

If your space is long and narrow, consider renting a long, skinny table, sometimes referred to as a conference table. To facilitate talking across the table, the ideal width is 18 inches. If the 18-inch table isn't available, use the standard 30-inch wide banquet table. Fill the gap with wide, low center-pieces.

A long narrow table is most effective if you have enough guests to crowd around it, almost elbow to elbow — especially fun for large family feasts and holiday dinners.

If you're a mathematician, you may be able to figure out how many tables you need and how many of what size can fit in your space. But if numbers aren't your strong suit, do some prearranging to make sure that everything fits. Table 5-1 lists standard table shapes and sizes and the number of people you can actually plan to seat at those tables. (Rental companies may not agree with these numbers.)

Table 5-1	Standard Table Sizes
Rounds	
36-inch	Seats 4-5
42-inch	Seats 6-7
48-inch	Seats 7-8
60-inch	Seats 8-9
72-inch	Don't use this size. Because of the distance across the table, conversations are limited to the people directly to your right and left.
Rectangles	
6-foot	Seats 8-10
8-foot	Seats 10-12

Pay attention to the table legs and the size of the chairs, as well. A pedestal table seats more people than a table with legs. Armchairs obviously take more space than bistro chairs.

Decorating

A little imaginative redecorating can also help transform a small room into an intimate setting or a fun place to be. Hang something unique on the walls for guests to look at while dining. (Some large public libraries lend out art.) But the art doesn't have to be a van Gogh; it can be a pop-art poster, your three-year-old's finger-painting masterpieces, your collection of baskets, or your grandmother's handmade quilt-turned-wall-hanging.

Never be intimidated because your house is small or your decor is plain. Your guests are there because they like you, not your house. If you're comfortable with your surroundings, chances are your guests are, too.

Little thoughts for big houses

Just because you live in a castle on a 20-acre estate or in a comfortably-sized home with plenty of room for company doesn't mean that you don't have space problems. In fact, you may need to be even more careful with your use of space than the guy who lives out back in the garage apartment.

The number one concern for the host with a large setting is figuring out how to confine the party so that the atmosphere isn't lost in space. If you spread the guests too thinly, the party fizzles before it gets started.

Five good reasons why tiny apartments are fabulous for entertaining

Just because you live in a two-by-four space that doubles as an obstacle course doesn't mean that you can't entertain. Granted, you may have to limit the number of people you invite at one time. But miniscule spaces do have their advantages for guests as well as hosts:

✔ They're cozy, comfortable, and non-intimidating.

✔ They force the host to organize, clean-up, and de-clutter for entertaining.

✔ They encourage guests to get up close and personal.

✔ They contain all the delightful cooking aromas.

✔ They remind people of simpler times. (Sitting on steps, eating off trays, and using fewer than three utensils is fun.)

No matter how much space you have to spare, start your party in a small area and force a little closeness. You can move guests to your grand ballroom for dinner and dancing, and they can tour your house later. But be sure to get people together in the beginning.

If you live in a large house, plan a big party once a year and take advantage of all the space you have.

Mansion dwellers, beware: Large dining rooms can be stiff and cold. To warm up the atmosphere, dim the chandelier with a rheostat. Seat an extra guest or two around your table or use several tables close together. (See "Choosing a table," earlier in this chapter, for appropriate table sizes.)

For a large dinner, use several tables in different rooms. But be careful when you use this strategy; put two or more tables in each location so that guests don't feel isolated or out of place. Do *not* put one table in every room. This grave error kills your party faster than arsenic in the appetizers. Guests may feel like they're stranded in Siberia or not at the best table, and they aren't able to eavesdrop on another conversation or catch the laughter of the party.

Alternative spaces

Regardless of where you live or the size of your home, no space is off-limits. You can use every room of your house, including the bedroom, the bathroom, the deck, the roof, or the elevator to enhance the atmosphere or expand your capacity.

The kitchen

Dinners in your kitchen allow you to enjoy the company from beginning to end. For guests, the atmosphere is warm and friendly and may even be a trip back in time to the pot-watching, spoon-licking days of another era.

Two things are essential when you serve in your kitchen:

- Keep the sink clean.
- Keep the light on the table, not the dirty countertops.

Do not wash dishes during the party. Washing dishes can make guests feel uncomfortable or obligated to help. Put the dishes in a small soapy tub or right into the dishwasher.

Setting the scene

Certain moods prevail, depending on the surrounding space. For example, if you want people to dance, choose a small space, such as a front hallway for the dance floor. People love to be crowded together for dancing. If the space is too big (or the lights are too bright), no one will dance. Think of how you want guests to feel and choose a setting to support that vision.

For Guests to Feel	Choose This Setting
Elegant	Candlelit dining room
Cozy	Library, den, or any room filled with books
	Table in front of the fireplace
	Kitchen
Energized	Space too small for the crowd
	Every room of the house
Relaxed	Outdoors on a perfect day
	Deck with a view of mountains or water
	Anywhere the sun sets
Breathless	A rooftop in a big city
	House-to-house progressive dinner
Romantic	Any room of the house where you don't normally dine
	Hotel suite
	Anywhere under the stars
Surprised	Bedroom
	Bathroom
	Elevator (get permission to use the Stop button)

The kitchen is a cool place to hang out, even if you never cook. In a few big-city restaurants with well-known chefs, the most sought after table is one set up in the kitchen. A top publisher frequently uses his kitchen for dinner parties. The informality of the setting disarms people and immediately makes guests feel comfortable and relaxed.

The bedroom

Unless your goal is matchmaking and you're sure that both parties are good sports, don't banish guests to the bedroom without a little forethought. Again, setting up more than one table is important. Even if you're only sending a few guests to the bedroom, two tables are better than one. Your aim is not to inspire kinky thoughts but to make people comfortable.

The bathroom

Sending guests to the bathroom only works if your bathroom is fabulous and (scrupulously clean) and if you have more than one bathroom. If the room is spectacular — with a claw-footed tub, imported marble, or mirrored walls — then you have a reason to show it off.

Creative ways to entertain in the bathroom include

- Putting the bar in the bathtub (fill the bathtub with ice to keep drinks cold)
- Setting up a buffet on the long sink counter with candles reflecting in the mirror

Some people may think that entertaining in the bathroom is crude or totally inappropriate and may not find the thought funny at all. But it's your party, and you're entitled to a little fun. Just be sure to point the way to another functional bathroom for the usual purposes.

The roof

Sitting above the traffic with an overview of the city lights, rooftops, parks, and rivers is wonderful. The key to a successful rooftop party is organization and simplicity. Make sure that you have everything you need on the roof: bar, ice, grill, food, and bathroom facilities nearby. You don't want guests climbing up and down dangerous stairs, especially after more than one drink.

Space-wise

A woman we know who lives in a small house gave a large Christmas party. She set up a buffet and tables with placecards in every room of the house. One of her guests was an over-bearing man who got along with no one. She invited him because he was a "big shot" (CEO of a Fortune 100 corporation), and because his wife was her tennis partner. She seated him at the table in the marbled, mirrored, orchid-filled bathroom. His seat was closest to the toilet — maybe a hint to relax. He may have been shocked and surprised, but we admire the hostess for her clever use of space.

Keep the menu simple. You can serve fancy deli food or have guests contribute their favorite dishes while you provide the drinks and ice. Put all the food on one table and have guests help themselves.

Don't forget to dust off soot before guests arrive. Provide trash containers and ashtrays so that people don't feel compelled to fling garbage or flick butts over the side.

If your chosen roof is a multifamily dwelling or public building, you may want to check city ordinances and regime rules before planning a "top of the world" party.

The great outdoors

Don't forget your outdoor space. Whether your party is formal or casual, consider having some part of the party outdoors if the weather is nice: cocktails on the patio, dancing on the deck, tea in the garden, and so on. Or plan the whole party outdoors. Your own backyard can be the perfect setting for a cookout or picnic.

If you're planning a picnic and want to get away from home, or if you don't have a yard, the possibilities are endless. Half the fun is finding a place. Use your critical eye and inventive brain. Drive around and discover perfect places for picnics. The ultimate picnic is near water. If you can watch birds, listen to streams, and smell the woods, you've found utopia. Here are some more places to picnic:

- A clearing in a forest
- The side of a mountain
- A field of wildflowers
- A courtyard
- A public park
- A lake or riverbank
- A dock
- A beach

Picnics don't have to be daytime events. Wait until after dark and use the magic of moonlight to transform your chosen space into a romantic setting.

Whatever setting you choose for your outdoor party, be sure to visit the site beforehand to determine how you can set up and serve. Determine where people can sit. Are picnic tables or benches in the area? If not, are logs or stones available for sitting? Do you need to bring folding chairs, blankets, pillows, or quilts? Do you have an alternative setting in mind in case of bad weather? For more ideas on planning a perfect picnic, see Chapter 13.

Renting Space

Sometimes you need more space than you have available in your home or neighborhood. When you search for space to rent, the first and most crucial consideration is the reason for the party and the formality of it. A setting appropriate for a company barbecue or family reunion may not be the best place for a wedding reception or your great-grandmother's 100th birthday party.

Finding space

When you choose a space, take time to find something different, such as a diner, barn, boat, museum, lobby, historic home, aquarium, or zoo. Or you can take over a restaurant if it has the right feel. An eccentric setting can be perfect.

Next, consider the size of your party: You want everyone to fit in one room. But if you rent a palace, make sure that you invite enough people to fill it. Too much space is the kiss of death to your party. By the same token, don't rent a space that is divided into several little rooms. Even if they connect, the party is disjointed and dull. Huge doors or columns dividing the space can be fine, as long as people aren't cut off and the traffic can flow.

Noise level and sound are also important considerations. Your choice of settings can be the difference in a comfortable buzz of conversation and an ear-splitting, nerve-shattering racket. The best way to check the acoustics is to go into the room when it is in use. If that isn't possible, check to see that the room has rugs, drapes, or fabric on the walls to absorb sound.

Renting a tent

Renting a tent is another way of creating and expanding your available space. A tent is also a perfect solution for large outdoor parties when you want protection against the weather. There are tents, and there are *tents*. Some have beautifully designed roofs and/or special clear sides for views. This type of tent may be just what you want for a wedding or other formal event. Other tents are nothing fancy, but are exactly what you need for a barbecue or other casual event. Of course, you pay for what you get, so expect an elaborate tent to set you back more than a plain one. But for a once-in-a-lifetime special event, the difference in the tent can be what makes the party extraordinary and unforgettable.

To find tent companies, ask people who entertain frequently, consult the Yellow Pages of your telephone directory, or research tents on the Internet. Just because the company is not based in or near your town doesn't mean that you can't rent their tents. Many companies deliver and set up tents throughout entire regions. If you live in a small town, look for a tent company in the nearest big city.

If you are planning to rent a tent for your party, start looking for it months in advance, especially if your party is during wedding season (spring or summer). When you contact tent companies, request a brochure with sizes, types, photographs, formulas for figuring out how many people the tent can accommodate, and a price list. You can also ask about choices of siding. Choose a solid tent to block the view of the surrounding area. Otherwise, you can opt for a tent with French windows or stripes of solid and clear material.

Most tent companies offer at least three sizes. The size you need depends on the event and whether guests will be standing or seated at tables, and/or if you plan on including a dance floor. For a canopy over the bar, rent a small tent (10 feet by 10 feet or 3 meters by 3 meters).

Rental companies tend to overestimate the size you need and recommend the biggest tent they have to offer. People are happier closer together than too far apart. Unless you're bringing in Ringling Brothers for entertainment, erring on the small side is better than going for the big top. (Ditto for dance floors. Too small is better than too big.)

Give extra thought to the weather, how you can heat or air-condition the space, what kind of flooring you need, and how you can decorate. Many tent companies can provide everything. (When you rent the tent, be sure to understand exactly what services are included in the price and what costs extra.) Other companies specialize in tents only. Ask them to recommend other specialists who can help you with flooring, lighting, sound, temperature, decorating, and any other service you may need. Any professionals you have hired for lighting or sound should be present throughout the party in case anything goes wrong. Ask someone from the tent company to be there as well.

As with any party, lighting is a key factor. For a fancy party, hire a professional lighting expert if you can. Inform him of the colors of the tablecloths, flowers, chairs, and so on. Discuss the type of event you are having and ask for advice about lighting. If you can't afford to hire someone or if no lighting expert is available, have the tent set up the day before and experiment with the lights that night. The tent company may be able to offer advice.

If restroom facilities are not available nearby, or if you don't want people going into your house, rent a portable toilet, sometimes called a Port-O-Potty or Port-O-Let. They don't all look like the miniature outhouses you see at construction sites. Some are beautiful, with sinks, privacy doors, and toilets that flush. Look under "Toilets-Portable," in the Yellow Pages of your telephone directory and call to find out what's available.

Moving People through Space

Creative use of space can mean the difference in crowded or cozy, dull or delightful. When you plan how to use your space, keep two things in mind:

- ✓ The kind of mood you want to create
- ✓ How you want your party to progress

Using your space isn't about two rooms or 20, but about how you divide your space and move people around.

When you choose a setting for your party, picture how you can use the space to move people around. You don't have to be a rocket scientist to move people through space. The trick is to create a natural progression that promotes mixing, mingling, and moving. To do so, think about dividing your party and your space into two or three segments so that your guests aren't stuck in one spot all evening. For example, if you're having a luncheon or dinner party in your home, you can divide the segments like this:

- ✓ **Drinks:** It's a universal law that people bunch together at the bar, front door, or kitchen at the beginning of a party. Crowding together this way makes people comfortable, giving them a chance to find their niche and figure out whom they want to talk to. So set up the drinks in the area where you want people to congregate before the meal. Depending on the formality of your party and the atmosphere that you want to create, you may choose your living area, outside on a patio, or in your kitchen with guests watching you cook. Guests may take a while, but they settle into the space you want them in sooner or later. No need to issue orders — they will come.

- ✓ **Meal:** Move guests away from the drink area. Even if you live in an efficiency apartment or have a combination kitchen/living/dining area, you can create the illusion of a different space. One of the easiest and best ways to accomplish this illusion is with lighting: Use electric lighting during drinks and then lower the lights and use candles during the meal. If guests have been standing, the simple act of seating them and changing the lighting makes the space seem different.

Low lights and flickering candles can transform a dump into a cozy den. See Chapter 6 for more tips on effective use of lighting.

✔ **Coffee:** If you want to liven things up a bit and prolong the evening, get the guests up and moving to a different area for coffee. Move them away from the mess of dinner into a clean space with a different atmosphere — a patio, terrace, or living area. Ideally, you want to move your guests to a different space from where they had drinks (which is still a mess — unless you hired help, bribed the children, or quickly threw it all under the sofa). If your space is limited (you have nowhere else to go) and your party is large, consider moving one guest from each table — an effective tactic for refreshing conversations and changing the pace without having to move the entire party. See Chapter 2 for more tips on how to pull off this maneuver.

If you want to shorten the evening, stay at the table for coffee. Guests can relax and continue their conversations. But after a while, when their fannies begin to ache, they will have the urge to get up and stretch. If you don't offer to move the party somewhere else, the guests will leave.

Be careful not to move the whole group so many times that you begin to look and feel like a traffic cop. Three moves is a good maximum.

If you're having a cocktail party, buffet, large tea, or any other party with no sit-down meal, get guests moving by serving food in one room, drinks in another, and coffee and sweets in still another. Alternate dim and bright lighting for a different atmosphere in each space.

Be sure to provide seating in some areas for people who are in deep conversations or who may just be more comfortable sitting down. This tip is especially important if any of the guests are elderly or handicapped, drinking too much, or wearing very high heels.

For the ultimate use of space, open up your whole house. Don't make any room off-limits. By doing so, you create a sense of freedom and fun. A large party becomes intimate and cozy as you open your home, your life, and yourself to your guests.

Chapter 6
Creating the Atmosphere

● ●

In This Chapter

▶ Imagining the atmosphere you want

▶ Zeroing in on guests' senses

▶ Offering a welcome touch

▶ Adding visual appeal

▶ Engaging ears

▶ Stimulating the sense of smell

▶ Waking up the taste buds

● ●

A successful party is more than the sum of the food and drink. It's the atmosphere and ambiance you create with a warm welcome, soothing lights, compelling aromas, and absorbing conversations.

The good news is that any person in the world can give dazzling parties. Whether you spend a pittance or a fortune, live in a two-room apartment or a penthouse, you have the same tools available (free of charge) to create the atmosphere and make your party unforgettable: your own imagination and the guests' five senses.

You may be thinking, "Oh no, not five more things to worry about." Don't worry, because your guests' senses become involved naturally, whether you plan it or not. But with a tiny bit of extra thought, you can make a good party better or a great party sensational by enthralling each sense of every guest.

In this chapter, we show you some simple ways to create the atmosphere you want by involving all five senses. Guests won't be aware that you knowingly stimulated their senses, yet they can be affected subtly but powerfully. An hour, a week, or a year later, they will remember your party because their senses were captivated.

It's All in Your Imagination

Just because you're serving smoked salmon imported from Nova Scotia or are pouring expensive liquor does not mean your party automatically will be a success. It takes more than handling the details (such as buying a beautiful tablecloth or sending fancy invitations) to give an incredible party. A few flowers alone do not make an "atmosphere."

Creating the atmosphere for a party begins in the mind and imagination of the host. It requires a vision and an overriding view. The people are the stars of your party and should not be outdone by any props. But that doesn't mean details don't count. They do. The key is to use the details to appeal to guests senses. From the guest list to the music, from the cutlery to the lighting, and from the raw ingredients to the final food presentation, approach every detail with a sense of excitement and adventure. Only by using your own imagination can you create an atmosphere that taps into the minds and imaginations of your guests.

Targeting the Five Senses

The beginning of all human knowledge is through the senses. We interpret life through what we see, hear, smell, taste, and feel. The pleasure of a party depends to a great extent on how the senses are stimulated.

When organizing your party, think for a few minutes about how you can involve guests' senses easily, directly, and purposely.

- ✔ Will you greet them with a warm touch? Will they have something to do with their hands?
- ✔ Will their eyes linger on something?
- ✔ Will their ears hear fascinating conversations?
- ✔ Will the aromas tantalize their appetites?
- ✔ Will their taste buds be awakened with something delicious?

If your answer to each of these questions is, "Yes, sort of, or maybe, " then you are on your way to a successful party. You don't have to plan all of this. In fact, you don't have to do any of it because the senses respond to your party automatically.

But if you want your guests to have an unforgettable memory of your party, delve a little deeper and think of ways to zero in on each sense. Use the senses like a secret weapon. Plan to attack your guests' senses, not in a forceful way, but more like a stealth bomber. People will leave your party knowing they had a great time but won't quite be able to put a finger on what made it so wonderful.

When planning your assault on the senses, consider all angles. People are attracted to different things in various degrees. A guest with a highly developed sense of taste may focus on the food. Someone with a finely tuned sense of hearing most likely picks up on conversations, music, and other sounds of the party. The visually oriented eye their surroundings and may be drawn by things others hardly notice. To appeal to all guests, it is important to target each of the five senses.

Using the Sense of Touch

One of the simplest and best ways to make guests feel at ease is to reach out and touch them at the beginning of the party. To create a lasting memory of warm affection and a welcome heart, use the sense of touch when guests arrive. Besides telling guests you are glad to see them, let them *feel* how thrilled you are that they're there.

Making guests comfortable

Planning a secret assault on the senses is great fun for the host, but your most important consideration is your guests' comfort. From the moment they walk in your door, your number one objective is to make people feel comfortable inside and out.

If you don't do anything else to engage the senses, use them fundamentally to establish a comfortable atmosphere:

- ✔ Greet guests warmly
- ✔ Offer them something to drink right away
- ✔ Introduce them to others to start conversation
- ✔ Provide comfortable seating
- ✔ Keep room temperature comfortable

By setting up the surrounding so that people are comfortable, you give guests the opportunity to relax and be themselves. They leave thinking how attractive and charming they were, not knowing that your genius had anything to do with it.

In order for guests to be truly comfortable, you must be comfortable yourself.

- ✔ Get organized so that you can relax and feel good on the inside.
- ✔ Wear something that makes you feel comfortable on the outside.

If you're a natural toucher, go ahead and greet your guests with a hug, squeeze, or kiss.

Take the touchy-feely approach only if you are a natural born toucher and if your guests know you to be that way. Otherwise, hugging and kissing can seem insincere and awkward.

If hugging and kissing are not your style, you can still use touch effectively. Touch the small of a guest's back, touch his sleeve — any gesture that lets that person know you are delighted to be with him. At a loud party, when talking to a guest, you can put your hand on his elbow and lean in to say something. Most people are receptive to that kind of touch — it's not intrusive.

Following are a few more ways to add more touching and feeling to your party:

✔ Seat too many guests at one table so elbows and shoulders touch. (Do this at a casual party, not a formal affair or business dinner.)

✔ Feed a bite of food directly into a guest's mouth with your fingers. (Save this for family, close friends, or lovers — those you are sure will not be offended.)

✔ Put on some music that makes people feel like dancing. Watch all the senses go wild.

Beyond people touching people, demand that guests use their sense of touch in other ways. Force them to get actively involved.

Creating opportunities to use the sense of touch helps people relax and can smooth out awkward lulls at the beginning of the party. Offer guests a drink when they arrive so they have something to do with their hands.

Here are some other simple ways to involve your guests' sense of touch:

✔ Let guests help make drinks, pour cocktails, or mix up their own concoctions.

✔ Solicit someone to pass hors d'oeuvres.

✔ Choose someone to stir a sauce.

✔ Ask a guest to help put food on a plate.

✔ Let guests serve themselves (from your kitchen or a buffet).

✔ Serve food that must be attacked with a fork and knife, slurped with a spoon, or eaten with the hands.

People love to get involved in creating the meal. Let guests make homemade pizzas or pasta. You may end up with a migraine and a huge mess, but everyone will be best friends at the end. (See Chapter 13 for details on how to pull off a "make it yourself" meal.)

Appealing to the Sense of Sight

Think of the sense of sight as an open opportunity. You can use anything to appeal to guests' visual sense. Silver, crystal, and flowers draw eyes, but so does a sunset, a campfire, the view out the window, the color of the room, the pictures on the wall, and the excited, receptive look of other guests.

Bewitch guests' eyes with the total surroundings. Use everything around you as a possible attraction:

- Candlelight
- Centerpieces
- The food on the plates
- A sunset
- Your clothes

One of the easiest but most powerful ways to affect the sense of sight is by adjusting the light. Although the wrong lighting won't necessarily deem your party a total disaster, the right lighting can work wonders for the atmosphere.

Spend a few minutes the night before your party deciding how lighting can work for you. The goal is to flatter people and create an aura of magic. Offer eyes a break from bright sunlight or the harsh fluorescence of offices and stores. Soften the atmosphere by lowering the light.

In addition to enhancing the atmosphere, lowering the lights

- Calms nerves.
- Softens appearances. (Nothing is more aging than fluorescent light.)
- Makes any room look more beautiful.

For dinner parties, turn down the lighting. Turn off or dim overhead lights. Use lamps and/or candles to adjust to a happy medium. Guests should be able to see their food, but crows feet and laugh lines should fade to the background. For maximum control, fine-tune your lighting with dimmers or rheostats. If your lights don't have dimmers, you can purchase them at your local hardware, lighting, or discount store. The cost is minimal and you can install the devices yourself.

Not into do-it-yourself home improvement projects? If you can change a light bulb, you can adjust your lighting. Simply buy some low-wattage (25–40 watt) bulbs. Experiment by using the bulbs alone or combining them with candlelight.

Choose colored bulbs to achieve special effects:

- ✔ Pink or peach soften faces — makes people look healthier and younger.
- ✔ Amber gives a warm glow like candlelight — makes eyes and jewelry sparkle.
- ✔ Red can be dramatic in the right space — a ceiling lighted red looks sensational.

Blue or green lights make people look tired. Use them only when you need to feign illness. Save yellow for zapping bugs outdoors.

Cocktail parties or large gatherings can stand to be a little brighter. The level of energy goes up with the level of lighting. Use brighter lights to highlight areas where you want people to congregate.

However, increasing the lighting does not mean you should use lights so bright they could foil a prison escape. We said a *little* brighter, not a lot.

For an atmosphere of mystery, intrigue, or romance, dine outside under the stars. Use glowing candles to illuminate the tables and a few flares to define the space. Let the full moon work for you. You save electricity, but your party is fully charged.

Engaging the Sense of Hearing

The most effective way to enchant guests' ears is by inviting interesting people so that stimulating conversation becomes the main attraction. If you invite the most fascinating people you know, guests ears will get a wonderful workout. (See Chapter 2 if you need some pointers on how to shape a guest list.)

The magic of candlelight

Nothing surpasses the quality of light that you get with candles. Candlelight is muted, yet alive, flickering and dancing, not static. It adds instant intimacy and can transform the atmosphere of an ordinary room to a world of enchantment.

Advantages of candlelight:

- Guests look fabulous and feel more comfortable
- Food looks more appealing
- Dust disappears

All candles are glorious. For elegance, choose tall tapers. Keep the candles in proportion to the candlesticks (the same height as the candlesticks or shorter). For a less formal effect, use columns or votives.

You can adjust the amount of light with the number of candles you use. Place candles in front of mirrors to reflect more light, or behind beveled glass to refract and subdue it.

For a night no one will ever forget, turn off the light switch and use a zillion candles instead. Eyes will sparkle, and guests will glow. Short of pulling a rabbit out of a hat, this is the best magic you can perform at your party.

If you prefer dripless candles, put them in the freezer for 24 hours. You can then remove and store them at room temperature until ready to use. It doesn't matter how far in advance you do this. After the candles have been through the freezing process, they should never drip.

Take precautions when using many candles. Position them so that they are not likely to get bumped into or knocked over, and keep them away from flammables such as drapes, dried flower arrangements, and other decorations. Snuff out candles before you leave the room. Keep a few fire extinguishers on hand, and keep the fire department phone number near the phone just in case.

Other sounds that can enhance your atmosphere include:

- The pop of the cork from the champagne
- Meat searing in a hot pan or on a hot grill
- Wood crackling in a fireplace or a bonfire
- Music

Music can be a wonderful addition to a party. You can use it as entertainment or as a simple background effect. If your party is large and music is a main attraction, see Chapter 15 for tips and suggestions.

When using music as a background for smaller parties, be careful that it doesn't become overwhelming. It should never be so loud that it interferes with conversation.

Choose music carefully. Consider your guests and the atmosphere you intend to create. Snoop Doggy Dogg may be all right for your teen's birthday bash, but not necessarily appropriate for dinner with your in-laws. Use your own taste in music combined with what you know about your guests to create the desired atmosphere.

Classical music is lovely for a special dinner party. In fact, Georg Philipp Telemann wrote music especially for banquets in the first half of the eighteenth century.

For a cocktail party, you can't go wrong with jazz. Actually, jazz is appropriate for most any party, especially when guests are arriving and during the cocktail hour. Jazz can set up a lively atmosphere.

The most spirited and fascinating parties require no music at all. If guests are intrigued by the company, they won't notice the lack of music. A lively party makes its own music, with the harmony of many voices and the steady rhythm of laughter.

Take a moment to listen to your party. Your ears can tell if guests are enjoying themselves and if the party is a raging success.

Don't panic if you hear a lull. Parties generally have a sound pause about a half hour after starting, almost as if the guests are taking a collective deep breath. While the sound of silence can seem like forever to the host, it's really only a moment before guests get right back into it. Expect volume to fluctuate — it's part of the natural noise rhythm of the party.

Delighting the Sense of Smell

The quickest way to whet an appetite is to plan a strategic assault on the nose. Tantalize with the sense of smell from the moment your guests walk in the door. Think ahead when planning your party. Get something in the oven as guests are arriving. You want them to start inhaling.

- ✔ Open the kitchen door.
- ✔ Let guests hang out in the kitchen so the aromas excite them.
- ✔ Bake dessert while guests eat dinner.
- ✔ Reheat cookies during the meal to serve with coffee after dinner.

At most parties, you want the food and wine to be the major olfactory attractions. Aromas are especially important when serving fine wines. The nose (smell) of a fine wine unfolds throughout the meal as it changes temperature. Some wines are light, some full-bodied, some ethereal and delicate, others powerful; but all can be camouflaged or overpowered by strong odors in the room. You want guests to get a good whiff of a great wine.

Aromas that drive guests to distraction

Any of the following will entice guests' sense of smell as they arrive at your party:

✔ Bread baking

✔ Meat roasting

✔ Onions/garlic simmering in olive oil

✔ Anything sweet baking

✔ Oranges and cinnamon simmering

✔ Coffee brewing

Fully ripe fruit also emits a wonderful sweet aroma. Use it as a decoration or centerpiece in a basket, bowl, or on a platter.

Rich chocolate cakes and some citrus cakes emit a heady perfume when cut. For the full effect, allow the cake to come to room temperature and slice it at the table.

Use extreme care with any scents other than the food and wine. Flowers can be delightful, but too many flowers can make a dining room smell like a funeral parlor. (Most white flowers emit a particularly strong smell.) Choose unscented candles and flowers for the table.

Be extra cautious when using artificial fragrances:

✔ Don't wear so much perfume or cologne that guests need a gas mask.

✔ Reschedule pest control.

✔ Stay away from overpowering room fresheners.

✔ Don't use incense right before your party.

A crackling fire in winter is a scent enhancer with an added bonus of sound, warmth, and light. If you have a gas fireplace, toss in a handful of pine cones to add fragrance and add some snapping sounds to the flame. The front of a lit fireplace is the perfect place for cocktails, coffee, or a cozy afternoon tea.

Bombarding the Sense of Taste

What looks good and smells good should taste like heaven on earth. You can choose from many methods to awaken taste buds.

✔ Excite the mouth with something spicy or exotic.

✔ Surprise the throat with cold and hot foods.

  ✔ Soothe the palate with down-home comfort food.

  ✔ Arouse the taste buds with a sensual meal.

If you need help choosing foods, see Chapter 18, which offers a wide variety of menus or look back at Chapter 8 for ways to balance out your menu selections.

Naturally, you want the guests to enjoy the taste and smell of the food you serve. But with careful planning, your menu can affect all the senses; the menu in Figure 6-1 is one example.

The aromas produced by the Grand Marnier soufflé in Figure 6-1 permeate the whole house, and the presentation amazes guests. (For an easy-to-follow, delicious recipe, check out *Cooking For Dummies,* by Bryan Miller and Marie Rama, IDG Books Worldwide, Inc.)

You don't have to serve a four-course meal or complicated food to delight all the senses. The simplest menu can just as easily have the same effect. Serve:

  ✔ The very best bread, homemade or fresh from the bakery (touch)

  ✔ Crisp crackers (sound)

  ✔ Perfectly ripe fruit (color, shape, smell)

  ✔ Rich cheeses served at room temperature (texture)

  ✔ Fabulous wine (color, aroma)

This is a portable feast that can work in any setting. It is a refreshing change from the menu of overabundance, allowing guests to linger and enjoy every sensation.

Menu for All Senses

Puree of corn soup garnished with strips of
Smithfield ham

(smooth in the mouth, salty on the tongue)

&

Fresh artichokes

(a tactile experience)

&

Poached salmon served on a bed of spinach
Saffron Rice

Roasted red peppers

(a riot of colors; a feast for the eyes)

&

Grand Marnier Soufflé

(permeates the whole house with a tempting
aroma and amazes guests with its
presentation)

Biscotti

(guests use fingers to dunk in coffee)

Coffee

(emits a delightful aroma while brewing—
a warm way to end the meal)

&

Champagne

(The pop of the cork will perk up guests' ears.
Delicate bubbles will tickle and lighten heads
and attitudes.)

Figure 6-1:
This menu
is an all-out
assault on
guests'
senses.

"Come quickly. I am drinking stars." — Dom Perignon, upon drinking his first
creation

Part II
Eating and Drinking

In this part . . .

There's no denying that eating and drinking are a big part of entertaining. But whether you love to cook, hate to cook, or simply refuse to cook, we have the perfect solution for feeding your guests. We begin this part by suggesting several starting points for making a menu. Then, we help you flesh it out and balance it. You find ideas to fit your busy lifestyle and your budget.

Next, we guide you through your drink selections from cocktails to coffee. We show you how to set up a complete and functional bar, giving you tips on how and when to serve what. We even offer advice for what to do about the guy who is staggering across the room with his car keys in hand.

Chapter 7
Dreaming Up the Perfect Menu

· ·

In This Chapter

▶ Making menu choices

▶ Clueing in to the weather

▶ Indulging individuals

▶ Using the occasion as a guide

▶ Developing a central theme

▶ Turning out a meal without turning on the range

· ·

There are as many ways to approach menu making as there are imaginations. A starting point can be the season or the weather, your favorite food, a guest's special request, the occasion for the party, or something totally playful, such as a theme. The fun and joy in making menus is finding different solutions to the same puzzle. In this chapter, we give you some tried and true methods to help you get started. In the next chapter, you delve deeper and discover how to balance your menu. We even have suggestions for those of you who hate, dislike, or simply refuse to cook.

Decisions, Decisions

Does the thought of making the menu paralyze you with fear and indecision? Maybe you feel insecure about your cooking skills, or perhaps the number of choices is overwhelming. Maybe you just aren't sure which foods go together well.

Before you consider canceling your party, remember two things:

✔ **No one is expecting a five-star meal at your house.** You are not competing with your guests' favorite restaurants.

✔ **Menu-making can be fun.** In fact, making menus can be one of the most wild and creative diversions you can find without leaving home or breaking the law.

Making a menu requires you to make a few decisions. *When* you begin to make those decisions depends on what kind of party you are giving and what kind of person you are. If you are giving a large and/or elaborate party or if you are inexperienced or unsure of yourself, start thinking of a menu when you invite your guests. If you are giving a small and/or casual party, or if you are a relaxed, laid-back person, you may be able to throw together a menu at the last minute. (See Chapter 3 for tips on organizing your time.)

Sometimes, getting a start on your menu depends on what inspires you. Any one of the following may be the perfect time to make your menu:

✔ When you invite your guests and think of what they like

✔ When you stop at the food store and see what looks good

✔ When you see a recipe you want to try

If you are still stuck for a menu idea and just can't seem to get started, read on for more inspiration.

Considering the Season and the Weather

One of the first things that hits people everyday is the weather. Climate affects attitudes and appetites, so why not use it as a starting point for your menu? You can either match the food to the weather or add an element of surprise by contrasting it.

To match the weather, approach making the menu the same way you decide what to wear in the morning: Take a look outside. You certainly wouldn't wear a wool sweater in a heat wave or a bikini in a snowstorm. By the same token, people don't want to look at a steaming bowl of chili when the temperature is 90 degrees, and sorbet doesn't seem right if it's cold and wet outside.

Ask yourself the following questions, and build the menu around your answers:

✔ What does the weather make me feel like eating?

✔ Which foods are associated with the current season?

✔ What foods are freshest this time of year?

You can never go wrong choosing foods appropriate for the season. That's when they are available, ripe, fresh, and beautiful. Specific foods come to mind during certain times of year, and taste buds are conditioned for them. The following are some examples of seasonal foods where we live; they may not be seasonal for you:

- **Spring:** Lamb, salmon, artichokes, asparagus, sweet peppers, zucchini, rhubarb, raspberries, strawberries

- **Summer:** Lobster, grouper, arugula, scallions, watercress, eggplant, tomatoes, squash, peas, basil, corn, watermelon, peaches, apricots, blackberries, cherries

- **Fall:** Steak, game, cabbage, garlic, cauliflower, mushrooms, pumpkins, apples, chestnuts, cranberries, figs, grapes, pears, walnuts

- **Winter:** Beef, pork, ribs, clams, scallops, broccoli, Brussels sprouts, potatoes, oranges, grapefruit, pineapple, collard greens, fennel, parsnips, radishes, spinach, turnips, dried fruits, kiwi

To find out what food is at its best in your area, just take a quick trip to your local grocery store and check out the produce section. What looks the freshest and is most plentiful? If you can get only tiny, weird-looking strawberries that cost $5 a pound, you may want to use oranges in your menu instead.

Of course, in some places, some foods are simply not available during certain seasons. There is no point in planning to make a peach pie in the middle of the winter.

However, if your heart is set on a particular ingredient that isn't in season, you can consider the freezer section. Foods that have been flash-frozen at their peak can taste wonderful — sometimes better than "fresh." For example: corn on the cob, when flash-frozen, can taste better than non-frozen fresh corn that was picked a few days earlier.

Different seasons conjure up not only different foods, but different cooking methods as well. In cold weather, warm up by roasting, baking, and slow simmering. In warmer months, cool off by chilling, grilling, and poaching.

Year-round choices

Some foods are available all year. You can match them to any season, depending on your choice of cooking method and accompaniments.

For example, you can find chicken anywhere anytime. By changing the method of preparation and the side dishes, the taste can change to match the season. The following are four simple menus based on chicken with seasonal accompaniments and a fresh fruit of the season for dessert:

✔ **Spring:**

- Chicken kabobs marinated in mint and yogurt, basmati rice, asparagus

- Raspberry sorbet, raspberries, and shortbread

✔ **Summer:**

- Fried chicken, corn on the cob, tomatoes and basil, green beans, biscuits

- Fresh peach and blueberry cobbler

✔ **Fall:**

- Roast chicken, garlic mashed potatoes, red cabbage

- Baked apples

✔ **Winter:**

- Chicken pot pie, endive and walnut salad

- Pears poached in red wine

Get fresh

By taking charge of menus, you take control of your health by limiting salt, preservatives, and chemicals in your choices. Gathering food, whether it's picking vegetables in a field or finding fresh produce in the grocery store, connects us to the earth. What foods of the season are readily available in your area? Create a menu that celebrates what is fresh and what is around you.

✔ If you are a fisherman, the best freshness guarantee is to reel in your own dinner.

✔ If it's hunting season, treat your guests to a stew of quail, game pie, or spaghetti sauce made with venison.

✔ If your garden grows something other than weeds, use your best-looking vegetable as a theme. Use the produce as a centerpiece; puree it in the soup; toss it in the salad; and make it a part of the main course. That's creative. That's using your imagination.

Note: If you are not into baiting hooks, hiding out in tree stands, or getting your hands dirty, you can accomplish the same thing at the fish market, the butcher shop, or the farmer's market. Whether it is fruit, vegetables, meat, or fish, you can never go wrong when you go for the freshest food in town.

Ground beef is also a practical, year-round choice that you can serve in a number of ways.

- ✔ **Spring:** Taco salad
- ✔ **Summer:** Hamburgers
- ✔ **Fall:** Meatballs
- ✔ **Winter:** Chili

Just because a food is available doesn't necessarily mean you want to serve it off-season. For example, winter-gassed tomatoes never taste ripe and juicy, no matter what you do to them.

Tricking palates

To put a different twist on a seasonal menu, trick people's palates by serving food that doesn't necessarily match the weather but goes with the season. Surprising people's taste buds can bring back memories or create longings. For example, if you live in Florida and your guests are from a place where it is normally cold in the wintertime, beef stew cooked in red wine will taste delicious and appropriate to them in January, even if it's a warm, sunny day. The guests will associate the food with winter months and winter memories.

In the dead of winter, when the air is cold and the skies are gray, people may not feel like leaving the house. So why not surprise them with a menu to uplift their spirits? No one will expect the combination of lime daiquiris, grilled pineapple, pork loin, and coconut mango tart. That menu, however, can turn a freezing night in Minnesota into a three-hour tropical vacation. Tricking guests' tastes can be just what the doctor ordered.

Pleasing People

A common saying is "the fastest way to the heart is through the stomach." For a completely different approach to your menu, try planning it to make a particular someone happy. You can please yourself, your guests, or one special guest.

The easiest choice and one of the most common ways to make a menu is from your own viewpoint. What foods make *you* happy? What do you like to cook? What do you want to experiment with?

Choosing foods that you love to cook and eat is a practical and delightful solution to making a menu. This approach makes perfect sense because you know what you like and you know what you are comfortable cooking. If you enjoy eating the food you serve, most likely, the guests will, too. A menu that pleases you will always be successful.

Do you have a secret recipe for lasagna? Is your cheese soufflé the envy of the neighborhood? Are you the best barbecue chef in town? There is nothing wrong with serving your specialty every time you have guests. Rather, it is a brilliant idea because it simplifies your life. People will adore eating your famous dish and will look forward to having it again.

If repeatedly using the same recipes bores you — and if you are a confident cook, take the plunge and experiment. Trying new foods on your guests is exciting — it's a challenge for you, and it's fun for the guests. When you enjoy cooking, your guests can be happy guinea pigs.

While pleasing yourself is certainly gratifying, you may find it even more rewarding when you plan a menu with your guests' pleasure in mind. Think about who you are serving. Suppose that you are entertaining very sophisticated world travelers who are accustomed to eating exotic foods. Consider serving them "comfort food" — plain, ordinary home cooking, such as chicken soup, beef brisket, meatloaf, apple pie, and chocolate chip cookies. Your cosmopolitan guests will be surprised and grateful for the familiar tastes of home.

On the contrary, if you are serving someone known to be the meat and potatoes type, serve what he likes, but give him a little jolt by offering one course that is unusual, such as cold kiwi soup, edible flowers, sea urchins, or cardamom ice cream.

Don't worry that everyone will not like everything on the menu. A guest with dietary restriction or allergy will select the foods he can eat. A picky eater will stop at McDonald's on the way home.

The same applies if you are a vegetarian or vegan. Treat your meat-eating friends to your favorite dishes. You may introduce them to foods with which they are unfamiliar. Many guests will be surprised and delighted to see how satisfying a meatless meal can be.

If the thought of trying to please all of your guests seems overwhelming, you may want to concentrate on pleasing one particular guest — a special guest, someone you adore, or someone you really want to impress. A unique way to make a menu and one of the best ways to honor a guest is to offer to serve his or her favorite foods. Call the guest and tell her you want to cook her favorite meal. Ask her to provide the menu.

The fact that you are willing to take the time and trouble to create someone else's favorite meal is a gesture that person will never forget.

Guests' requests

When you ask someone what he wants for dinner, you may be surprised by the answer. The following are a few we've heard:

✔ **A meal my grandmother used to cook.** This person is after old-fashioned taste (cream, butter, eggs), not slimmed-down, updated versions. You may have to find some older cookbooks for recipes. The guest will re-live an evening of long ago and gain a new memory of a special evening with you.

✔ **Champagne.** This answer calls for a menu built around champagne. Get help from your wine merchant. Serve a different champagne with each course. Some recipes even call for champagne as an ingredient. The meal doesn't have to cost a fortune, but it will be an extraordinary one.

✔ **Exotic foods.** If a guest's request includes items that are impossible to find, local restaurants may be able to help you. If the menu totally intimidates you, prepare one of the items and forgo the rest.

Most people are very surprised when asked for their favorite menu and may not answer right away. However, don't take their reticence for displeasure. Instead, they are taking your question seriously and are already getting excited about coming to your party. Give them a little time to think about their special menu.

Some answers may relieve you. Others may intimidate or make you anxious. People are looking to recall a certain taste or feeling. The feeling may be easier to recreate than the specific taste because of a "secret ingredient" from an old family recipe that you don't know about. If the dish is so retro that you don't have the foggiest idea what it is and cannot even find a recipe for it, you may have to adapt something you are familiar with and know how to cook. The key is to listen to what the person wants and to match the meal as closely as possible with the guest's specific requests.

Suiting the Occasion

The reason for the party is another excellent starting point for making your menu. What is your party all about? Is it business, a celebration, or a gathering of friends? Sometimes the occasion itself is the best guide to what kind of food you should serve.

The following are some tips to help you evaluate the situation and the role you may want the food to play:

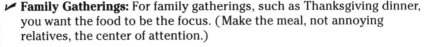

✔ **Family Gatherings:** For family gatherings, such as Thanksgiving dinner, you want the food to be the focus. (Make the meal, not annoying relatives, the center of attention.)

✔ **Business meals:** Food should not be the focus of business entertaining. Business meals are about communication, not pretentious or fancy food, which can distract from conversations. In business situations, the menu should be simple. Choose food that is easy to manage and doesn't require an array of utensils. Guests should not have to give the food a thought besides putting it in their mouths and enjoying the taste. Take a look at Chapter 17 for help with business entertaining and a list of "forbidden foods" for business meals.

✔ **Special occasions:** To celebrate and honor the people and events that have meaning in your life, choose foods that are special, luxurious, or favorites.

   • **Birthdays:** Plan to serve the birthday person's favorite meal.

   • **Anniversaries:** Serve champagne and everything that goes with it.

   • **Holidays:** Let tradition dictate, but don't be afraid to add a little something extra or different. (Look for holiday tips in Chapter 14.)

✔ **A gathering of friends:** If your guests are your favorite friends, you can do anything with the menu. You can serve sloppy food, finger food, or attention-getting food. You can go all out with the menu, serving multiple courses, and your best friends won't think that you're showing off. They'll be flattered that you went to so much trouble to please them.

If cooking is not your thing, serve sandwiches and beer. True friends don't care. The point to having a party is getting together and having fun.

Creating a Theme

If you really want to have some fun with your menu, consider developing it around a theme — not Mardi Gras, a birthday, or a holiday, but something more original. Think of a theme that is playful, such as a certain food, color, or nationality. When you approach menus this way, your own creativity may surprise you.

Highlight one food or flavor

An easy way to create a theme is to build the menu around a particular food or flavor. The menu can revolve around any food that lends itself to multiple methods of presentation. This technique is not something you would do every time you entertain. It's not obsessive, but a unique way to add a little fun and humor. Figures 7-1 through 7-3 show examples of menus that revolve around a food theme.

Salmon Four Ways

Smoked salmon on toast

Salmon mousse on cucumber rounds

ે

Salmon cakes

ે

Poached salmon

Peas

New potatoes

ે

Fruit tart

Salmon cookies

(Just kidding! Enough is enough...)

Figure 7-1:
Salmon is a
versatile
food that
you can
present in
many ways.

Garlic Lovers' Menu

Raw vegetables with garlic sauce (aioli)

ે

*Linguine served with garlic, olive oil,
and black pepper*

ે

Chicken stuffed with whole garlic

ે

Salad drizzled with Caesar dressing

ે

Vanilla ice cream

Figure 7-2:
If everyone
eats garlic,
no one will
notice
everyone
else's garlic
breath.
(Besides,
garlic does
not produce
dragon
breath
when it is
cooked.)

To get the most flavor out of garlic and to make for easier peeling, lightly smash the clove with the flat part of a knife before you peel and chop.

A Twist of Lemon

Greek lemon soup (avgolemono)

ða

Veal scallopini with lemon and capers

Spinach

Risotto

ða

Salad with olive oil and lemon

ða

Lemon mousse served in a hollowed out lemon

Lemon nut cookies dipped in chocolate

Figure 7-3:
The lemon is one of the most widely available and useful fruits. Always have a few on hand.

To get the most juice out of a lemon, roll it firmly on the counter with the palm of your hand before slicing.

Focus on color

Colors are also fun menu themes. Suppose that someone special finally gets a well-deserved and long-awaited raise? Why not celebrate the good news with a *green* menu? Take a look at color-themed menus in Figures 7-4 and 7-5.

Unless it's Saint Patrick's Day, don't artificially color all the food green. You are playing with food, not food coloring. The point is to show off the real color of the food, not to add something artificial. Guests may not notice your theme unless you point it out. Those who do will be in awe of your creative genius.

You don't need a specific reason to base your menu on a particular color. You can choose a color arbitrarily based on what stands out at the market, what looks good on your china, or just on a whim.

Figure 7-4:
Green is the color of money and of many delicious foods!

Green Menu

Spinach and scallion frittata

 za

Grilled marinated shrimp
Green rice with toasted pine nuts
Asparagus

za

Kiwi, green grapes, pistachio ice cream
Mint tea

Figure 7-5:
An all-red menu looks stunning on plain white china.

Red Menu

Tomato soup

za

Red snapper
Rosy mashed potatoes
(puréed red peppers mixed with
mashed potatoes)

za

Rhubarb pie with strawberry ice cream

Explore international avenues

Making a menu around an ethnic theme or a nationality can be a rich and rewarding experience. You can use your own roots as a starting point. Go back to your grandparents and beyond to discover your cultural heritage. Make a menu to reflect who you are.

If one grandparent came from Europe, one from Asia, one from Africa, and another from Mars, choose one of those cultures as a theme for your party. When you plan your meal around an ethnic theme, it's best to stick with one cuisine. Italian, French, Mexican, Chinese, or South American foods taste best on their own rather than mixed and matched.

If your relatives loved to cook, maybe you have some of their treasured recipes. If you're really lucky, your relatives passed on their skills and taught you their cooking techniques. But even if your ancestors never mastered the art of cooking, you can still find many sources (cookbooks, magazines, television, and Web sites) for menu ideas and recipes from different cultures.

If you have a computer with Internet access, the World Wide Web is an abundant source for recipes of all kinds. For recipes, food history, and food lore from all regions of the world, consult the Global Gastronomer at `www.cs.yale.edu/homes/hupfer/global/gastronomer.html`.

(For more information on recipe sources, see the section on choosing the right recipes in Chapter 8.)

Almost every culture features at least one fabulous casserole (not the kind made with leftovers and a can of soup, but real, authentic casseroles made with fresh ingredients). Casseroles are terrific for entertaining, because they can be made far in advance, can go from oven to table, and are perfect for family-style or buffet service. The following is a sampling of casseroles from around the world:

- Indian curry
- Ghanaian ground-nut stew
- Greek moussaka
- French cassoulet
- Spanish paella
- Brazilian black-bean stew

Holidays are the perfect opportunity to incorporate your past. By passing on traditions of your ancestors, your menu can be a living legacy — a gift to your children and to all future generations.

If delving into your past doesn't especially interest you, you can develop ethnic menus just for the fun of it. Here are a few ideas:

- Honor a friend with authentic dishes from his cultural heritage.
- Make a menu that centers on a country your child is studying in school.
- Browse through cookbooks that feature ethnic foods. Experiment with dishes that look or sound appealing.
- When you travel in foreign countries, take note of the different foods you enjoy. Ask for recipes from waiters and cooks. Then you can share the experience by duplicating these dishes for your guests back home.

No-Hassle and No-Cooking Menu Approaches

All this menu-planning may sound easy if you love (or even like) to cook. Some people use fear of cooking or a strong dislike for cooking as an excuse not to entertain. But even if you hate to cook or don't have time to cook, you can still invite friends over and serve them delicious food.

One solution is to serve something so simple (as in Figure 7-6) that anyone can prepare it — and so simple your guests are totally surprised.

Figure 7-6:
Your guests will love this menu, but it takes a confident party-giver to do something so unexpected.

An Astonishing Menu

Grilled cheese sandwiches

Ice cold beer

If you are not comfortable with such a simple offering, thousands of menu items are available for the totally hassled or non-cooking host. In the following sections, we offer some of the best solutions, from the very expensive to the practical and still wonderful.

Mail order

Call your favorite restaurants around the country or favorite mail-order food suppliers. Have gourmet items delivered overnight. (Restaurants and mail-order houses are happy to oblige. Dollar signs will reflect in their eyes as the money flies out of your bank account.) Just in case you don't already get enough catalogs in the mail, you can often find mail-order suppliers listed in the back of food magazines. See Appendix C in this book for a few of our favorites.

All the items on the menu in Figure 7-7 can be ordered through the mail and delivered to your door overnight.

Figure 7-7:
Try this
menu for
your next
party. You
may never
want to go
grocery
shopping
again!

Mail-Order Menu

Benne wafers

Smoked salmon

Buffalo steaks

Key lime pie
Champagne truffles

Caterers

Catering is a convenient option when you want to keep your kitchen and your hands clean. Hiring a caterer doesn't have to be costly. In fact, if your life is already jam packed with responsibilities, catering may be your most economical choice when you consider the value of your time. Contact someone you've heard of or who catered a party you attended. Know your budget and be explicit about what you want. If you are unsure about the items you want to put on your menu, some caterers offer taste tests for a minimal fee.

Good caterers can cook anything and can accommodate a party for two or two thousand. For more help on communicating with caterers, see Chapter 15.

Take-out and delivery

Let a menu beget a menu. If you have an impromptu party to prepare for, then make a beeline for your take-out-menu file. Call your favorite local restaurant or restaurants. Most can prepare take-out orders on request. You can order the entire meal from one restaurant or get the courses you love from different places. Pick it all up on your way home from work.

If you can't stand the thought of running all over town or simply don't have time to pick up the food, call your favorite restaurant that offers delivery service. Transfer the food to your dishes and no one will ever have to know that you didn't cook. It's up to you whether to tell the truth or take the credit yourself.

If the restaurant offers take-out but does not deliver, you can always charge the food to a credit card and pay a taxi driver to pick it up and deliver it to your door. Better yet, bribe your teenager, a neighbor, or significant other to go pick up the food from the restaurant. There's no reason why you should have to take care of all the details. Delegate, delegate, delegate. . . .

When you're really in a pinch, don't hesitate to swing by the drive-through at your favorite fast-food establishment. One wife of a Fortune 500 chief executive officer serves Kentucky Fried Chicken at all her dinner parties, regardless of whether her guests are close friends or her husband's business associates. Her secret? She bakes the chicken another two hours in a 250 degree oven (121 degrees Celsius). Everyone raves and asks for the recipe. She never tells.

Convenience foods and grocery store services

With today's convenience foods, you don't have to cook anything from scratch. If you can preheat an oven or set the microwave, you can prepare an impressive meal straight from the freezer case. You can add fresh fruit, prepackaged salads, or cut vegetables from the produce department to round out the meal.

The grocery store deli is another source of no-fuss, already prepared, heat-and-eat entrees, side dishes, breads, and desserts. You can use them to supplement your home-cooked meal or get the entire meal from the deli.

When you purchase food from a deli, ask how fresh it is and ask for a taste. Most delis are happy to oblige. A good friend of ours learned this lesson the hard way. She purchased some fancy-schmancy dip at the deli. It looked great, but tasted like plastic. She removed it from the table when no one was looking. Now she always samples before she serves.

A simple menu solution

If you are short on time, forget the whole meal. Simplify your menu planning by inviting friends over for drinks and hors d'oeuvres, followed by a meal in a restaurant. Or do it the other way around: Have the meal in a restaurant followed by dessert and coffee at your house. Whichever way you do it, you get the credit of inviting people into your home with very little work.

If you need to entertain a lot of people but don't have a lot of time to prepare, a cocktail party or dessert party is the way to go. You can have a fun and relaxing party with food prepared almost entirely in advance, so why bother with anything in between?

Jump over to Chapter 15 for more about cocktail parties and Chapter 8 for dessert parties.

Chapter 8

Balancing Menus

• •

In This Chapter

▶ Deciding which foods go together

▶ Determining the number of courses

▶ Finding good recipes

▶ Figuring out how much food to fix

▶ Suiting your lifestyle

• •

*A*fter you determine the way to approach your menu, you still have to decide what to serve, which foods go together, how much to cook, and what your limitations are. The two most valuable words to remember as you prepare your menu are *simplicity* and *balance*.

When making menus for company, most people go astray by trying too hard — serving too many courses, using recipes that are too complex, and choosing foods that are too rich. The result is overkill.

You can avoid a fizzled affair by balancing your menu. Naturally, you want to choose foods that taste and look good together. You also want to balance the number of courses with the amount of food you serve. A perfectly balanced menu does not leave guests hungry or stuffed.

But making sure that the food looks and tastes good and serving the right amount is only part of the formula. Other, equally important factors include matching preparation time with the time you have available, keeping the level of difficulty within your range of ability, and choosing menus that suit your lifestyle. A perfectly balanced menu does not overpower your energy level.

In this chapter, we show you how to find the right balance for your menu so that everything is in harmony.

Figuring Out What Foods Go Together

When you mull over recipes to decide what foods to prepare, your main objective is to achieve a balance by alternating and juxtaposing the following characteristics:

- ✔ Color
- ✔ Size
- ✔ Texture
- ✔ Temperature
- ✔ Taste

The contrasts between these elements bring out the character of each specific food and make the menu sparkle. Start by choosing one item you really want to prepare or serve. Your selection can be the main course, a vegetable, a dessert — whatever excites you most. Then build the rest of the menu around it.

If walking this menu-balance-beam seems difficult, play a simple game of fill-in-the blank:

If one course is (A) _____, make the next course (B) _____.

A	B
complicated	simple
rich	lean
spicy	bland
smooth	crisp
large	small
hot	cold
heavy	light
fresh/uncooked	prepared/cooked

Playing around with different characteristics of food is like putting together a puzzle — it's fun. Here are a few examples of creative ways to combine foods in your menus.

- ✔ For a riot of colors, serve curried carrot soup, sauteed spinach, yellow (saffron) rice, roasted whole garlic cloves, grilled red peppers, sauteed eggplant, and chocolate mousse with whipped cream and strawberries for dessert.

- ✔ Choose tiny shapes for a first course, such as small pastas. Next, serve a large, whole roasted fish to contrast size.

- ✔ Follow a smooth soup with a crisply sautéed chicken breast to contrast texture.

- ✔ Contrast temperature by serving a steaming-hot first course (soup or spring rolls) followed by a room-temperature entrée (such as poached fish) and a chilled or frozen dessert (key lime pie or parfaits).

- ✔ Use simple and complicated recipes in the same menu. Alternate unaltered (raw, uncooked) food with an elaborate recipe. Sliced raw fennel tossed with lemon juice and olive oil is a fine contrast to a fancy pork presentation, such as a marinated and stuffed pork loin. Serve a plain green salad before or after a flavorful, complex stew. These two courses contrast many characteristics — lean and rich, simple and complex, light and heavy, uncooked and cooked — offering a variety of tastes.

Pop quiz: What is wrong with this menu?

> *New England Clam Chowder*
>
> ❧
>
> *Chicken with creamy mushroom sauce*
>
> ❧
>
> *Vanilla pudding*

The preceding menu ignores all the menu-planning principles. As a whole, the courses are too soupy, too bland, too white, and too repetitious.

This menu cries out for color, texture, and lightness. You can improve it in a number of ways:

- ✔ **Change the chowder to Manhattan clam chowder.** This soup is tomato-based rather than cream-based and adds color.

- ✔ **Update the creamy mushroom sauce with a sauce of wild mushrooms with white wine and garlic.** The original sauce is too creamy and soupy to serve after a soup course. For a different twist, serve the

(continued)

(continued)

chicken with an herb pesto, fresh salsa, or chutney to lighten it up and add color.

✔ **Add crunchy roasted potatoes and a green vegetable with the chicken.** These elements add more color and texture.

✔ **Serve crisp cookies with the vanilla pudding.** Better yet, banish the pudding and change the dessert to sectioned oranges marinated in Grand Marnier with chocolate truffles alongside (to add freshness, color, flavor, and luxury).

Here's the new-and-improved version of the menu:

Manhattan clam chowder

❧

Chicken with wild mushrooms, white wine, and garlic roasted potatoes

Green beans (or your choice of fresh green vegetable)

❧

Marinated orange sections

Chocolate truffles

Deciding How Many Courses to Serve

There is no correct number of courses to serve at a party today. Any number of courses can be appropriate. When deciding how many courses to serve, you may want to consider the following factors:

✔ **The occasion.** A business meal is not the occasion for multiple courses. Keep the focus of the meal on yourself and any business at hand rather than on the food by serving no more than two or three courses. (See Chapters 7 and 17 for help planning a menu appropriate for business.) When you don't know your guests very well, you may also want to serve fewer courses so that you can spend more time getting to know your guests rather than running back and forth in the kitchen. A meal for close friends is a perfect opportunity to serve many courses.

✔ **The number of guests.** If you are having a large number of guests, you may want to consider a buffet, a cocktail party, or a dessert party. (See Chapters 7 and 15 for tips.) A party with a lot of people is complicated enough. Uncomplicate it with the food. With a small number of guests, you can serve an unlimited number of courses, but you may need some help in the kitchen.

✔ **How much help you have.** If you can get help, you can serve any number of courses to any number of guests. (See Chapter 15 to determine how much help you need for the size and type of party you are having.) However, even with help, it is not practical to serve a large number of courses to a large number of guests.

✔ **Your ability and interest.** If you have not mastered the art of cooking or if what you eat is not a major interest in your life, serving two or three courses is more realistic for you than attempting a multiple-course meal. Even if you hire a caterer, guests may think it odd if you serve them a meal that is out of character for you.

✔ **Your time and energy.** Fewer courses take less time and energy to prepare. If you have limited time, put your energy into preparing one course and make it wonderful rather than exhausting yourself over many courses.

Limiting the number of courses

Unless you are a Martha Stewart clone, have multiple servants, or are suicidal, you may not want to attempt a six-course dinner. For most parties and for most people, two or three courses is plenty.

Limiting the number of courses you serve has many advantages over serving a full six-course dinner:

✔ Fewer courses make everything less complicated and more manageable.

✔ Fewer courses mean fewer chances for things to go wrong.

✔ Fewer courses are easier on guests' stomachs and fannies.

✔ Fewer courses can be easier on your budget.

A two- or three-course meal can be quite elegant. Two courses can consist of Beluga caviar and lobster. Three courses can be jewel-colored soup, grouper en papillote, and flaming crêpes suzette. (Some examples of jewel-colored soups are carrot orange soup, pea and mint soup with red radishes floating on top, and cream of red pepper soup.) Figure 8-1 shows examples of other two- and three-course menus.

Simply Delicious Two-Course Menu

Fish stew

❧

Chocolate tart

A Delightful Two-Course Menu

Spicy grilled chicken

❧

Tropical fruit sundaes

Easy as 1-2-3

Wild mushroom soup

❧

Seared tenderloin

❧

Espresso

Figure 8-1:
Three
simple
menus
guaranteed
to wow
your guests.

A limited number of courses is mandatory if

- ✔ You are serving a large number of people. (Take a look at Chapter 15 for big-party menu suggestions.)
- ✔ You are serving large amounts of food (such as at Thanksgiving or a family reunion).
- ✔ You are doing all the work yourself (shopping, cooking, cleaning, and so on).
- ✔ You have anything else to do besides plan a party.

For a no-fuss solution, consider serving a one course meal, such as home-made pizzas. Buy a dozen small pizza rounds from your local pizzeria and store them in your freezer. When you are ready to have a party, thaw them out, throw on some toppings, and slide them in the oven. Boom! You have an instant one-course meal that your guests are sure to enjoy.

Another way to simplify your menu is to focus on a course other than the main course, such as hors d'oeuvres and cocktails or desserts and coffee. You can prepare or purchase most of these items in advance.

If you plan to serve just hors d'oeuvres or desserts, aim for variety. Use the same principles of balance that you use to plan for a main course: Pair hot with cold, crunchy with smooth, salty with sweet, dry with moist. Have fun playing with guests' taste buds by alternating the textures, temperatures, and tastes of the morsels of food.

When to serve many courses

Serving many courses may not be such a crazy notion if you love cooking, enjoy entertaining, have a comfortable place to seat your guests, and have the luxury of plenty of time or plenty of help. Handled with care, such a meal can be delightfully different.

Small parties provide the best opportunity for multiple courses. At small parties, people are likely to pay more attention to the food, and your big effort won't be a big waste.

The goal is not to emulate or compete with a five-star restaurant. Add courses for a particular purpose:

- ✔ **To lengthen the evening.** If you want your guests to hang around for a long time, keep the courses coming. This tactic also works well for special evenings, such as New Year's Eve, while guests are waiting for midnight.

- ✔ **To spotlight a particular food.** If you find an astonishingly beautiful vegetable at the market, separate it from the rest of the meal. Highlight it by serving it on a plate by itself as a separate course.

- ✔ **To show off your culinary skills.** If you want your guests to be awed, do something different: Serve many small courses.

Serving many courses is foolhardy if the foods are too complicated or too rich, or if you serve too much food on the plate. Resist the temptation to overdo it. Don't unbalance the whole meal by offering so much food in one course that what follows doesn't stand a chance. If you overstuff your guests with one course, they won't be able to enjoy the rest of the meal.

Simplify your work and keep courses in balance by serving some foods uncooked. Perfectly ripe yellow and red tomatoes sliced and drizzled with olive oil and basil or perfectly ripe cheeses with grapes and country bread are good examples. *Perfectly ripe* is the key term. When an uncooked food has the spotlight, it should be as close to perfect as possible. Figures 8-2 and 8-3 show examples of well-balanced multi-course menus.

Choosing the right recipes

Recipes are everywhere: in magazines, newspapers, cookbooks, and grocery store flyers; in your grandmother's kitchen drawer; on package labels, television, videos, and Web sites. The difficulty is in choosing the right recipes. Most published recipes have been tested. If you measure ingredients and follow directions, the outcome probably won't be a total disaster. But being diligent doesn't guarantee the food will be wonderful. The combination of ingredients may sound better than it tastes. Some recipes have no impact. Some recipes are easily forgotten.

Figure 8-2:
This seven-course menu has a nice balance of flavors, textures, colors, and tastes, yet is not overwhelming for the host to prepare or the guests to digest.

Seven Perfectly Balanced Courses

Turkish olives, carrots, cucumbers, radishes

❧

Corn soup

❧

Red and yellow tomato salad

❧

Roasted loin of pork
Green vegetable

❧

Assorted cheeses

❧

Fruit tart

❧

Coffee

Five Palate-Pleasing Courses

Goat cheese and crackers

❧

Grilled leg of lamb

Mint pesto

Potato cakes

❧

Green salad and olive oil rolls

❧

Angel food cake

Strawberries and peaches

❧

Chocolate crunch cookies

Coffee

Figure 8-3:
This menu, featuring two dessert courses, is sure to delight your guests.

For the same amount of time and trouble it takes to make the wrong recipes, you can make recipes that linger in people's memories and make you look like a genius. Select the right recipes by considering the following:

1. **Are the ingredients fresh?** Beware of recipes that call for *all* packaged foods, canned goods, or frozen items. Truly unforgettable recipes start with fresh ingredients. Use prepared foods sparingly.

   - Use nothing imitation or artificially flavored.
   - Use no ingredient that is beyond its freshness date or that has developed a strange odor.
   - Use fruit and vegetables that are fresh and in season.
   - Use unsalted butter (often referred to as "sweet" butter).

2. **Do the lists of ingredients and directions read like a short story or a novel?** Run away from recipes that require you to prepare four or five different parts for the whole. If you have to take the day off to make it, consider looking for a recipe with a shorter list of ingredients and fewer steps.

3. **Are the explanations clear?** Read recipes completely. Make sure that you are familiar with and like all the ingredients, have all the equipment you need, and understand the procedure.

4. **Does the recipe include directions for advance preparations and storage?** Choose recipes that you can begin preparing in advance. Beware of recipes that require too much last minute preparation.

5. **Does the recipe include words that are unfamiliar to you?** Think twice about a recipe if the ingredients are foreign to you and/or you don't understand the directions. If you are an accomplished cook or a very confident host, you may have fun trying out new recipes on guests. Otherwise, stick with ingredients and procedures with which you are comfortable.

Now that you know what to look for, have some fun on your search for recipes. Besides traditional sources, look into what's available on the Internet. You can always use your web browser to conduct a general search. Type the word **recipes** into any search engine, and you may be astonished. If you find the number of offerings too overwhelming, narrow your search by adding a specific cuisine, food category, ingredient, or name of the recipe you would like to find.

You can find tons of recipes of every kind at Mimi's Cyber Kitchen (www.cyber-kitchen.com). You may also want to check out the Yum Yum Archives (www.yumyum.com) where you will find over 10,000 recipes. You'll also find a link there to Amazon.com, a giant bookstore with a good selection of cookbooks to order online. For cooking demonstrations as well as recipes, tune into *The TV Food Network*. Get the recipes from the shows you like free on the Internet at www.foodtv.com/recipes.

Pacing the Meal

Regardless of how many courses you serve, how you pace the meal can make an enormous difference in your guests' enjoyment of it.

Guests have only a certain amount of energy to spend on an evening out. If you wait too long to serve dinner, they may have used up too much of their energy on conversations; they may have drunk one too many alcoholic beverages; or they may just be tired of waiting for the meal. Thirty to forty-five minutes is plenty of time to serve hors d'oeuvres and cocktails before a meal.

Pacing the courses is especially important when you serve a long meal. You are not in a race. Give guests a comfortable amount of time to enjoy each course without feeling rushed. The whole purpose of serving multiple courses is to stretch out the evening and relax.

The key to pacing multiple courses is to have them prepared in advance (soup already re-heating on the stove, salad or cold seafood course prepared and chilling in the refrigerator). If you take too long between courses, guests may end up dozing off. On the other hand, if you jump up and down from your seat like an overworked, disorganized jack-in-the-box, guests cannot relax.

How do you find the right pace? Trust your intuition. Wait until guests are finished or almost finished eating before you casually leave the table to make final preparations for the next course. Do not begin clearing until everyone finishes eating.

Each course can lengthen the meal by 15 minutes to a half hour, depending on conversations, slow or fast eaters, clearing plates, last-minute food preparations, and arranging the next course on the plates.

On a rare occasion, you may have one guest whose slow pace of eating is devastating to your timing. Unfortunately, you cannot control or change that person's behavior, and she may be totally oblivious to the fact that everyone else is finished. If you see that the other guests are very restless, you may want to start clearing. Most likely, the slow guest will get the hint and finish up.

Most people don't have enough china and silver to serve a multiple course meal without re-using some of the plates or utensils. Before serving the first course, fill a plastic tub or sink with soapy water. Slip dishes in the water to soak between courses. When you are ready to use them again, rinse and dry. Try to plan your courses so that you alternate between the kinds of dishes you need to serve them on. For example, if you serve the first course on plates that you need to wash and use again, serve the next course on a different plate. This way, you will have time to wash the dishes you need before the next course. Depending on the size of your party and the number of dishes to be washed, you may need to solicit some help. If you don't have hired help, ask a guest you know well, one of your children, or a significant other to pitch in.

First and Last Impressions

No matter how many courses you serve, what you serve first and last may have the greatest impact on your guests. Hors d'oeuvres/appetizers or desserts can stand alone as the sole food for your party or elevate an ordinary meal to a higher realm. They are irresistible treats — an invitation to pleasure — and people adore them. The first and last courses are the ones guests are most likely to remember.

Taste teasers: hors d'oeuvres and appetizers

Hors d'oeuvres are served with cocktails, before guests are seated. Ideally, they are small bites full of savory flavor. Plan on three to four bites per person.

Appetizers are served as a first course at the table. An appetizer should contrast with the next course, but not overwhelm it. Appetizers are taste teasers, not appetite killers. However, if the rest of the meal is light, you can serve something small and rich — rich as in foie gras (liver pâté) or rich as in the sauce (béarnaise or hollandaise) for a starter.

Good choices for hors d'oeuvres include:

- ✔ Fresh vegetables — marinated, raw, or grilled
- ✔ Smoked fish
- ✔ Chilled clams, squid, shrimp, and so on
- ✔ Special olives
- ✔ Roasted nuts

Good choices for appetizers include:

- ✔ Cold or warm salads
- ✔ Cold or hot soups
- ✔ Soufflés or tarts
- ✔ Pastas
- ✔ Grilled or fried vegetables
- ✔ Cheese biscuits
- ✔ Stuffed vegetables

The grand finale: dessert

Dessert is the *pièce de résistance* — the final little food gift you present to your guests. Dessert can be the saving grace of a meal that didn't turn out quite right or the finishing touch for the perfect meal. Make this course memorable, but keep it in balance with the rest of the meal. Or make dessert the only course. For example, if you just baked a pan of brownies and don't trust yourself not to gobble them all up in one sitting, invite some friends to divide the calories.

After a very rich or heavy meal, serve something light — fresh fruit, sorbet, angel food cake, or meringues. After a low-fat entreé, serve something indulgent — cheesecake, mousse, or French layer cake. Coffee-flavored and chocolate-flavored desserts are always a hit.

The only thing better than one dessert is two desserts. People may diet all week, but when they go out to a restaurant or a party, they indulge. When people see two desserts, their brains immediately register "This is a vacation."

To serve more than one dessert without upsetting your carefully balanced menu or overstuffing your guests, consider offering dessert as two separate courses. Serve the main dessert first, and then coffee and a plate of cookies later. Refer to Figure 8-3 in this chapter for an example of a menu incorporating two desserts.

Fruit desserts

Fruit is always a welcome dessert. Fresh fruits are colorful and beautiful — they decorate themselves. You can serve fruit any number of ways: whole, sliced, or puréed; poached, flamed, or baked; and in tarts, cobblers, or crisps.

Notice what's fresh and ripe every time you shop, and plan your dessert around it. You can decorate a fruit tart with almost any chosen fruit or combination of fresh fruits. Change the dessert with the season, serving what's best and beautiful in any given month.

The cookie advantage

One of the most delightful desserts you can offer is a beautifully arranged platter of cookies.

✔ Such an offering is a light and elegant ending to the meal and is visually interesting.

✔ Easy preparation is ideal for the less experienced baker.

✔ You save time and labor with advance preparation. (You can keep most cookie dough a week in the refrigerator or up to three months in the freezer.)

✔ Guests can eat as few or as many as they want.

Form cookies on a baking sheet a day before the party, cover, and refrigerate. Bake at the last possible moment before serving — as guests are arriving or during the main meal. The aroma will drive guests to distraction, and the cookies will taste heavenly. You can also bake the cookies a few weeks ahead and freeze them if you're pressed for time. For more timely tips, take a look at the section in this chapter called "Time-saving do-aheads."

Variety is king of the cookie platter. For an elaborate presentation, choose different shapes, colors, textures, and flavors. Add truffles, candied grapefruit peel, espresso beans, glazed apricots, spiced nuts, toffee, peanut brittle, or chocolate-dipped strawberries.

Here are a few stunning and delicious ways to serve fruit for dessert:

✔ Sliced fresh peaches tossed with a little brown sugar and topped with a dollop of sour cream is a dessert that takes two minutes to create and tastes terrific.

✔ Strawberries with a little freshly ground pepper or a splash of balsamic vinegar on top is surprising, delightful, and easy.

✔ Bowls of red cherries, orange apricots, and purple plums look like paintings and taste like summer.

✔ Poached pears in red wine with sabayon sauce is a luxurious ending.

Your dessert will be only as good as the fruit you select. To make the best selection, use the touch and smell test. If the fruit is too hard, it isn't ripe and won't smell or taste good. If the fruit is too soft, it may smell wonderful, but it's not in condition to use as the main part of the dessert. Purée it and use it as a sauce instead.

Ice creams, yogurts, and sorbets

Ice creams, yogurts, and sorbets are fabulous desserts — refreshing, but not too sweet. Serve them alone or put two flavors together. A scoop of ice cream becomes opulent with a special sauce and homemade cookies. Even the fanciest guests love ice cream sundaes, ice cream sandwiches, or ice cream cones.

Here's a way to add a touch of sophistication to your ice cream sundaes:

1. **Start by making chocolate leaves.**

   Wash and dry ivy leaves (or any other pretty leaf), and paint on one side with melted semisweet chocolate.

2. **Refrigerate until chocolate sets.**

3. **Peel off carefully and refrigerate the chocolate leaves until ready for use.**

4. **When the dessert course arrives, fill your best crystal goblets with ice cream.**

5. **Drizzle with homemade caramel, fruit, or fudge sauce.**

   Stick in a few chocolate leaves.

6. **Present all the goblets on a large silver tray.**

   Guests will think that you're a genius.

For homemade ice cream sandwiches with a gourmet touch, spread your favorite ice cream between two large homemade, bakery, or store-bought cookies. Freeze until serving time.

Wow your guests with an all-dessert party

If you want to save yourself some trouble and add some pure, unadulterated joy to your guests' lives, have a dessert party. All you need are a few drop-dead desserts and some top quality coffees, teas, and other drinks. If you enjoy baking, prepare a few of your favorite desserts. If baking's not your style, buy an assortment of desserts at the best bakery in town. Choose a variety so that each guest can sample several. Include desserts to cut, such as cakes; desserts to scoop, such as mousse; and desserts to pick up, such as chocolate-dipped strawberries.

For a large party, as an added entertainment bonus, hire someone to make crêpes and fill them to order. Or hire an ice cream store, such as Ben & Jerry's, to set up a dessert station at your party. They can provide all flavors of ice cream on sticks or in cones along with toppings to roll sticks in or to spoon onto cones or sundaes.

If you want to feature special coffees, hire someone to make cappuccinos and espressos. See Chapter 9 for more details.

Show stoppers

Layer cakes, dessert terrines, parfaits, and tortes are special desserts for special people or special occasions. They are time-consuming desserts, calling for two or three different stages of preparation. If you have access to a fabulous bakery, go ahead and buy this type of dessert. Otherwise, spread the preparations over a few days. The finished dessert will be fine in the refrigerator for a day or two before the party.

If you want to make a lasting impression, anything that's flaming does the trick. If you are a former flame-thrower, pyromaniac, or are otherwise proficient with alcohol and a match, you may want to consider cherries jubilee, crêpes suzette, bananas Foster, or Christmas pudding. Be sure to dim the lights before setting the pan ablaze.

Guests are especially appreciative if you can do this without setting the house on fire. You may want to keep an extinguisher nearby just in case. If you would rather not risk an unexpected visit from the fire department, a safer way to fire up the atmosphere is to stick sparklers all over the cake or pudding. Turn off the lights for your blazing entry.

For more ideas and suggestions about desserts, try reading *Desserts For Dummies*, by Bryan Miller and Bill Yosses (published by IDG Books Worldwide, Inc.).

Determining How Much Food to Prepare

When deciding how much of each food to cook, you must use common sense. Cooking for an army looks ridiculous if only ten people are coming. Outsiders may assume that most of the guests didn't show up. On the other hand, it's embarrassing to come up short on food. Coming up with the right amount of food allows you to offer guests seconds (count on half the guests or fewer wanting seconds) and also feeds you the next day.

As a rule, the more courses you serve, the less food you need to prepare for each course. The sum of all the courses should not equal more than a whole meal. You want to strike a balance between starved and stuffed.

Never overload a person's plate. Some guests will feel obligated to eat everything on their plates and may go home feeling more sick than satisfied. Others won't touch half of it. Throwing away mounds of food that guests couldn't finish is heartbreaking for the cook — and a waste of time and money. Serving small to moderate portions is best. Guests can always ask for second helpings, and what finer compliment to the cook?

Suggested serving sizes on written recipes are good guidelines for how much to cook for a three- to four-course menu. If you serve only two courses and have six guests, use a recipe designated to serve eight. Conversely, if you are serving more than four courses, a recipe for eight can easily serve ten.

But serving counts are only general guidelines. People's appetites differ for many reasons. Use the suggested serving count along with any additional information you have about your guests to help determine whether you need to prepare more or less food than suggested by the recipe. Following are a few clues to consider:

- **Your guests' ages, sizes, genders, and activity levels.** Older people generally eat smaller portions. Teenagers are bottomless pits. In most cases, women eat less than men, unless they've just exercised.

- **Where the guests are coming from.** Are they coming from the symphony where they haven't had anything to eat for a few hours, or from an outdoor sporting event where they have probably been snacking all day?

- **The richness of each course.** If the foods are rich or heavy, serve smaller portions than you would light foods.

- **What time you are serving.** If you are serving at 9:00 p.m., consider smaller portions than you might serve at 7:00 p.m. At a large ladies' luncheon, because of diets and conversations, expect less food to be consumed than at any other time of day or for any other party.

If you are serving family style or setting up a buffet, always prepare extra. As food dwindles on a serving platter, guests often take less, because no one wants to take the last helping. For ten or more guests, make enough to fill two trays or platters. After half the people are served, bring out a fresh platter so that the food doesn't look picked over or unattractive.

Suiting Your Lifestyle

No matter how perfectly balanced your menu seems, it's all wrong for you if it doesn't suit your lifestyle. Suiting your lifestyle means your schedule, your ability, your budget, and your personality.

Perhaps your life is already one giant juggling act and the thought of adding one more thing can throw you completely off balance. No matter how much or how little time you have to spare, no matter how much or how little money you have to spend, and no matter how much you love or hate to cook, there are menu solutions to suit every lifestyle.

Balancing the menu with your time and ability

Unless cooking is your hobby and you have time to kill, you probably want to prepare the meal for company in a relatively short amount of time. Even if you are an accomplished cook, if everything you have on your menu is complicated and time-consuming, chances are, nothing will turn out just right.

Having time constraints doesn't mean that some dishes cannot be complex. The key to balancing is knowing your time limits and planning ahead.

When planning your menu, follow these guidelines:

- Decide how much time you are willing to devote to preparation.
- Read recipes carefully to ensure that the preparation time meets your time constraints. Get a head start on anything complicated.

    (For help with your timing, go back to Chapter 3 and review the tips for getting organized. Plan your menu and your timetable so that you don't wind up in a last-minute crunch.)
- Make sure that your cooking ability matches the level of difficulty of the menu.

If you've never made a homemade pie crust before, give yourself time for a possible failure. (Don't hesitate to throw away failed crust. The ingredients add up to about 25 cents — a small amount to waste in the interest of getting it right.) There's nothing wrong with starting over, but you don't want to be caught in a panic the day of the party.

If you are a beginner cook, choose simple dishes or recipes you've already tried successfully. Practice complex preparations and experiment on your family first.

Save time by:

- Selecting foods that can you can prepare ahead. Save only one or two cooking tasks for the last minute.
- Starting early — as much as several days in advance.
- Choosing recipes that don't have a full-page list of ingredients.
- Including foods that can you can serve at room temperature.
- Planning to serve dishes that you can bake or reheat at the same oven temperature.
- Using pans attractive enough to go straight from the oven to the table.

Time-saving do-aheads

A little advance preparation goes a long way toward elevating your party from ordinary to extraordinary, not to mention saving your sanity. Many recipes include directions for freezing and defrosting. Following are examples of a few no-fail, do-ahead items that can release you from the pressure cooker on the day of your party:

- **Appetizers.** Most hors d'oeuvres freeze beautifully. Prepare them up to a month in advance of your party. Defrost them the morning of your party. Follow recipe directions for any further preparation, such as heating.
- **Creole.** Make the sauce up to a month in advance and freeze. Defrost in your refrigerator the day before the party. Reheat slowly, and add shrimp or chicken with enough time to cook just before serving. (Cooking time will vary depending on the meat. Check your recipe.)
- **Curry.** Ditto.
- **Stew.** Whether it's beef, lamb, or Brazilian black bean, cook the stew up to a month in advance. Defrost it in your refrigerator the day before the party. Reheat slowly just before serving.
- **Breads.** You can freeze most homemade rolls, breadsticks, or whole loaves up to a month in advance of your party. Defrost them at room temperature the day of the party. Wrap them in tin foil to reheat.

✔ **Cheesecake.** Many recipes freeze perfectly — up to two weeks before your party. Defrost in the refrigerator the day before the party. Don't try to zap it in the microwave unless you fancy "cheesecake soup." (See warning, below, for more microwave advice).

✔ **Pie and tart crust.** Homemade crust is much more delicious than store-bought. Make it, roll it, press into pie pan, and freeze it a week ahead. On the day of the party, it's ready to thaw, pre-bake, or fill and bake.

✔ **Cookies.** Bake them two to four weeks before the party and freeze. Defrost them at room temperature the day of the party.

✔ **Layer cakes.** Bake the layers up to two weeks in advance. Cool to room temperature, remove from pans, and wrap in plastic wrap to freeze. Defrost at room temperature and frost on the day of the party.

Balancing no-cook menus

If time is not on your side or you don't feel like cooking, you can have a perfectly balanced menu using the grocery store/convenience food approach. (See the section called "No-hassle and non-cooking approaches to menus" in Chapter 7.)

Figure 8-4 shows a menu that requires very little preparation. Have guests munch on veggies with a drink while you set the table, boil corn, reheat spareribs, heat rolls. Dig in!

Tips for freezing and defrosting

To avoid unexpected disappearing acts, freeze foods as soon as they reach room temperature — before spouses, children, or *you* get tempted.

Also, make sure that your freezer is set at the proper temperature for storing frozen food. The temperature in most freezers falls within a range of 5 to 20 degrees below 0 (Fahrenheit). If you have a chest freezer that is separate from your refrigerator and that you don't open and close often, 5 degrees below 0 is cold enough. Set the temperature lower in your refrigerator's freezer compartment to compensate for frequent opening and closing.

Don't worry about your freezer being too cold. The faster the food freezes, the more flavor it retains. But if you have an older freezer that doesn't keep food as frozen as it should, food absorbs moisture and gets freezer burn. You may have to do more last-minute cooking.

Take extra care when wrapping foods for the freezer. We recommend an airtight layer of plastic wrap followed by freezer paper or a double layer of tin foil. Remember to label the packages clearly!

For most foods, we recommend slow defrosting either in the refrigerator or on the countertop. Be extra cautious if you use a microwave for defrosting. Carefully follow the instructions for your microwave and your recipe. The whole point of making dishes ahead is to avoid last minute haste. Don't take a chance on ruining the food by over-microwaving it.

Instructions for the menu in Figure 8-5: Set table, melt butter for dipping lobster, indulge. If any guests are unfamiliar with how to pick the lobster out of the shell, you may want to demonstrate. You may also want to provide guests with plastic bibs and finger bowls or moist towels. Lobsters can be messy to eat, but the taste is worth the effort.

This menu is perfectly balanced because it begins and ends with the rich and extravagant but has something plain and simple in between. Best of all, it's in balance with your busy life.

Figure 8-4:
The colors, textures, and temperatures in this menu are so balanced they could walk a tightrope.

Simply Scrumptious Menu

Pre-cut carrots, celery and cherry tomatoes

❧

Spare ribs from the deli

Corn on the cob from the grocery store's freezer case

Fresh rolls from the deli

❧

Chunky pistachio ice cream (to add green in your menu)

Figure 8-5:
A classy menu that's short on preparation time and long on enjoyment.

Extravagantly Easy Menu

Steamed lobster (choose a lively one and have it steamed and split while you finish your shopping)

❧

Pre-packaged lettuce, bottled vinaigrette

❧

The most luscious dessert you spy in the deli case

Chapter 9
Cocktails to Coffee

. . . .

In This Chapter

▶ Basing the party on the beverage

▶ Matching the wine to the menu

▶ Serving cocktails before dinner

▶ Setting up your bar

▶ Making toasts

▶ Offering coffee, tea, and drinks after dinner

▶ Avoiding lawsuits

. . . .

Question: *What are the six most welcome words guests can hear after you greet them?*

Answer: *"May I offer you a drink?"*

Greeting your guests is the first step to a successful party. The second important step is offering them a drink. Drinks start your party off on the right foot by making people comfortable. Even if it's a glass of water or a tonic with lime, the first beverage is an important icebreaker. It gives guests something to do with their hands and helps them relax.

But making guests comfortable is just the beginning. From that first cocktail to the last cup of coffee, you can use drinks to enhance the food you serve and make your party flow. In this chapter, you find suggestions on selecting and serving the right beverages for your menu and your guests. You figure out how to set up your bar, and if you're tongue-tied, you get some tips on making toasts. This chapter also offers some guidelines on how to serve alcohol without having people pass out on the floor or weave dangerously down your driveway on the way to jail.

You also discover how drinks can play a much larger role in your party plans. Most people think of drinks last, almost as an afterthought. But you can actually plan your entire party around a special wine or a particular drink, using it as a basis for the menu, the mood, the setting, or the theme. Why not start there?

Planning Your Party around the Drinks

If you're stuck on your party plan (the thought of making a menu makes your head spin; the setting is dullsville; Oprah can't make it, and the other guests don't excite you), then consider approaching the whole thing from a different angle: Think drinks. Use a beverage as a starting point and build your party around it. Begin with

- ✔ A special wine or wines
- ✔ Various champagnes
- ✔ A keg of beer
- ✔ New microbrews
- ✔ Special cocktails
- ✔ Frozen blender drinks
- ✔ Homemade lemonade or limeade
- ✔ Special teas or coffees

When deciding which drink to serve, ask yourself:

- ✔ Does this make sense with the weather, the number of people, and the ages of the guests?
- ✔ Are the ingredients available?
- ✔ Does it fit my budget?

If you answered "yes," to all these questions, ask yourself what menu would go best with your chosen drink. The menus in Figures 9-1 through 9-6, for example, are based on the beverage.

If you want to spotlight the drink, the menu should complement but not outshine it. Keep in mind the principles of balance that Chapter 8 outlines. If you serve an exotic beverage, don't be so daring with the food, and vice versa. Balance the unfamiliar with something familiar.

A Menu for Martinis

Chicken livers wrapped in bacon

Miniature pizzas

Quesadillas with mushrooms

Grilled portobello mushroom strips on toast

Spring rolls

**A Menu for Tropical Blended Drinks
(with or without alcohol)**

Coconut shrimp

Fried plantains

❧

Whole fish fried in a wok

Creole sauce

Flat breads

Spicy black beans

❧

Grilled pineapple and papaya kabobs

Mango mousse

A Menu for Microbrews

Boiled crabs

Steamed shrimp

Breaded catfish

Sausages

Fruit and fruit beer for dessert

A Menu for Champagne

Oysters on the half shell

Cheese soufflé

Lobster

Chocolate truffles

A Menu for a Keg of Beer

Barbecued pig with choice of sauce (spicy or mild)

Stewed tomatoes

Coleslaw

Cornbread

Rolls

Brownies and cookies

A Menu for Warm Ginger Tea

Cold chicken with rosemary

Potato salad with olive oil

Crusty peasant bread

Fresh figs

Gingersnaps or fancy-cut gingerbread cookies

When your party is about a special drink, don't worry about likes and dislikes. If it's a part of your menu, encourage each person to sample the drink. A guest may think he doesn't like sake until he tries it. He may love it; but even if he hates it, he will always remember the experience.

Be sure to provide alternatives for the guest who politely declines. Offer choices of bottled waters, nonalcoholic beers, and diet and regular sodas. Soda water with a few drops of bitters and a twist of lime is a refreshing change, and it looks like a cocktail.

Wining and Dining

When you serve wine with dinner, carefully choose the wine to enhance the food. You can choose separate wines for each course or one wine that will carry throughout the meal. The idea is to keep the wine in balance with the meal. Choosing food and wine that go well together heightens the flavor of each. If your selections clash, neither the food nor the wine tastes good.

Evan Goldstein, Master Sommelier and Director of the Sterling Vineyard School of Service and Hospitality, says, "First and foremost, avoid culinary crash. If the wine is the star, keep the food simple. When the food is the whizbang, the wine should be simpler."

If you base your menu on the wine, consider the following basic principles:

- ✔ To show off young red wines, serve stewed meat or meat that has been significantly altered through cooking.
- ✔ To complement older wines, serve simply cooked, rare, juicy meats — no fancy sauces to compete with the wine.
- ✔ For dessert, serve wine that is equal in sweetness or sweeter than the dessert; otherwise, the wine tastes sour.

If you are a wine connoisseur, making the selection will be easy for you. If you are not familiar with wines, making your selection can still be easy. Just ask an expert for help.

Here are three ways to choose wines:

- ✔ Go to a wine shop and ask for help. (Provide the proprietor with your menu and budget.)
- ✔ Consult *Wine For Dummies*, by Ed McCarthy and Mary Ewing-Mulligan (published by IDG Books Worldwide, Inc.).
- ✔ Use the eenie-meenie-minie-moe method. (Not recommended.)

Following are three ways to serve wines at your party:

✔ Serve a different wine with each course. Your wine merchant can help you choose appropriate red or white wines for the food you serve.

✔ Serve the same type of wine from different regions. Start by choosing a Chardonnay, Cabernet, Riesling, or Merlot from California. Next, select the same varietal from your state or from different countries such as France, Australia, Germany, or Italy. Your wine merchant can help with the selections.

✔ Serve three or four different wines throughout the meal, like a wine tasting. Set out three or four wine glasses for each person. At the beginning of the meal, pour some of each wine for each guest. This allows guests to sip the different wines throughout the meal, noticing how their tastes differ with different foods.

When estimating how many bottles of wine you need, count on about five glasses per bottle. Plan on $2^1/_2$ glasses or one half bottle per person. If you are serving a very fine wine, you may need less, because people will usually drink more slowly and savor the flavor. Then buy one or two more bottles than you think you need. Overestimating the amount is better than coming up short at your party. You can always use the unopened bottles for your own enjoyment or another party.

Always serve water for those who don't drink or those who may want to limit their wine consumption. Those who don't drink alcohol won't feel left out if they are drinking something special. You can offer sparkling water, water with citrus slices, gourmet bottled waters, water with berry essences, or even imported ice cut from actual Antarctic glaciers.

Serving wine

You don't need to pour a taste test before serving wine. Offering a tasting can seem pretentious and may make the taster feel uncomfortable if he or she is not sure what to do. Under the following special circumstances, you can offer a taste test:

✔ If the guest of honor is knowledgeable about wine, offer him or her a tasting.

✔ If a guest brought a rare or expensive wine (not an ordinary table wine), it is appropriate for you (the host or hostess) to do the tasting or to let the guest who brought the wine do the tasting.

When all guests have been served, you can keep the wine bottles on the table and tell your guests to help themselves when they want more. Or, if you have a bartender or someone helping you serve the meal, you can ask that person to touch up guests' glasses as needed.

Guests don't care how you serve the wine. Don't fret over formalities. Keep the focus on having a good time.

How many glasses do you really need?

You don't need to spend a fortune on stemware to serve wine elegantly. (Any glasses are fine. In Italy, table wine is served in tumblers.) For most occasions, unless you are serving rare or expensive wines, you can use one all-purpose glass to serve the different wines throughout the meal. If wines are one of the main features of your meal, however, use red wine glasses and white wine glasses. (Special glasses for different wines make a difference in the taste.)

Here are some guidelines for serving wine:

- ✔ Serve champagne in flutes so that the bubbles can rise up and aromas are funneled to the nose.
- ✔ Serve wine in clear glasses so that guests can see its luscious color.
- ✔ Serve expensive wine in delicate glass. (It really does taste better that way.)
- ✔ Serve wine in glasses large enough to swirl and sniff. Noses should fit in the glass to inhale.

If you have a set of gargantuan goblets, serve wine in them, but never fill them to the brim. No matter what type of glass you use, fill it about one-third or less. This amount keeps the wine at the right temperature and leaves plenty of space to swirl the wine and allow aromas to escape and rise. Figure 9-7 illustrates just the right amount of wine to pour in the glass.

Put the "Happy" in Happy Hour

You don't have to serve alcohol to make people happy. It's not the drink that makes them happy; it's the welcome. A warm genuine welcome puts guests at ease, and that's when the party begins. When people are comfortable, they won't need a stiff drink. "Happy" doesn't mean getting drunk; it means being at ease.

Right after you greet and welcome your guests, offer them a drink. Whether it's a cocktail or a cola, giving them something to do with their hands can help them relax.

Figure 9-7:
Leave enough space in the glass for guests to get a good whiff of the wine.

If you serve alcohol, be careful not to let your guests get too "happy" on an empty stomach. You don't want them knocking back three drinks before a great meal. You want them to be able to walk to the table on their own accord and be able to taste the food.

Although the term is "Happy Hour," that doesn't necessarily mean 60 minutes. For a small dinner party (fewer than ten people), 30 minutes is plenty of time for cocktails. For a larger party, you may need more time. Forty-five minutes is enough time for any size party. Otherwise, guests may drink too much or begin wondering if they are ever going to get anything to eat.

Don't make your guests do a juggling act. If you are passing hors d'oeuvres with the drinks, serve tidbits of food that guests can pick up with one hand and eat in one bite.

Be careful of the kind of food you serve. You may want to avoid:

✔ Anything saucy that may drip down guests' arms

✔ Anything that leaves a film of grease on their hands

✔ Foods with bones or shells that must be discarded.

✔ Foods on skewers or picks

For guests with a drink in hand, ending up with an empty pick or searching for a place to park the debris is frustrating. If you want to serve food that needs skewers or picks, place a cup or other receptacle on the serving tray so that guests can eat the food and deposit the picks right away, or have someone circulating to collect them.

What's in a name?

Ever wonder who comes up with all those names for cocktails? Creative minds have given us classics such as Gimlets, Gibsons, Screwdrivers, Bloody Marys, Manhattans, Mint Juleps, and many more. Some that may not be as familiar are:

- Bees Knees: Gin, honey, and lemon
- Bay Breeze: Vodka and pineapple juice
- Fuzzy Navel: Vodka, peach Schnapps, and orange juice
- Greyhound: Vodka and grapefruit juice
- Rusty Nail: Scotch and Drambuie
- Pink Lady: Gin, lemon, sugar syrup, cream, and grenadine
- Angel Tips: Amaretto and cream

Sex with the Boss may sound a little risqué, but it's a delicious drink. We like it because it uses fresh ingredients and a top-shelf liquor.

Sex with the Boss

Squeeze a fresh blood orange, honey tangerine, or orange and 1/2 lime over ice.

Add a shot of gold Patron. ("Patron" means "boss" in Spanish.)

Pour over ice.

This hot drink comes from a cool bar — Fifty-Seven, Fifty-Seven bar in the Four Seasons Hotel, New York City:

Cosmopolitan Martini

6 ounces vodka
2 tablespoons cranberry juice
Juice of 1 lime
1 tablespoon Cointreau

Stir ingredients in shaker with ice. Strain into glasses; garnish each with a lime twist.

Serves 2. Note: For best results, make only two drinks at a time.

For more terrific drink ideas, see *Bartending For Dummies*, by Ray Foley (published by IDG Books Worldwide, Inc.).

Barring Everything

If you are focusing your party around a certain drink, you don't need to set up an elaborate bar. Create a simple bar that works with the event and your budget instead. For example, if your whole party centers on a keg of beer, you don't need liquor or wine. If you're serving blended drinks, you won't need much more. If it's a wine tasting, you don't need a bar at all. But if you plan to offer a variety of drinks, give some thought to what kind of bar you need.

Here are three kinds of bars you can set up:

- ✔ A self-service bar where guests can make their own drinks
- ✔ A bar where guests can go to order drinks
- ✔ A service bar where you, a helper, or a bartender can make drinks and deliver them to guests

When deciding which way to serve, consider how formal the party is and who the guests are. When the party is casual and the guests are good friends, a self-service bar can add to the fun. People love having their fingerprints on their drinks, creating their own wild concoctions, and sharing their specialties. Really close friends can make their own drinks right out of your refrigerator.

In other instances, guests may not be comfortable making their own drinks. You are better off pouring the drinks or having them served in the following situations:

- ✔ When the party is formal
- ✔ When the event is related to business
- ✔ When you don't know the guests well, or they don't know you

After you decide what kind of bar you need, you need to decide how to stock it. Figure out what your budget can stand. Take into account all the drinks, mixers, condiments, and ice.

If your bar is not self-service, you also need to figure out who is going to make the drinks. Can you do it yourself? Do you have a partner who can make drinks, or do you need to hire a bartender?

Where to set up your bar

If you plan to use a service bar that is hidden from guests, put it anywhere that's convenient for the person doing the serving. Otherwise, you need to set up the bar in a place that's easily accessible to guests.

You can set up a bar on almost any kind of table. Just cover it with a white cloth that reaches the floor to camouflage bottles, ice, and garbage underneath and behind it. Make sure that there is plenty of room behind the bar so that the bartender can maneuver easily.

If you are setting up a self-service bar, make sure that there's enough room for guests to gather around to mix and pour their own drinks. Everything you have to offer should be in plain view. Guests should not have to ask, "Do you have such and such?" Consider providing a cooler full of soft drinks and another for beer and wine. If you are offering mixed drinks, set out the liquor, mixers, and equipment. Be sure to provide plenty of glasses and ice.

When deciding where to put the bar, think about where you want people to be. If you are making the drinks yourself while trying to finish cooking, it may be easier to set it up in the kitchen and let guests watch what you're doing. If your kitchen is in chaos and guests would be in the way, find another area.

Place your bar in a visible area, but don't put it anywhere that can create a bottleneck. Think about how you want traffic to flow. Don't put the bar in the front foyer or hall. Guests can get stuck there like a rush-hour traffic jam.

If your house is very small, there may be only one place where the bar can fit. But with a little imagination, you may be able to create some new spaces: A pantry, a dining nook, or any tucked-away place is a possible bar site. You can set up the bar in a doorway of a room guests won't need to enter.

If you need a second bar, use it to draw people to places in your home where they may not go otherwise. That location can be any area — the living room, the den, a bedroom, or the garage. If the weather is nice, think about setting up the bar on the porch or patio so guests can breathe some fresh air or enjoy a view. See Chapter 5 for more tips on effective use of space.

Stocking the bar

If you need help stocking and setting up the bar, you can hire a catering service to do the whole shebang — provide linens, fruit, mixers, and complete bar set-up. The bad news is that this type of service can be expensive; expect to pay a per-head fee. The good news is that you can also expect no hassles and no headaches.

The most economical way to set up a bar is to buy your own liquor and wine. Take an inventory of what you already have before shopping. You can also save money and trouble by doing a little behind-the-scenes investigation.

Before you stock a complete bar, do a little sleuthing. You can get a good idea of what and how much to buy if you consider the following clues:

- ✔ **Ages of guests.** A 50-and-over crowd prefers drinks that are different from what a younger set favors. Older guests generally choose martinis, gin, and drinks on the rocks. For younger groups, pay attention to trends. If you've fallen behind the times and don't know the trends, just ask any bartender what's fashionable to serve.

- ✔ **Who your guests are.** Some professionals may drink at home but may be more socially conscious about drinking in public. Your doctor, lawyer, or business associates will drink differently at your party than will your bowling buddies, college fraternity brothers, or friends from aerobics class. Use what you know about people and their professions to estimate what kind and how much alcohol will be consumed.

- ✔ **Statistics.** According to liquor store owners, bartenders, and caterers we polled, about 65 percent of people who drink order vodka or scotch. (Most order vodka.) The remaining 35 percent order a combination of gin, bourbon, or rum. What does this mean to you? If your party is small or you don't entertain frequently, you don't need to buy the biggest bottle of rum in the store.

- ✔ **Personal preferences.** If you have invited close friends and you already know what they like to drink, other items on the bar are optional.

Many people have preferences for special drinks. If you know a particular guest always drinks Old Grandad, Campari, or Diet 7-Up, you may want to have it on hand. It's a personal gesture, and the fact that you remembered makes a lasting impression. (Double brownie points if you remember your boss's favorite drink.)

If your party is large and/or you want to offer nearly every known drink, you need to stock all or most of the following items:

Liquor

❑ Vodka   ❑ Scotch   ❑ Bourbon

❑ Gin   ❑ Rum   ❑ Vermouth

❑ Apéritifs

Wine

❑ Red wine   ❑ White wine

Beer

❑ One or two premium brands   ❑ Light beer   ❑ Nonalcoholic beer

---

Soft drinks

- ❏ Cola
- ❏ Ginger ale
- ❏ Lemon-lime

Waters

- ❏ Spring water
- ❏ Tonic water
- ❏ Club soda

Liqueurs

- ❏ Brandy
- ❏ Cognac
- ❏ Grand Marnier

Juices

- ❏ Fresh lemon and lime
- ❏ Orange
- ❏ Grapefruit
- ❏ Cranberry
- ❏ Tomato

Fruit

- ❏ Lemons
- ❏ Limes
- ❏ Oranges

Condiments and garnishes

- ❏ Olives*
- ❏ Coarse salt**
- ❏ Tabasco sauce
- ❏ Worcestershire sauce
- ❏ Bitters
- ❏ Celery stalks
- ❏ Grenadine
- ❏ Mint leaves †

Equipment

- ❏ Jigger
- ❏ Shaker
- ❏ Strainer
- ❏ Blender
- ❏ Pitcher
- ❏ Ice bucket
- ❏ Tongs
- ❏ Corkscrew
- ❏ Bottle opener
- ❏ Stirrer
- ❏ Cocktail napkins
- ❏ Knife
- ❏ Cutting board
- ❏ Bar towels

Glasses

- ❏ Wine glasses
- ❏ Champagne flutes
- ❏ Highball glasses
- ❏ Old-fashioned glasses
- ❏ Martini glasses ‡
- ❏ Beer mugs ‡
- ❏ Brandy snifters (for brandy or other liqueurs)
- ❏ Cordial glasses

* Try some large green olives from a local deli. Warn guests if the olives still have pits.

** For blended drinks with salted-rim glasses.

† For Mint Juleps or other summer drinks.

‡ Try freezing glasses and mugs for frost.

Figure 9-8 shows a collection of glassware for serving various drinks. No one we know owns them all. You can serve drinks out of glass jars, use the kind of glasses you already own, rent or borrow some extras, hire a bartender who will provide them, or start a collection. Using non-traditional glasses can add to the atmosphere of the party.

Half gallons, liters, or fifths?

When deciding what size bottles of liquor you need, consider not only what and how much you think your guests will drink but also which size looks best, is easiest to handle, and is most economical. Liters look best on bars and usually result in fewer open bottles remaining at the end of the evening. Half gallons may be slightly less expensive per ounce, but they are awkward to handle. At a self-service bar, guests tend to pour stronger drinks from half gallon bottles than they would from smaller ones. Fifths or pints are fine for cordials.

If you are serving mixed drinks or cocktails, do not buy cheap liquor. Buying the best quality pays off. Good liquor catches people's attention. Believe it or not, top-shelf brands smell and taste better than the bargain brand. Guests will drink less because they will savor, not guzzle, their drinks.

If you are serving blended drinks such as margaritas or daiquiris, however, most guests will not be able to tell a difference in taste. Buy a less expensive brand of liquor and spend the savings on good-quality mixers and fresh fruit.

Frozen water

Remember the old saying, "You can never be too thin, be too rich, or have too much ice?" We added that last part because we want you to overstock. How can you expect guests to chill out at your party if you run short on ice? You need ice to chill the drinks, to put in the drinks, and for guests to suck on when they've have had one too many.

Figure 9-8:
Traditionally, certain drinks are served in certain glasses. Don't worry if you don't own them all.

Here are some of the coolest tips for chilling drinks:

- The fastest way to chill anything (ten minutes flat) is to submerge it in a bucket filled with half ice/half water.

- If you own the kind of ice cream maker that you store in the freezer, take it out of the freezer and set a bottle of wine inside the chamber. The wine will be chilled in ten minutes.

- If there's no room in the fridge, fill the bathtub with ice and bury the beer.

- Do not put carbonated drinks (canned or bottled) or champagne in the freezer. If you forget about them, they will explode and make a royal mess.

When, why, and how to hire a bartender

Whether you are having a barbecue in your backyard or hosting a 25th anniversary party in your dining room, hiring a bartender is a great way to save your sanity. For informal parties, the bartender is a godsend, allowing you to spend more time with your guests. For formal parties, a bartender takes the burden off you and lends an air of elegance to the affair.

Looking for a bartender?

- Call a catering or staffing service.

- Ask a friend who entertains frequently for a recommendation.

- Go to your favorite restaurant or bar and ask the bartender if he/she is for hire to tend bar.

When you hire a bartender, you can arrange for her to do it all, from setup to cleanup and everything in between. You don't need to worry one iota about your bar. All you have to do is put away the table and the booze.

But don't just assume the bartender knows what you want. Tell her exactly what you expect and ask how much the charges are for the service you want. Most bartenders charge an hourly wage that varies depending on where you live.

If you have gone to the trouble to hire someone and have been clear with your instructions from the outset, there's no need to micromanage. Let the bartender do the job. She can advise you on everything from where to put the bar to what and how much to buy.

The bartender is not the caterer, the coat-checker, or the hors d'oeuvre passer. But she should be willing to serve wine with dinner. Make sure that everything is understood before the guests arrive.

How to make a toast

Toasts can be expressions of recognition, appreciation, or affection. They are sometimes funny, sometimes sentimental, and sometimes a bit corny.

Toasts are a tradition that can link generations, end family feuds, and create an air of closeness. They are also an awkward custom, according to Reid Buckley of the Buckley School of Public Speaking in Camden, South Carolina. "They open up the field for windbags and other attention-seekers. Guests are at [the speaker's] mercy unless you have strict and absolute rules," he says.

If you are giving a toast, whether it's at your own party or someone else's, avoid canned stories unless extremely funny or hot off the press. *Remember:* Be gracious, be funny, but be brief. More than two minutes is too much.

We once heard this toast at a party:

"If the soup had been as warm as the wine,
If the wine had been as cold as the chicken,
If the chicken had been as tender as
    the waitress,
If the waitress had been as willing as
    the duchess,
then the dinner would have been divine."

Obviously, you would not want to make such a toast at a private dinner. Someone might take it seriously. But in the context of a large catered function, it was brief, humorous, and appropriate (so much so that we still remember it years later).

At dinner parties, toasts begin after dessert, with coffee and brandy. If a long program will follow, you can give the toast when dessert dishes are being removed from the table rather than waiting until the coffee and/or after dinner drinks are served. Doing so is less elegant but will keep the event moving along.

At non-dinner parties, the toast (there should be only one, rarely rarely rarely more) begins after the first drinks are served, before second drinks. Ask bartenders or waiters to hold the service.

One of the best toasts is a funny anecdote about a person that does not wound or embarrass. Take extreme care not to touch on any sensitive or off-color subject such as race, religion, age, or sex. You do not want to risk offending even one guest.

Here's a simple toast a host might offer to his friends:

"To my friends who know the worst about me but refuse to believe it."

The host/hostess or a close friend should give the toast. (If you plan to ask a friend to do it, give that person advance notice. Calling on someone by surprise is a dirty deal.) If the audience is seated, the person giving the toast may choose to stand or remain seated. The person being toasted and the other guests usually remain seated. The person giving the toast lifts his glass, raises it to the person being toasted, and leads with the first sip.

In a small group, guests may want to clink glasses after the toast and before taking the first sip. The clinking of glasses is a lovely sound. Julia Child refers to it as "the bells of friendship." In large crowds, clinking glasses can be unwieldy. Guests can simply raise their glasses or touch glasses demurely on the right and left. Don't encourage daring reaches across the table lest a guest fall into the flan.

If you are the person being toasted, say a simple thank you. The most marvelous and direct response to a toast was that of Jim Thorpe, the great track star, to King George V of Great Britain, when Thorpe was being presented with his third (or was it his fifth?) Olympic gold medal. "Thanks, King," he said.

Be sure to discuss the dress codes. The bartender should look professional and neat. Khaki pants and a white shirt are fine for casual parties. A black and white uniform is appropriate for any party. (Black pants and shoes, a white shirt, and a black bow tie or a long black tie is suitable attire for men and women.)

It's understood that the bartender doesn't drink on duty. If you have an open bottle of wine at the end of the night, it is a nice gesture to offer it to her. Gratuities are not included in the hourly wage, and tips are always appreciated. Tip as you would the wait staff at a restaurant. You may want to give more generously if the service was exceptional or you plan to hire the bartender again.

How many bartenders do you need? Make sure that you have enough to do the job. Hire one bartender for every 50 guests or one bartender for each bar. For formal affairs, hire two bartenders: one to make drinks, and another to take drink orders.

Coffee, Tea, or Cordials?

The coffees, teas, and drinks served after dinner are the last things your guests put in their mouths. When you have served a delicious dinner and a wonderful dessert, you want the magic to linger. So make sure that your final offering is as good or better than the meal. If you are having a coffee, tea party, or cocktail party, the drinks are the focus. You want them to be delicious.

With a meal, coffee is traditionally served after dessert and stands on its own. However, you can serve coffee anytime a guest asks for it. For example, we have one friend who drinks coffee whenever he comes over — any time of day, with or without a meal. We have another friend who always serves Turkish coffee when he entertains. People love his get-togethers because of his warm personality and because of the delicious Turkish coffee they have come to expect at his house.

If you are not a big coffee drinker, specialty coffee shops can help you make selections. You can pick up brochures that outline the origins and characteristics of the coffees they sell. Smell and taste different varieties to discover what you like.

Buy your coffee beans in a place where there is a high product turnover. (You don't want the stuff that's been sitting around for six months.) Don't buy coffee beans in bulk. For maximum freshness, buy only what you can use within a few weeks, and store the beans in an airtight bag in the freezer.

Invest in a coffee grinder, which is inexpensive. The difference in taste makes up for the cost and for the extra step of grinding the beans yourself. If you can't afford a coffee grinder (preparing for a party can be expensive enough!), borrow one from a friend for your party. Grind the amount you need just before brewing.

Set up your coffee machine and arrange cups hours before the party so that offering guests coffee is not a big deal. (Any kind of coffee maker is suitable.) Allow enough time for the coffee to brew before it's time to serve it. Most household coffee makers take approximately ten minutes to brew a full ten-cup pot. Make two pots, transferring the first one to a thermal serving pot, so that you can give guests a choice of regular or decaffeinated coffee. Provide sugar, low-calorie sweeteners, and cream.

If you are having a large party and do not have the equipment to make the amount of coffee you need, you can rent a commercial coffee maker that brews up to 100 cups of coffee. Allow a full hour before you intend to serve it for the coffee to brew.

If you don't need quite that much coffee or don't want to bother with rentals or spend the extra money, you can try one of the following solutions:

- ✔ Brew the coffee ahead of time and transfer it to separate thermal containers. Most thermoses hold their heat for two to three hours.

- ✔ If you have an instant boiling water unit in your home, speed up the brewing process by passing the hot water directly over a plunger-style coffee pot or a regular coffee filter and pot.

- ✔ Use your everyday coffee maker, but make the coffee extra strong. When you are ready to serve it, add boiling water to the desired strength.

If you can't get extraordinary coffee, you may want to consider offering grated nutmeg, cinnamon, chocolate shavings, pure vanilla powder, and a bowl of fresh whipped-cream. Guests can choose to drink their coffee plain or make it into a second dessert.

You may also want to offer liqueurs such as Kahlúa, Tia Maria, Irish Cream, or Sambuca. Some people like to add them to their coffee.

Offer espresso or cappuccino only if your party is small. Most home machines make only two to four cups at a time, making it impractical to serve more than six or eight guests.

If you want to serve special coffee drinks to a larger crowd than you can handle yourself, you can hire someone to make lattes, espressos, cappuccinos, and so on. (Call specialty coffee shops or caterers or look in the Yellow Pages under "coffee.") Companies that offer this service usually charge a per-head fee, and some have a minimum. The person you hire provides all the ingredients and equipment, including the cups for serving and the water for brewing. All you have to provide is a power source. Hiring someone to make coffee drinks is a special addition for a dessert party or a large charity function.

Guests who like to drink tea after dinner usually want something decaffeinated and soothing like an herbal tea. Chamomile, mint, and Japanese teas are excellent choices. For a more exotic offering (so that guests truly feel like they're on vacation), serve a plum tea. Cinnamon tea is also a good choice, adding a delightful, fresh aroma to the room after a meal. All these teas are so flavorful that guests rarely need to add milk and sugar.

(For more information on how to brew and serve tea or plan a tea party, see Chapter 16.)

You may want to serve another selection of drinks after the coffee and tea. After-dinner drinks are appropriate with any meal, but they are especially wonderful for more intimate parties where guests can sit around in small groups sipping and sharing conversation. Consider an assortment of single-malt scotches or a selection of grappas. (Each has a distinct flavor and different characteristics.) Port is an elegant selection, or you might consider cordials such as Cognac, Grand Marnier, or B&B.

Swimming in the Bathtub with Jim Beam

When you serve alcohol at your party, you may discover that some guests can't hold their liquor or don't know their limits. You want your guests to enjoy themselves, but you do not want to end up with a roomful of swaggering, slobbering, soused strangers. (Even your best friend can become a stranger when in a drunken stupor.)

To avoid inebriated guests hanging their heads over your toilet or sacking out on your sofa for the night, keep an eye out for signs of too many high-octane cocktails, and start weaning them off before it's too late:

- Close the bar/cut off all alcohol before words get slurred and vision gets blurred.
- Serve plenty of food. Make sure that guests are eating and not simply subsisting on liquids.
- Serve lots of water — enough to dilute liquor and get guests going (to the restroom).

Contrary to popular belief, coffee exacerbates the problem. Coffee dehydrates the body, just like alcohol, and does not help guests sober up.

If it's already too late (an obviously drunken guest is staggering about with his car keys in hand), you must take action:

- ✔ Ask your spouse, significant other, or someone sober to drive him home.
- ✔ Send him home in a taxi.
- ✔ Put him to bed or let him sleep it off on the sofa.

Inconvenience is only a part of the reason you don't want your guests getting drunk and driving home. A lawsuit may be lurking in your punch bowl. Yes, you (the host) can be held legally responsible if the guest you have filled with liquor has an accident on the way home. Even if he steps off a curb and breaks his own ankle, the medical bill can turn up in your mailbox.

According to trial lawyer Parker Barnes, of Beaufort, South Carolina, three things are predictable:

- ✔ It is 100 percent predictable that some people will over-imbibe.
- ✔ It is 200 percent predictable that the one who has over-imbibed has already accepted an invitation to be the main character in a lawsuit, whether it's with his spouse, his hosts, another guest, or any other person outside the house.
- ✔ It is 400 percent predictable that lawyers will sue anybody for anything and that they will ask for damages in excess of ten times what the case was not worth to begin with.

The one thing that is unpredictable is a jury.

Be especially careful about providing teenagers with beer or liquor (at prom or graduation parties). Serving alcohol to minors is illegal. "You are liable. It's called 'aiding and abetting' or 'contributing to the delinquency of a minor,'" says Barnes. "Nothing is simple except this: Don't do it!"

Even if you are not concerned about lawsuits, consider your moral obligation to your guests. If a person is a good enough friend to invite to your party, you should be a good enough friend to make sure that he returns home safely.

Part III
Minor Details, Major Impressions

In this part . . .

This is the closest we come to setting rules. Yes, we show you how to set a "proper" table. But we also encourage creativity and show you how to make the most of what you have. We help you make decisions regarding entertainment based on the size and type of party you are having. We also discuss the basics of good behavior for hosts and guests. But we're not just talking table manners. For the host, we offer tips on how to get guests to the table and how to get them to go home. Whether you are the host or a guest, we help you create and foster lively conversations and give you some pointers on how to keep your cool in a crisis.

Chapter 10

Table Settings and Food Presentation

- -

In This Chapter

▶ Deciding how to serve

▶ Setting a beautiful table

▶ Presenting the food

- -

You're having 12 people over for dinner and you have only 8 plates, your knives are so dull they won't cut butter, and you wouldn't know a champagne flute from a shot glass. And what do you mean you don't have time to carve the potatoes into palm tree shapes?

Before you get carried away worrying about the dishes you don't have or waste time performing major surgery on food for decoration, ask yourself, "Does anybody really care?"

Although there is a right place to put the wine glass and a correct way to line up the forks, table setting is more than just the way to arrange things. More important, your table setting should make guests physically comfortable and visually excited. The same is true for the way you present the food. Arranging food and embellishing plates can be minimal and simple but still pack quite a punch.

In this chapter, we help you decide on a serving style and show you how to set the table accordingly. You find out where everything goes, but you also get tips on setting the table and presenting the food so that it enhances your party without overwhelming the people.

Deciding on a Serving Style

Before you can figure out how to set the table or how to present the food, you must decide on a serving style. Will your party be a buffet or a sit-down dinner? Will it be casual or formal?

Many factors determine the way you choose to serve the food: the kind of party you are having, the space you have, the food, the number of guests, how much help you have, the atmosphere you are trying to create, and your own personal traditions and preferences. The following are a few ways to set up and serve:

- **French service:** Guests are seated at tables. Waiters serve one course at a time from platters to guests' plates. This is the most formal and elegant service — the style of the rich and famous. If you get an invitation to dine at the White House, expect to be served in this manner.

  Very few occasions call for French service. It can seem pompous, and the formality can make people uncomfortable. French service is appropriate on a cruise ship where the whole experience is about show.

- **Plated:** Plate the food in the kitchen. You can arrange food so that it looks beautiful on the plates. Depending on the size of your party, you may need help. If you don't need or want professional help, recruit your spouse or child, a friend, or a helpful guest.

  For a small party, you can easily plate the food yourself. Or you can ask guests to come into the kitchen and get their plates as you fill them. Asking guests to get their plates is a good way to get people involved in the party. Guests feel uncomfortable while you are slaving away in the kitchen. See Chapter 15 for tips on plating food for a larger group.

- **Family Style:** Pass platters around the table. Guests helps themselves.

  Family style service is the best all-around serving style for any type or any size of party (even a fancy wedding). It is the easiest way for the host to serve, it encourages people to interact, it makes people feel more relaxed, and guests can take as much or little as they want to eat.

- **Buffet:** Set up the food on a table or sideboard. (Or if you're short on space, you can serve a buffet effectively and attractively right from the stove or kitchen counter.) Guests help themselves. Buffets are perfect if you have a small table or a large crowd.

  Keep an eye on the platters. When one starts looking shabby, replace the platter with a fresh one. Use warming trays or chafing dishes to keep food hot.

  Buffets get people moving. Besides a good stretch of the legs, buffet service allows guests to move around and talk to more people than if they were stuck sitting in one place for the entire meal.

- **Combination:** Sometimes the most effective service style of all is a combination of the preceding. You can take advantage of the best features of each style. Guests enjoy the variety, too. For part of the meal, they are royally served and for part of the meal, they can move around and serve themselves. Here is an example of how you can use a combination of serving styles:

- **Main course:** Serve French style. No need to hire help: You can be the old woman who lived in a shoe and serve like they do in the White House. You can handle serving one course yourself or use your children as waiters. Or you can hire out a few neighborhood kids. Ages 8 to 16 are ideal. Make sure that the kids are strong enough to hold platters for a length of time so that the entire contents doesn't end up in some unsuspecting guest's lap.

- **Salad:** Toss and plate in the kitchen.

- **Dessert course:** Lay out a dessert buffet.

Setting the Table

You know how many guests you invited. Now that you've chosen your style of serving, you have some idea of how many tables you need to set. Do you have to set up a buffet table? A few tables to seat guests? One big table? Before you get hung up on the minor details, go back to your big picture. What feeling do you want to convey? Pay attention to the basics: lighting, color, music, and so on.

Put your energy into creating the mood rather than worrying about what you don't own. People will notice the actual items on your table a lot less than the overall ambiance.

Mix, match, and make do

When you plan your party and your menu, you consider the atmosphere you want to create. Now you need to carry through that atmosphere to your table. You don't need to go out and buy an expensive linen table cloth or a matching set of crystal, nor should you have to spend a fortune on flowers or other elaborate table decorations. In fact, not owning everything can actually help make your party successful. By making do with what you have, you are saying to your guests, "I am enjoying what I have. There's no pretense here."

Whether you own an abundance or practically nothing, approach the table as a blank canvas — you're painting the picture. You can add, subtract, and do whatever you want.

To decorate your table, choose something that goes with your personality or plan. You may choose a color, a flower, or a vegetable. Or the table can be totally bare, if that's your style. You can use something you collect, such as shells, dolls, model cars, or hats. Scrounge around your house for things you love. You'll find something just right for decorating your table.

If you are serving family style, don't clutter up the table with collections. Save space for platters and bowls of food.

You may want to set the table using one theme, such as all glass, all pottery, or all baskets. Or, maybe you would rather mix things up a bit. Nothing has to match. In fact, a too-matched setting can be dull.

Mixing styles is exciting as long as all the elements are the same quality. You can mix antiques with contemporary pieces, rustic with fancy. What you don't want to do is mix a van Gogh painting with left-over packing crates or use paper cups with a silver tea service.

"Making do" does not mean you cannot use your beautiful things. If you've ever had a bridal shower, you've probably got more china in the closet than stars in your eyes. If you've been collecting silver for 20 years, chances are that your silver is a major chunk of your net worth. Or maybe you inherited china, linens, flatware, or crystal from a grandparent. Don't let your treasures collect dust. Get them out of their hiding places and use them for entertaining. Your attitude makes the difference in how guests respond. What's really important is your joy in using and sharing your best.

The great cover-up

Whether you own an antique pedestal-base mahogany table, an old, beat up, hand-me-down dinette, or an ordinary card table, you can dress it up or dress it down to suit your taste and your purpose. Guests will never guess that they are eating off a cable spool or a cardboard box if it's covered with a lovely fabric.

A plain ivory table cloth is most flattering to your guests — people's faces stand out and look beautiful without too many competing patterns. A colored undercloth with lace overlay is another elegant option. Bright, dark, or patterned tablecloths look most stunning if your china is plain (not patterned). To measure for a tablecloth: Add 24 to 30 inches to the dimensions of your table for a 12 to 15 inch overhang.

If you don't own a tablecloth, there is no need to go out and buy expensive linens. Use what you have available:

- ✔ Bedspreads
- ✔ Burlap
- ✔ Colored paper
- ✔ Curtains
- ✔ Flat-weave rugs

- ✔ Palm leaves
- ✔ Quilts
- ✔ Taffeta

Sometimes less is more. Silver reflected on a bare mahogany table looks stunning. Enhance — don't hide — the natural beauty of the wood by using linen or lace place mats rather than a tablecloth.

Place mats take up more space at each place setting. If you are squeezing extra guests around your table, go ahead and use a tablecloth. For buffets, where people are seating themselves randomly and may want to sit close together, tablecloths work better than placemats.

It's a bird, it's a plane . . . it's a napkin

Cloth napkins are nicer than paper for any kind of entertaining. But that doesn't necessarily mean starched linen damask. Cloth napkins can be dishtowels, fabric remnants, bandannas, or even washcloths. They can be cotton or chintz. Choose a fabric that goes with the atmosphere of your party.

Of course, there is absolutely no reason why you cannot use paper napkins for a casual party, picnic, or buffet. Many gift shops and paper companies offer good quality heavy paper napkins in a variety of beautiful colors and designs.

Forget about fancy napkin folds. Leave the fans, flowers, and birds to the restaurants. For home entertaining, keep it simple. All you need to do is fold the napkin in a traditional rectangle or triangle. You can place the napkin in the center of the plate, to the left of the forks, or under the forks, stuff it in the wine glass, or drape it over the back of the chair. For a looser look, grasp the center of the unfolded napkin between your thumb and forefinger; lay it down beside the fork.

For a slightly more decorative touch for your napkins, try these tricks:

- ✔ Pull the napkin through a napkin ring.
- ✔ Roll the napkin up diagonally.
- ✔ Roll the napkin up diagonally and tie a knot in the center.
- ✔ Roll the napkin up, tie a ribbon around it, and add a sprig of flowers.

China versus Chinet

Dinnerware comes in a huge array of colors, patterns, and prices. You don't need a full set of fine china to entertain. You can set a table with mismatched china and serve out of your pots and pans. Most people couldn't care less about the price of the plate.

When you do decide to invest in fine china, think through your selection. You want to be happy with this decision for a long time. If you can buy only one set, choose all white. Classic white never becomes outdated; you are not likely to tire of it; and best of all, it's versatile. All food looks good on white china, and it goes with everything.

Maybe you enjoy collecting china and own entire sets. Or perhaps you have just a few plates from several sets. To create visual excitement, try using different plates for different courses, or use a different pattern at each place setting. For a large party, use a different set on each table. You need not ever invest in a matched set of china for twenty four.

Don't worry if the only plate you own is the one you use for your microwave meals. That's why paper and plastic were invented. Go to your favorite gift shop or paperware company. You can find a startling array of colors, shapes, and patterns to suit almost every occasion and match most any mood.

If you don't feel comfortable using paper plates, you can rent or borrow what you need, or even serve a meal without plates. See Figure 10-1 for a sample menu.

Figure 10-1:
With a little imagination, you don't need plates.

> ### A Dinner with No Plates
>
> *Crab meat served in ½ honeydew melon*
>
> *Homemade mayonnaise in hollowed out lemon halves*
>
> ❧
>
> *Turkey salad in iceberg lettuce cups*
>
> ❧
>
> *Ice cream cones*

What to do with forks, knives, and spoons

Have you ever sat down in a fancy restaurant only to face six forks, four spoons, an entire set of knives, and goblets galore? Each item has its intended function, but all that glass and silver can be a little confusing.

If your dinner requires more than one fork per person and you don't have enough to go around, aim for one apiece and wash them between courses. (Most people don't know what to do with all those extras anyway.)

According to Ed Munves of James Robinson, Inc., in New York (one of the world's most elegant silver stores), "Nothing is wrong as long as it's done neatly, cleanly, and politely. Too much emphasis is put on rituals that had to start with someone making up rules. People should do what is comfortable for them and their guests."

When it comes to utensils, how many you put on the table is insignificant. What counts is that each guest has just what is needed to eat and enjoy the food. The following table shows uses for each utensil.

Utensil	Use
Small fork	First course, salad, breakfast, lunch
Large fork	Lunch, dinner
Large spoon	Soup, dessert
Small spoon	Stir, dessert, fruit
Knife	Cut, spread

For buffets, you can either set the dining table with silverware at each place or set up the utensils on the end of the buffet table. If guests are sitting randomly (or in places other than tables), you can roll up a set of utensils (fork, knife, spoon) inside each napkin. Stand the rolls up in a basket or bowl for a presentation that looks like sculpture.

Glasses

Chapter 9 shows glasses in all shapes and sizes for every beverage under the sun. If you've stocked your home bar with glasses for every type of drink, use them. But you don't need to buy a collection of glassware for a party. All you really need is an all-purpose wine glass for each person. The glasses don't even have to match.

If you are having a large cocktail party and plan to set up a bar, expect guests to use more glasses. You can borrow or rent sets of glasses or have your caterer or bartender provide them. To avoid any separation anxiety, never mix your own glasses with those you have rented or borrowed.

For an elaborate meal that calls for a different wine with each course, four glasses per person is usually enough: one for white wine with the soup and fish course, one for red wine with meat, a champagne flute for dessert, and a water glass. If you plan to serve a separate sherry or Madeira with a soup course, add a fifth glass.

At a buffet, don't expect guests to hold their plates, utensils, and glasses. If you have set tables, put the glasses on the tables along with bottles of wine and/or pitchers of water. If guests are seating themselves around the room, walk around and hand out glasses and pour drinks. Leave open bottles near guests so that they can refill their own drinks. For a large or formal party, you may need help to distribute and refill drinks.

Putting It All Together

After you round up all the plates, silverware, and glasses you need to set your table or tables, your next step is figuring out where it all goes. Know a few basic rules about "proper" place settings, such as where to put the water glass and the salad fork. Place settings are standardized not just for the sake of having a set of rules, but for everyone's comfort. For example, whether you eat in a five-star restaurant or in someone's home at a sit-down dinner or a buffet, table settings are the same. Any plates in front of you or to your left are yours, and any glasses to your right are yours as well. Set your table in logical order so that guests are not confused.

All you really need to serve a great sit-down meal (a buffet, a sit-down dinner, a picnic, a barbecue, and so on) is one plate per person, one fork, knife and spoon per plate, and one all-purpose glass per person. Figure 10-2 shows a simple table setting.

If your table is crowded, conserve space by using only two utensils: a fork and a knife. You can save more room by putting the napkins under or on top of each person's plate or by draping them over the backs of the chairs. Take out dessert utensils when it's time for dessert.

If you are serving an elaborate meal and have the space and enough silverware, go ahead and put out all the utensils. If you have them, why not use them? Your table will look spectacular. The utensil to be used first goes on the outside, continuing in toward the plate in order of intended use. Line up utensils evenly at the bottom.

Figure 10-2:
This simple table setting is easy for you and comfortable for your guests. No one has to guess which fork to use first.

A Simple Table Setting

If you are using the menu shown in Figure 10-3, set the table as described in the following list. Figure 10-4 shows an elaborate table setting.

Side of the plate	Utensil
Left	Fish fork, salad fork, dinner fork. If you are serving European style (serving salad last), reverse the dinner and salad forks.
Right	Outside in — soup spoon, fish knife, dinner knife.
Top	Dessert spoon and fork. If you prefer, you can bring the dessert utensils in with the dessert instead of putting them on the table at the beginning of the meal.

Unless you don't mind people smoking during the meal, don't put ashtrays on the tables. Smokers, unite — outside. (See Chapter 12 for more on smoking etiquette.)

Un-setting a Table

How you un-set, or clear, the table also adds to guests' comfort and enjoyment of the meal. Clear the dirty dishes and used utensils between courses. If you don't, the table looks sloppy and makes the next course look less appealing. Before you serve dessert, remove anything on the table that was used for the first or main course.

Lay It All Out Menu

Wild mushroom soup and tiny pepper biscuits

ès

Shrimp and bay scallops with herbs

ès

Salad of diced tomatoes, cucumbers, and yellow peppers; warm croutons

ès

Pork loin, braised with bourbon

Sautéed broccoli

Glazed shallots and carrots

ès

Frozen coffee mouse in meringue shells with warm chocolate sauce

Figure 10-3: If you are serving a menu like this one, use all the utensils you have.

Figure 10-4: Guests may not know where to start, but they will be comfortable when you lead the way.

An Elaborate Table Setting

Clear all of the following:

- ✔ Plates
- ✔ Dirty flatware
- ✔ Platters
- ✔ Salt and pepper shakers
- ✔ Bread basket
- ✔ Butter

Leave wine and water glasses on the table so that guests can continue sipping.

Blooms and Beyond: Center Attractions

You don't have to be a floral designer or interior decorator to create an attractive centerpiece. In fact, centerpieces look best when they are spontaneous in spirit — not too perfectly arranged. You want to choose something pleasing to look at, but not something so ostentatious that it distracts from the food and conversation.

Nowhere is it written that you have to have a centerpiece. If you don't have time to arrange anything and don't feel like forking over the money for a florist, go for a bare look. Bare can be especially effective on a small table. Unscented candles are good additions and substitutions for flower arrangements.

Be careful not to place tall candles or a candelabra directly between two people, obstructing their line of vision. Move them slightly to the left or right so that guests can see each other, or choose low candles such as votives that guests can clearly see over.

On a buffet table, where you are not concerned about guests' line of vision, you can use tall candles, a candelabra, or a tall flower arrangement. Just be sure that the table decorations do not create an obstacle for guests when reaching for food.

The key to a great centerpiece is doing what's comfortable for you. If that means calling the florist, then do it. If you enjoy creating your own arrangements, then have some fun with your centerpieces.

Flower power

Sometimes, calling a florist is the easiest and best option. For the best chance at getting the flowers you want, order them a few days before your party. You can specify the type of container (or bring your own) as well as the colors, height, and density of the arrangement. If you don't know exactly what you want, give the florist some information about your party and your table setting. The florist will be able to make suggestions and work within your budget.

Don't build a forest in the middle of your table. Keep the arrangement low or sparse (or both low and sparse) so that guests can see over or through it. If you prefer something large and dramatic, go for effect. Use the arrangement as a decoration, but remove it when guests sit down to eat.

Stay away from strongly scented flowers at the table. You don't want the sweet smell of the flowers to overwhelm the aroma of the food. If you can smell the flowers from across the room, they are too overpowering for the table.

Choose any flower you love. Although people sometimes associate certain flowers with certain occasions such as funerals or weddings, most people appreciate any flower for its beauty and are not likely to question its function at your party. If your favorite flowers have an over-powering smell or if you just want them to stand out, use them near the entrance to your party rather than on the table. A striking arrangement gets attention at the door, and guests may not notice any arrangement later when they are engrossed in conversations and concentrating on the meal.

If you prefer to arrange your own flowers, you can buy them from the florist or pick them from a garden or field. Use Oasis, pin holders, or chicken wire for stability. If these terms are foreign to you, ask a friend to show you some flower-arranging basics or get a book on the subject. Vary the heights of the flowers for interest.

Don't be afraid to take a new approach. If your party is formal, throw a few garden flowers in a bowl and let them fall loosely to liven up a perfectly ordered table. If your party is casual and you're serving something simple like meatloaf, use roses or orchids for a striking contrast. Remember, more isn't always better. One exquisite flower can be as beautiful as a roomful of flowers.

For a stunning arrangement in less than two minutes, all you really need is a bunch of daisies and a 4-inch crystal vase (or a tea pot, pitcher, or watering can). Strip the leaves off the bottom of the stems, cut the stems under water, fill the vase with warm water, and Voilà! You have your centerpiece.

The following are a few more easy ways to arrange the flowers:

- Use baskets of zinnias.
- Arrange sets of flowers in small containers. Use three sets per table, each a different color. Use white linen and white china to show off the bursts of color on the tables.
- Line up wine bottles or silver cups down the center of the table. Put one stem in each.

If you've gone to the trouble or expense to get flowers for your party, make the most of them. Here are some tips to help extend the life of your flowers:

- Buy the freshest flowers available.
- Re-cut the stems under water.
- Strip the leaves from the stem so that no leaves are touching the water.
- Put flowers in a container of fresh water as soon as possible.
- Change the water every day.

Weeds, twigs, and other natural wonders

You can find some of the best materials for your centerpieces in your backyard or on the side of the road. Develop an eye for nature, and you will open up a world of ideas for your table. Wildflowers, rushes, tall grass, small cattails, eucalyptus, ferns, Spanish moss, milkweed, foxtail, pine straw, and pine cones are just a few possibilities.

Other items to consider:

- Leaves
- Driftwood
- Rocks
- Shells
- Birds' nests

Be careful what you pick. Some plants are pretty, but endangered. (The lady's slipper is one example.) Other plants serve a specific purpose — picking sea oats is illegal in many coastal areas because they protect the sand dunes. If in doubt about a plant or flower, leave it. And make sure that the bird's nest is abandoned before you take it home.

Never try to improve on nature. You have no need to enhance flowers, twigs, weeds, or pine cones with spray paint. Unless the decoration is expertly done, it has the potential to look tacky. Save the glitter and gold spray paint for your "totally tacky" party. See Chapter 20 for a complete plan.

Good enough to eat

If you are looking for a beautiful and economical way to decorate your table, turn your eyes to the food. A basket of homemade breads, breadsticks, rolls, and biscuits makes an attractive and scrumptious centerpiece. (If you've gone to the trouble to make them, why not show them off?)

Fruits and vegetables make colorful centerpieces, and you can turn the produce into a course for the meal or a meal for the next day.

Make a simple but elegant arrangement of whole, perfectly ripe fruit. Use all one fruit or choose a variety of colors, shapes, and sizes. Mound up the fruit in a basket or bowl or build a pyramid on a platter or on the table itself. Bring out cheeses, breads, and port, and serve the centerpiece for dessert.

Pile different textured vegetables such as eggplant, artichokes, and pomegranates on a platter. Or, stand stalks of asparagus or several bunches of green onions in a small tureen. Nothing is wasted if you cook the veggies for another meal.

For a dramatic approach, use a main course such as Beef Wellington or a whole fish on palm leaves as your centerpiece. After that course is served, remove the platter and leave the center of the table bare.

Odds and ends

The possibilities for centerpieces are endless. You may want to mix and match elements. For example, mix fall flowers with fall fruits or vegetables. Flowers and candles are also an effective combination.

Here are a few more ideas:

- Fill a clear bowl with as many whole lemons as you can fit in the container. Add water. Stick a few purple irises between the lemons.
- Cover straw hats with real flowers. (Use a glue gun to attach the flowers. The glue gun seals the moisture in the stem. Expect the flowers to last four hours. The hats can be party favors.)

✔ Wrap boxes like gifts and pile them in the center of the table and place real gifts wrapped individually in front of each place setting for guests to take home.

✔ Display framed photographs with candles (best for birthdays, showers, and anniversaries).

Presenting the Food

When you have made the effort to prepare good food, you certainly want to present it so that it looks as good as it tastes. The food you present should be a feast for guests' eyes as well as their appetites.

Food presentations need not be pretentious. A little food on a large plate is more attractive than too much food on a small plate. Food should not be so decorated that it looks like an entire kitchen brigade had their hands all over it before it got to the table. Leave the ice carvings and complicated displays to the five-star hotels. (Who has the skill or the time?) For home entertaining, take a simple and straightforward approach.

If you have planned your menu with balance in mind, making the food look attractive is easy. Make your presentations colorful with one of the following:

✔ **The food itself:** Put some color in your menu by serving foods such as peppers, spinach, and saffron rice.

✔ **The serving piece:** Use colorful dishes to serve plain foods such as white or brown rice, pasta, and bread.

✔ **The decoration:** Add a spot of color to meat platters with garnishes such as sliced tomatoes, arugula, herbs, or flowers. (See "To garnish or not to garnish," later in this chapter for more suggestions.)

Choosing a serving piece

One way to choose a serving piece is to match the personality of the food with the dish on which you serve it:

✔ Arrange elegant foods such as lintzer tortes, fancy cakes, delicate pastries, or chocolate truffles on crystal or silver platters.

✔ Present rustic foods such as stews, pies, or cobblers in pottery.

✔ Offer assortments of one item in baskets; for example, an appetizer of raw vegetables or desserts such as cookies.

✔ Serve colorful foods such as fruits, vegetables, or glazed desserts on or in plain white china or clear glass containers.

Or, have some fun and juxtapose the food's personality with a serving piece that's just the opposite of its perceived character:

✔ Pass everyday foods such as hamburger buns on a silver platter with an orchid.

✔ Put a delicacy such as smoked salmon on rustic pottery with branches of herbs. Make containers out of fruits and vegetables for a natural presentation.

✔ Use hollowed out pumpkins, squashes, and peppers as containers for other vegetables (asparagus, celery, radishes, or carrots) or fill them with dip.

✔ Halve cantaloupe, honeydew melons, avocados, or tomatoes to hold crab, shrimp, or any poached or marinated fish.

✔ Fill Belgian endive leaves with vegetable or fish mousse.

✔ Hollow out lemons, oranges, or tangerines for sweet mousses, or fill with sorbet, ice cream, or frozen yogurt and freeze until needed.

To garnish or not to garnish?

Many times, food looks lovely as it is and needs no embellishment. However, a little decoration can be the detail that makes the dish memorable.

The most natural decorations come right from your menu. If you are cooking with any fresh herb, such as basil, rosemary, or thyme, save a few sprigs for garnishing. Lay the decoration flat on the plate or stick it straight up in the food for a more dramatic effect. Use whole miniature vegetables, long strips of citrus zest, or thin strips of leeks or onions crisply fried.

If nothing from your menu strikes your fancy, go out into the yard and look for things you can wash and use as plate decorations — maybe a different wildflower for each course. Lining a plain white platter with food and adding one or two small flowers at the edge is elegant and easy.

Be careful when garnishing with flowers. Guests may automatically assume that anything on the plate is edible. Some backyard plants are poisonous. Sometimes the flowers are edible and the other parts of the plant are not. Also beware of commercially grown flowers that may have been sprayed with insecticides. Purchase edible flowers from a specialty grocer.

Here are a few examples of flowers that are safe to eat. You can choose them according to appearance or taste. Try tossing edible flowers in salads or candy the petals for a dessert garnish.

Acacias	Jasmine
Almond-scented broom	Lavender
Bergamot (good with poultry, pork, and curries)	Lilac
Carnations (clovelike)	Marigold (citrus flavored)
Dandelion (bitter)	Mimosa
Flowers of all fruits	Nasturtium (peppery)
Geraniums (scented)	Rose (candy the petals for a dessert garnish)
Hawthorn	Squash or zucchini blossoms (can be stuffed and then poached or fried)
Hibiscus	Violet (mild wintergreen)
Hollyhock	

If you enjoy playing with knives and creating sculpture, you can dress up dishes with interesting cuts of vegetables or fruits. Many cookbooks carry step-by-step instructions for commonly used garnishes. For more complex creations, you may want to invest in a book on garnishing, a good sharp knife, and possibly a set of garnishing tools.

A little garnishing goes a long way. Too much will ruin the effect. Spend more time on the food that is to be eaten than on that which will only be seen.

Drum roll, please!

What you serve and what you serve it on is only a part of the total presentation. You can add a little drama with your methods and madness.

✔ Pile trays with whole fruit; fill bowls with grapes dripping over the sides; offer plates of walnuts, almonds, cheeses, and breads.

✔ Bring tarts, cakes, or pies to the table whole so guests will be awed by the sight of them.

✔ Arrange platters with an assortment of bite-sized desserts.

✔ Add a sauce to dessert. Ladle it on the plate and set the dessert on top of it. Fruit sauces add color; creme anglaise and zabaglione add luxury, and chocolate adds decadence.

Light up guests' eyes and set their souls on fire with a flaming dessert such as cherries jubilee, crêpes suzette, bananas Foster, or Christmas pudding. (See Chapter 8 for more advice on "showstopper desserts" and how to avoid burning the house down.)

Presentation tips for the truly insane

If you really love cooking and have oodles of time to mess around in the kitchen, go ahead and knock yourself out — make yourself crazy. If you want to gild the lily, go over the top, and make a major impression, one of these extra details may be worth the time to set your party apart:

✔ Make tiny tarts or stuff mushroom caps for starters. (Guests will be salivating.)

✔ Make appetizers that puff up in the oven. (Guests will go wild.)

✔ Make handmade breads, rolls, breadsticks, crackers, or biscuits. (Guests will go ape over one, turn flips over two, and be totally stunned by an assortment.)

✔ Make butter curls and place them on top of each other in a triangular shape to pass with your homemade bread. (Guests will ooh and ahh.)

✔ Make soufflés. (Guests will swoon.)

✔ Make individual beef or veal Wellingtons. You can cheat and use frozen puff pastry or really go crazy and start from scratch. (Guests will be howling at the moon.)

✔ Make homemade ravioli. Appetizers will qualify you for temporary insanity. Dinner portions may just put you over the edge. (Guests will be crazy about this.)

✔ Fill snow peas with anything. (Guests will be dumbstruck. You may be ready for a straitjacket.)

✔ Make chocolate truffles with a fresh raspberry inside. Dip each truffle in melted dark chocolate for a hard, crunchy coating. (Guests may die and go to heaven.)

✔ Any adventure in filo pastry is a sure sign of madness. (Guests will go completely nuts.)

Chapter 11

Bring on the Entertainment

● ●

● ●

*T*he three-piece band is over your budget. Your yard's too small for pony rides. And everyone slept through the vacation videos at your last party. What's left for the entertainment?

First, start thinking of entertainment on a much more fundamental level. Parties are entertainment in themselves: They appeal to all the senses, create a mood, set an atmosphere, break the ice, and bring people out of their shells. Even if you are extremely famous or extremely wealthy, guests are not expecting an exotic striptease by Demi Moore or a whirl around the dance floor with John Travolta. If people can leave their worries at the door, relax, and have some fun, that's entertainment! For most small parties in the home, you need nothing more.

Big parties, in contrast, can handle hullabaloo. At a big party, entertainment may be just the extra something that puts the party over the top and makes it unforgettable.

In this chapter, we show you how to take advantage of the natural entertainment value of your parties — when it's enough, and when you need to add more. When the occasion calls for planned entertainment, we show you how to choose it, where to find it, and how to fit it in your budget.

Entertainment for Small Parties

Most small parties in the home do not need extra entertainment. In fact, entertainment can easily overwhelm a small party. Too many competing elements can cancel each other out, creating an atmosphere of chaos and confusion. These surroundings can make your party overstimulating instead of relaxing. But just because you haven't planned entertainment doesn't mean that your guests won't be entertained.

At a small party, the people are the focus. Your guests are a part of the entertainment — not in an obvious or planned way, but just by being themselves. For example, someone who captivates others with stories or someone who's naturally clever, witty, or just plain fun to be around can liven up the whole crowd. Never underestimate the power of a fascinating guest.

The natural attraction of other guests is a powerful factor in having a successful party. In addition, if you plan your party with the five senses in mind, people respond to the overall atmosphere: lighting, decorations, aromas wafting from the kitchen, attractive and delicious food, drinks, and party sounds. (See Chapter 6 for ways to create atmosphere through the senses.) When you stimulate guests' senses, moods change, spirits lift, and people become animated. Who can ask for better entertainment? It's free. And it's often all you need.

Most people are easy to entertain — all they really want is an escape from their normal routines. What people don't want is another dull evening to add to their lives. The key is to offer them a break — a change of scenery and a change of pace.

People can find entertainment in the simplest things:

- ✔ A guest whom others would love to meet
- ✔ A guest who is a born raconteur
- ✔ Delicious food
- ✔ A meal in which guests actively participate in the preparations (make their own pizza, pasta, tacos, and so on)
- ✔ A flaming dessert
- ✔ A daring cocktail or luscious wine
- ✔ A delightful child (greeting them and helping you)
- ✔ A lovely view
- ✔ A cool breeze
- ✔ A sunset
- ✔ A starry night, a full moon
- ✔ A knock-their-eyes-out outfit
- ✔ A fire — in the fireplace or in the oven (Yes, even a disaster or mistake can count!)

Music is a valuable element at a party, although at a small gathering, conversation may be enough noise. If you use music for a small party, play your favorite CDs or tapes to help create a mood. Make sure that you keep the volume at a level that doesn't interfere with conversation.

Don't let dead silence hit the airwaves midparty, forcing you to leave your guests in search of more music. Estimate the length of your party, and prepare your music ahead of time. If by chance you underestimate the amount of music you need, you can always start it over or put a CD on repeat.

Depending on the kind of party you are having, you can ask guests what they would like to hear. At most parties, people are not paying close attention to the music because they are listening to conversations. However, if the party is a large outdoor gathering or a dance where the music plays a more central role than mere background noise, you can take guests' requests.

Although a small soirée doesn't need extra embellishment, some hosts feel more comfortable with some form of planned entertainment. If you like staging games or other activities or if you feel more secure having something planned, use your intuition and organize something you think that your guests would get involved in and enjoy.

Use your guests' talents. Ask them in advance to:

- Make up a limerick
- Tell a joke
- Perform a magic trick
- Sing a song
- Play an instrument

Games are another option. In the right group of people, games can be loads of fun. Small groups can play board games or card games. For larger groups, word games or mystery-solving games can involve everyone at once.

Often, people are not in the mood to be told what to do or pushed into a structured activity. If you're planning your party around a particular activity such as swimming, lawn bowling, charades, or card games, let folks know via the invitation. People who hate those kinds of parties have the option to politely refuse. Those who love getting involved have something fun to look forward to.

Pop quiz

Which two activities have every potential to suck the life out of any gathering?

A. Home movies

B. Your child's cello concert

C. Truth or Dare

D. Charades

E. Pictionary

F. Trivial Pursuit

Answer: If you chose anything other than A and B, your party is in trouble.

Entertainment for Large Parties

Big parties are different from small parties in that large gatherings can handle more extensive entertainment. At a big party with dozens of guests, entertainment doesn't detract from other elements. In fact, it enhances the party atmosphere. With planning and imagination, entertainment can make the party fabulous, festive, and fun.

The first step in choosing entertainment for a large party is to figure out the mood you want to create. Entertainment can establish and carry a mood or a theme. For example, if you're trying to create an elegant or romantic mood, hire a violinist, harpist, pianist, and/or vocalist. If you want a more lively atmosphere, hire a jazz band, folk singer, interactive smaller band, or disc jockey (often called a *deejay*).

If you plan your party around a theme, match the entertainment to that theme: a jukebox for an "oldies" party, a fiddler or line-dance instructor for a western party, slot machines and a craps table for a gambling party. Or get a feel for the atmosphere you want, and look for entertainment to create or enrich that ambience.

After you decide on the atmosphere, you need to consider your crowd. If your guests are not the dancing type, a pianist and vocalist are more appropriate and more enjoyable than a dance band.

Tell the guests what the entertainment will be. This announcement not only builds excitement, but gives people fair warning about what you expect of them. People may not like being asked to do the tango by surprise.

Make sure that the entertainment you choose

✔ Is appropriate for the kind of party you are having.

✔ Suits your guests' tastes and ages.

✔ Is something you personally love.

✔ Works with the setting and the space.

Live music can certainly energize any party. However, most houses can't handle big bands, and most occasions don't call for them. If you do choose live music, think about what's appropriate for your space and what else is going on in that space (chatting, cocktails, dinner, or dancing). For small spaces, opt for one piece. A piano is a good choice. No need to worry if you don't have one. Many pianists have portable keyboards that they can customize to produce the sound you want.

A performer can easily control the volume of her instrument, but not so for a multipiece band. If your party is outdoors or in a rental space, you can choose larger, louder bands. The following are just a few examples of music and other forms of entertainment that may work better for home parties.

Outdoors

Fiddler	Bluegrass band	Reggae music
Calypso or steel drums	Guitarist/vocalist	One-man band
Small dance band	Disc jockey	Hay ride
Canoe rides	Fireworks	Bonfire
Oyster roast	Pig roast	Clam bake

Formal

String quartet	Cellist	Harpist
Pianist	Jazz band	Duo (two violins, violin
Keyboard player	Flaming desserts	and flute, flute and harp,
Disc jockey for	Limbo contest	and so on)
ballroom dancing	Espresso/cappuccino	Combo (an ensemble of
Casino with roulette	maker	three to five different
and craps tables	Crepe maker	instruments)

Informal

CDs	Disc jockey	Jukebox
Barbershop quartet	Guitarist	Belly dancer
Magician	Fortune-teller	Storyteller
Comedian	Caricaturist	Mime or clown
Square dancing	Handwriting analyst	Dance instructor (can teach the hottest new craze or anything from the tango to the two-step. Some dance instructors can also serve as disc jockeys).

Finding the Entertainment You Want

When you decide the type of entertainment you want, find it and reserve it. Good entertainment books up quickly, especially on Saturdays and holidays. You probably need to nail it down at least six weeks in advance of your party. Remember, the sooner you book entertainment, the more likely you are to get what you want.

The best way to find entertainers is to go to a reputable agent. You can locate agents listed in the Yellow Pages under "Entertainment," or "Entertainment Bureaus." Find out who's reputable by asking friends who give big parties or plan big events or by calling the best hotels in your area. Hotel convention and conference services can refer you to the most reliable companies.

After you find out what entertainment is available, the ideal way to make the final selection is to see the performance in person. Ask if you can observe them in a place where they perform regularly or at another event. That way, you're sure of what you're getting. If you can't see the entertainer in action, ask for references from people who have used them.

Some musicians have tapes and videos you can review. Tapes aren't always a true representation. A video is better, because you can see how the entertainer interacts with guests and maintains the mood of the party.

Other ways to find entertainment:

- ✔ If you see or hear great entertainment at someone else's party, at a nightclub, or at a public event, ask the performer for a business card or talk to the host or event organizer to see how you can get in touch with the performer at a later date. Keep your own file of names and numbers for future reference.

- ✔ Call local high schools and colleges to book their jazz bands or other musicians.

- ✔ Hire a disc jockey to make some party tapes. You can help tailor the music for dancing, cocktails, dinner, or any other kind of party.

- ✔ Check out music that you like from your public library.

- ✔ Call a local public radio station and order tapes of their programs. If you are unfamiliar with public radio, you can call the Public Radio Music Source (1-800-756-8742) for information about CD and cassette selections. You can order almost any music currently available in the United States, old or new, including jazz, classical, country, pop, rock, and so on. Prices are comparable to retail music stores. Because public radio is a non-profit operation, your purchase benefits continuing programming.

You can tape your own programs from the radio, but unless you have very sophisticated equipment, the quality of the sound is not usually as good as a professionally prepared tape. Also, if you don't sit by your tape recorder with one finger on the pause button, your homemade tapes will also include advertising and other vocal interruptions that are undesirable for your party tapes.

When booking entertainment for your party, ask for a written contract. Most agents want a contract for their own records and provide it automatically. While a contract may seem like a mere formality, it is the best way to avoid any misunderstandings. The contract spells out all the details, including the place and date, what the entertainer wears, the fee, the type of entertainment to be provided, the number and length of breaks the entertainer takes, and so on. It should outline the showing up time, starting time, and ending time.

Sometimes, guessing what time a party will end is difficult. If you schedule your entertainment for 7–10 p.m. and everyone is having a wonderful time, you may not want the band to pack up at 10:01. Ask your entertainers about their schedule. Depending on the time of your party, they may be booked for another appearance after yours.

You may want to ask for a stipulation in your contract stating that you have the option to pay more money and keep the entertainers longer, if needed. Realize that the performers may consider this overtime, so negotiate the price ahead of time.

Hiring a disc jockey or band

How much sound you need depends on your space and the number of people. If you don't want or need a band, disc jockeys are an excellent alternative. Disc jockeys are less expensive than bands and more flexible in the range of music they can offer, as well as volume control. Plus, people like to hear music they recognize performed by the original artists.

When hiring a disc jockey or band, ask the following questions:

- **How much space do you need?** Use this information to help you decide where you want them to set up. Entertainers can turn their speakers in any direction. In addition, speakers are powerful and don't need to take up a central spot in the party area.

- **What equipment will you be bringing, and what do you need from me to set it up?** Most performers need a 110-volt electrical outlet with a three-prong socket. Place the entertainment as near to the outlet as possible to avoid the danger of extension cords. If your party is outside, you may have to get an electrician to install the power you need for a large band.

> ✔ **Do you roll in your equipment or carry it piece by piece?** Inform the players of any stairs, carpet, or other obstacles.
>
> ✔ **How long does it take you to set up?** You want the musicians already set up and playing when the first guest walks in.

Instrumentalists and vocalists need to take breaks. Most bands supply their own taped music during breaks; one- or two-piece entertainers may not. Discuss this with your entertainers and be prepared with a little background music to fill the gaps. With disc jockeys, you don't have to worry about gaps in the entertainment — the music flows constantly.

Often, creating fun for others is not as easy as it looks. Remember that your entertainers are hard at work. Offering them refreshments is a good idea. Disc jockeys and bands generally do not expect tips beyond the contracted price. However, if the disc jockey or band has gone out of the way to play special requests or to otherwise make the entertainment better than you expected, you can offer a tip. The amount you give is entirely up to you.

Considering your budget

We haven't forgotten about your budget. Hired entertainment can be expensive. But entertainment at a big party can also be cost-effective. Divide the total cost of the entertainment by the total number of guests. Are your friends worth that much? If not, invite more friends and the cost per person diminishes accordingly. Of course, your food and beverage budget rises, but you can adjust that by what you choose to serve. Pop over to Chapter 15 for big-party food solutions.

If budget is your primary concern, you may need to rethink your entertainment options. Big-party entertainment doesn't have to be expensive to be wonderful — in fact, it can be absolutely free. A masquerade party is entertainment galore. So is a CD collection of fabulous dance music. If the occasion is a seated dinner with a few tables, have one or two fascinating guests move to a new table before dessert so that everyone is amused, delighted, and entertained.

Regardless of your choice of entertainment and how much you paid for it, guests at a party are not the same as a paying audience. They do not want to sit down, shut up, and listen. They want to be free to talk and roam. If you plan your party specifically to listen to a recital or singer, or if your entertainment is a trolley tour of the town, make that fact clear on your invitations. Guests will know what to expect, and you will not end up having to "shhh" the motormouths. Bossing people around is not what parties are about.

How long should the entertainment last?

Depending on the entertainment, you may choose to use it for all or part of your party. If you rent a jukebox, it will be there all night. Some guests will push buttons and dance all night. Others may prefer to stand around the bar or the food table. If you use three rooms for this party and invite plenty of people, everyone can find a place exactly where they want to be.

If you're having a large, sit-down meal, you may need only 20 or 30 minutes of entertainment. After the main course, when people may have run out of things to say, consider entertaining them with a comedian, a magician, a singer, or an activity related to your theme. (See Chapter 20 for help in developing themes.) The theme can be apparel-related. You can invite all the guests to wear hats. During dessert, have a hat-judging contest and give away a prize.

When you hire entertainers, you may use them before, during, or after the meal only, or throughout the entire evening. Decide how you want your party to flow. If you want to use them for the entire event, you can ask performers to play one kind of music during dinner and then switch to another kind during dessert. Changing the music can change the mood of your party. Musicians can tone down the volume and type of music so guests will feel like going home or crank it up so everybody feels like dancing.

If the entertainment is loud and the party lasts into the wee hours, you may be disturbing the peace. (Call your city or town hall or local law enforcement agency to find out if there are any local curfews.) If you prefer not to have the police shut down your party, consider inviting all your neighbors, the sheriff, and the mayor. (If everybody's there, no one is left to complain.)

Of course, inviting the entire neighborhood plus half the police force isn't usually practical or possible. As a courtesy to your neighbors who are not invited, let them know that you will be having a party on a certain day at a certain time. Ask them to let you know if the party gets too loud. Give them your phone number if they don't have it. They'll appreciate your consideration, and they'll probably call you before they call the police.

Getting guests to dance

Dancing can be ideal entertainment for large parties. You don't need a real dance floor. Guests are known to dance in hallways, on carpeted floors, and even outside on old broken-up brick. All you really need is a little open space, lively music, and willing participants.

The key to a successful dance is a crowded dance floor. The more the merrier, so to speak, so invite plenty of guests. To get people to dance, start way ahead. Remember to tell them in the invitation. Knowing that they are going to dance could affect the way guests dress, what shoes they wear, and maybe even what date they bring.

At sit-down dinners, people tend to get into a talk mode and get too sedentary to get up and dance. For a more successful dance, serve heavy hors d'oeuvres or set up a buffet. You don't have to fit everything in one room. Dancing can be outside, the food inside, and a bar in both places.

Disc jockeys and bandleaders can help you coordinate and keep the party flowing. These music mavens can help get people moving from cocktails to dinner and from dinner to dancing. Give the disc jockey or bandleader a schedule of the evening's activities so they can wait for a signal from you. Tell the bandleader or disc jockey when you're ready for the dance music to begin and have them pump up the volume. Ask a guest to initiate the dancing, and get out there yourself. If your party and music are appropriate, consider line dancing. The steps are easy to learn, and everyone can get involved, with or without a partner.

As you arrange all this joy for others, don't forget to amuse yourself. Have fun while you organize your party. Get in the mood by playing the music you love. Plan entertainment that you can enjoy as much as your guests.

Chapter 12

Manners, Conversations, and Coping Mechanisms

In This Chapter

▶ Hints for hosts

▶ Guidelines for guests

▶ Tips for making conversation

▶ Tactics for coping with disasters and mistakes

*T*he first step to being a good host or a good guest is knowing how to act. You know not to talk with food in your mouth, not to lean your elbows on the table, and not to reach across the table. However, not all the rules of etiquette are so obvious. In this chapter, you get a quick review of the basics. If you need more information, we suggest that you may want to invest in a complete book of etiquette. Some of the best manuals are written by Letitia Baldrige, former Chief of Staff for Jacqueline Kennedy Onassis and America's leading authority on manners and social relationships.

This chapter is not about developing an armor of behavior but about casting off fear and uncertainty. When we talk about manners, we're not talking about where to put your napkin or how to hold your tea cup. We are talking about the social skills you need to succeed in every situation: how to behave so that others feel comfortable, how to initiate and carry on conversations, and how to cope when things go wrong.

Be a Thoughtful Host

Good manners are never fussy or pretentious. Good manners put people at ease. If you are the host, manners begin with making your guests comfortable. But that won't happen if you're a bundle of nerves. So start with yourself. Forget about impressing people. Forget about what others may think. When you stop worrying about other people's opinions and judgments, you are suddenly free — free to serve the kind of food you enjoy, play the music you like, and invite the people who make you comfortable. When you clear out the worries, good manners come naturally.

Make your invitations clear

Good manners start long before the party begins. Making your guests comfortable begins with the invitation. Besides the obvious, such as the date, time, and place, the invitation gives all the information guests need: what kind of party it is, what to wear, how to get there, and how to RSVP.

Many people today forget their manners and do not respond. Calling those guests is perfectly acceptable. The trick is to find out if they are coming to your party without making them feel bad for not responding. You can always blame it on the mail system: "I'm not sure if you received my invitation in the mail." Then you'll get your answer.

Good manners do not dictate that you include all your best friends and neighbors in every invitation. It's your party. You are never obligated to invite anyone.

Your number one priority: greeting guests

If you want to bring out the best in your guests, start with a warm welcome. Greet guests as you would want to be greeted, with a firm handshake or a warm hug. However you choose to greet guests, tell each person how happy you are that they could come. When guests feel that you are thrilled to see them, you will get the most out of their personalities.

During the first ten minutes of your party, make each guest feel like a VIP:

- ✔ Greet each person enthusiastically.
- ✔ Put guests at ease by offering drinks.
- ✔ Introduce guests to each other.
- ✔ Initiate conversations and find common ground so that guests can continue talking without you.

At the beginning of the party, unless guests are good friends or you invite them to watch or help, beware of abandoning them and disappearing into the kitchen. If guests don't know each other well, they need you to keep conversations started and flowing.

Paying back invitations

When someone has entertained you, feeling obligated to reciprocate is only natural. However, payback invitations are not tit for tat. Just because someone had you over for a five-course meal does not mean that you have to do the same. Any invitation counts, whether you invite them for a cookout or take them to a restaurant for lunch. If another couple entertained you and your spouse or date, for example, your payback does not necessarily have to include them both. You or your spouse/date can invite either the host or hostess for tea or a round of golf. How you choose to fulfill the obligation is entirely up to you.

There is no set time limit for a reciprocal invitation. You don't have to do it in the next two weeks, but sometime within the next year is appropriate.

When you do decide to have a party, avoid inviting everyone you owe and no one else. Include others to whom you owe nothing. You want your guests to feel that you included them because you like them, not because you felt obligated to invite them.

If you were invited to a party that you did not attend, you do not owe the host an invitation. If you cancel at the last minute or forget to show up, however, you not only owe that person an invitation, but a huge apology as well.

When all the guests have been greeted and are engaged in conversations, refill drinks and pass hors d'oeuvres. Even if you have hired help, passing something yourself is a good way to ensure that you get around to talking with all the guests and a way for you gauge how conversations are faring. By passing food, you also give guests who are involved in conversations a polite way of indulging their appetites without having to interrupt the conversation and move to a food table.

If you serve it, will they come?

Getting people to the table can be one of the most frustrating parts of entertaining. You've made all this great food, it's hot, and no one is budging. Instead of getting flustered, try one of these people-moving strategies:

- ✔ At a small dinner party, ask a friend or two to take another guest and lead them to the table. Give the slowpokes a job. Ask them to pour wine or light the candles.

- ✔ At buffets or cocktail buffets, ask a female guest (the guest of honor, the oldest woman, or a close friend) to start serving herself. Then gather up some more guests. After a few people start moving in the food direction, others will follow.

- ✔ At large parties, moving 50 to 75 people to their tables can take 30 to 45 minutes. You and your help can tell guests, "Bring your drinks; it's time to go in; dinner's ready." Be prepared to repeat frequently.

Questions and answers

Q. What should I do if a guest arrives early?

A. Take the guest to an area where you feel comfortable — perhaps the kitchen, the living room, or your garden. Offer a drink. If the person is very early and you need to be making last-minute preparations, invite the guest into the kitchen to watch or help.

Q. What should I do if a guest is late?

A. If you are serving a meal, don't hold it up for one late person. Start the meal as planned. The late guest can either catch up or start with the course being served when he or she arrives.

Q. What should I do if a guest shows up with a date and I have not planned for the extra person?

A. Act like you are thrilled and go out of your way to be gracious. You can always squeeze in an extra place setting and divide the food in smaller portions. If you have prepared separate servings, such as individual Wellingtons or soufflés, divide yours with another guest who won't mind having a smaller portion. The trick is to divide the food subtly so that the extra guest never realizes your imposition.

Q. Is it okay to ask a guest to help with something?

A. Yes. Ask guests to pass a platter of hors d'oeuvres, mix a drink, help you carry something to the table, talk to a particular guest, and so on. Just don't ask them to stay and clean up.

The way you serve the food also plays a role in making your guests comfortable. Unless the party is casual, think twice before serving something messy or difficult to eat. At a cocktail or stand-up party, keep the hors d'oeuvres bite-sized so that guests can eat without making a mess of themselves. Serve drippy, greasy, sticky, or fishy foods on skewers or picks. If you do that, make sure that guests have a place to deposit the picks. You can provide a receptacle on the tray or have someone circulating through the crowd to collect them.

Following are a few tips on serving etiquette for sit-down meals. These guidelines represent traditional ways of serving. Most of these "rules" have a reason and are based on logic, common sense, and a desire for everyone to be comfortable. For example, because most people are right-handed, food is served from the left to avoid awkward body movements from the server to the guest and lessen the possibility of a plate of food landing in the guest's lap.

- ✔ Serving drinks from the right makes sense because the glasses are on the right side of each place setting. (If you slip up and serve a plate or pour a drink from the wrong side, or if you just like being a rebel, guests probably won't care.)

- ✔ Serve platters of food from the guest's left side.

✔ If you are plating food in the kitchen, you can have it on the table before guests sit down, serve it while they are sitting down, or wait until they are seated and serve it from the left.

✔ Pour drinks from the right.

✔ Don't begin clearing until everyone is finished.

✔ Clear the plates from the guest's right.

When the meal is over, whether or not you want guests to leave the table is strictly a judgment call. There is no right or wrong. When guests are relaxed, content, and engaged in conversations, there is no reason why you can't continue sitting around the table.

On other occasions, moving people away from the table can be desirable:

✔ If conversation is fading and you want to inject new energy into your party.

✔ If you want to create a transition between the dinner and time to leave. (Some guests may be uncomfortable leaving the party directly from the table.)

✔ If you have hired help and want them to begin cleaning up.

The most effective and polite way to get guests moving is to say, "Dessert and coffee will be served in the living room." If the dessert and coffee have already been served, say, "Let's move into the living room to talk."

Getting people to go home

After dessert and coffee, guests usually linger a while longer and start their good-byes. If you are tired and ready for guests to leave, make a big deal of the first guest leaving. Stay on your feet so others get the idea that it's time to go home. (If you plop right down and get another drink, the remaining guests may follow your lead.) If you want people to leave, you must send the right signals:

✔ Stop serving drinks.

✔ Turn the music off.

✔ Let the conversation gradually subside. (Stop initiating new topics.)

✔ If you are sitting down, stand up.

✔ Tell guests how much you enjoyed having them.

✔ Don't say "no." If someone suggests that it's late and they really must go, agree with them and usher them to the door.

Gifts for guests

If you want to do something to surprise and delight your guests, give out small gifts (party favors). The gifts can be funny, serious, or delicious. To make a lasting impression, choose a gift that matches your personality or the theme of the party — anything from chocolate truffles or lace handkerchiefs to disposable cameras or a deck of cards. At any sit-down meal, place tiny wrapped gifts at each place setting or stick them inside a napkin ring. Small bags of homemade goodies, such as cookies or English muffins, make special gifts for the guests at any kind of party. Tie the bags with ribbons and put them in a basket by the front door to give to guests as they leave. While munching on your food gift the next day, guests will remember your and your party.

If guests don't pick up on these signals, you may want to try something a little less subtle. You can look at your watch and say, "Oh my gosh. Look at the time! Let's do this again soon." Or say to your spouse, "Let's go to bed and let all these nice people go home."

Many times, all the guests will leave except one or two who settle in for the long haul. For some reason, they don't get the hint. If you are a night owl, perhaps you won't mind. But if you can barely keep your eyes open, you have every right to say that you are tired. You don't need to apologize.

 Don't start cleaning up until the guests have left. If it's late and you are too tired to do it all, put away the food. You can do the rest in the morning. Cleaning up makes the guests feel uncomfortable and ruins the atmosphere of the party.

Even if they offer or insist, don't let your guests wash dishes or clean up. You have made them comfortable from your invitation right up to the end of the party. Allowing them to participate in the dirty work can spoil the whole thing.

 The exception is if you have cooked a holiday meal, such as Thanksgiving dinner for family and close friends. You'd be crazy not to accept offers to help clear the dishes and clean up afterward. See Chapter 14 for more tips to survive the holidays.

Be a Great Guest

As an invited guest at someone else's party, you are expected to behave in a certain way, starting with the invitation. Your first responsibility is to respond promptly, preferably within a day or two of receiving it. Answer with "yes" or "no," not "maybe."

Most invitations clearly state who is invited. When the invitation is for a small seated dinner and is addressed to you only, don't ask to bring a date or friend unless the host is a very close friend. If you're invited to a cocktail buffet or large informal party, it is bold to ask, but you may. The host can always say no.

If you are already entertaining, decline the invitation. As an explanation, you may tell your host, "We are entertaining the Clintons that night." If the host then extends the invitation to include you, Hillary, and Bill, you may choose to accept or decline.

Even if the party is a casual event, never just show up with an extra guest. The host may have limited space, limited seating, and limited food. If the party is at a hotel and the host is paying a per-person charge, you can be sure that your extra guest will not be a welcome addition.

If you suspect that someone who makes you extremely uncomfortable may be invited, asking the host if that person will be there is acceptable. For example, you can inquire about an ex-spouse, someone you recently fired or someone who fired you, an ex-business partner, or a person with whom you are embroiled in a lawsuit. Because the situation can be uncomfortable for everyone, the host will be thankful to know and will understand if you decline.

Gifts for the host and hostess

Besides yourself, the one other item you may want to take with you to the party is a small gift for the host or hostess. Think of something that person would enjoy. If the host is a close friend, you can choose something personal like bubble bath, a book, his or her favorite brand of cigars, a flat of pansies, and so on. If your host is a business associate, choose something less personal: a bottle of wine, a special coffee or tea, homemade bread, fine chocolates, and so on. No matter who your host is, don't take a $1,000 bottle of wine or anything else expensive. The gift is intended as a token of appreciation for the hospitality, not a major contribution to the value of the host's estate.

Following are a few tips on what *not* to bring:

✔ Don't put the hosts on the spot by bringing wine you insist on opening or food you expect to be served.

✔ Don't show up at the door with flowers that must be arranged. Flowers are a lovely gift, but are best sent the day before or the day after the party.

✔ Never bring a permanent decoration for the host's house. It's embarrassing for the host if he or she hates the gift but feels compelled to display it. If you really want to give something special, think of a unique gift. A friend of ours snapped some pictures at a luncheon. A few days after the party, she sent the hostess a handmade photo album. It wasn't an extravagant gift, but it took some thought and effort. No host or hostess would ever forget a gift like that.

Preparing for the party

If you have accepted an invitation and are not sure what to wear, call the host and ask. If the answer is vague, such as "casual," ask how casual. You don't want to show up in jeans and a T-shirt if everyone else is wearing a jacket. Get clarification about what kind of party it is and how you are expected to dress.

On the date of the party, prepare your attitude. When you accept an invitation, you have a duty to make a contribution. This doesn't mean your tuna casserole. It means giving of yourself. You cannot be a great guest if you are preoccupied, self-absorbed, or in a bad mood. Get in the right frame of mind: To be a great guest, leave your worries at the door.

Every guest is a part of the entertainment. This doesn't mean that you have to be the life of the party. Think of what you have to offer (your wit, your charm, your smile, your attentiveness to others) and be willing to give that.

Coming and going: It's fashionable to be on time

For a dinner party, being on time is important. Forget about being "fashionably late." In most cases, if the invitation specifies 7:00, you should arrive no earlier than 7:00 and no later than 7:20. If you are delayed for any reason and think that you will be more than 20 minutes late, call the host.

In some areas of the country and in certain social circles, however, guests know that they are not expected to arrive at the designated time. A friend of ours who had just moved to a new town was invited to a party at 7:00. She arrived at 7:20, and was the first guest to show up. Others dwindled in between 7:30 and 8:00. Among this group, it is conventional to arrive 30 to 45 minutes late. Use what you know about the customs of the area and the people with whom you are socializing to help you determine the appropriate arrival time.

If you are invited to an open house or cocktail party, the arrival time is never rigid. The invitation may say "7:00 to 9:00," meaning that you are expected at some time between those hours. Showing up at 8:50 when the party is almost over, however, would be a bit presumptious.

Perhaps even more important than arriving on time is leaving on time. Never overstay your welcome. The party is over sometime after the meal is finished but before the host or hostess starts yawning. Seek a happy medium between "eat and run" and "eat and move in." In other words, don't leave while still gulping down your dessert, but leave before the host flicks the light on and off and goes to bed.

If you want to be remembered as a perfect guest, don't leave the party without telling the hosts their party was wonderful. Follow up with a note to tell them again. The thank-you note may be a lost art form, but it is still the most gracious way to express gratitude. Think about the party and mention something special about it so that the host knows that you noticed. The note doesn't have to be a dissertation. Even a three-line message will be appreciated.

If you don't want to write, do the next best thing and follow up with a phone call.

In between hello and goodbye

Modern manners are more flexible than in the prim and proper past. Female guests are no longer expected to leave the room after dinner so that the men can smoke cigars and drink in private. You are no longer bound to a single way of conducting conversation, and nobody really cares if you drop your napkin or use the wrong utensil.

This is not to say that etiquette should be forgotten. If you are unsure about what to do, watch the host or hostess and follow his or her lead. If you make a mistake, don't apologize or call attention to it. Your overall behavior is what people will remember, not that you ate your salad with your dinner fork.

Ten traits of a terrific guest

1. **Courteous:** RSVPs ASAP (responds promptly to the invitation).

2. **Thoughtful:** Sends flowers the day before or after the party or brings a hostess gift.

3. **Prompt, but not too prompt:** Arrives on time or a few minutes late — never early and never very late.

4. **Good conversationalist:** Fits in. Talks to people he or she doesn't know. Listens well. Never insulting. Talks loudly enough to be heard but not so loudly that others cringe.

5. **Humble:** Does not need to be the center of attention.

6. **Hearty appetite:** Eats (does not pick at) the food.

7. **Observant:** Notices the special things and compliments the host.

8. **Knows his or her limits:** Stops ordering refills before crossing the line to a drunken stupor.

9. **Knows when to leave:** Stays a reasonable time after dinner but leaves before asked to sleep over.

10. **Appreciative:** Writes a thank you note.

Relax and be yourself. Show respect for your host and the other guests, and you will fit in at any party.

✔ Never go on an uninvited house tour.

✔ Never hype up (over-excite) the host's children.

No one will want to shake your hand if it's cold, wet, or greasy from holding a drink or handling messy hors d'oeuvres. At cocktail parties or in other stand-up situations, hold your drink in your left hand. Try to choose the foods that are least likely to make a mess in your hand, and keep your napkin handy.

See "Making Conversation," in this chapter, for more tips on what to do between hello and good-bye.

Etiquette for Eating

When you are home alone, you can eat like an animal if that's what makes you happy. Go ahead and gulp your food, lick your fingers, and drink from the milk carton. No one will ever know. But eating in the presence of others is another story. Most of the time, you know what to do, but sometimes you may not be so sure.

For example, suppose that you have just been served a plate of fried chicken. You sit there staring at it, not knowing exactly what to do. Do you eat it with your hands like you would at home, or do you tackle it with a knife and fork?

When you are unsure, watch the host or hostess. If he or she picks up a drumstick or a chop, do the same. If the host is eating with a fork and knife, follow suit.

These foods are perfectly acceptable to eat with your hands:

✔ Chicken (at a picnic or barbecue)

✔ Pizza

✔ Fajitas

✔ French fries

✔ Asparagus (unless it's soggy, sauced, or too long)

✔ Artichokes (Eat leaves with hands, heart with fork and knife.)

✔ Corn on the cob (Eat in small increments, not straight across like a typewriter.)

Smoking etiquette

Many people who smoke particularly enjoy having a cigarette or cigar after a meal. However, non-smokers are often offended because they don't want to breathe second-hand smoke, they don't like the smell, or they are sensitive to smoke. If you are the host of the party, do whatever you want. You have every right to smoke in your own home or to ask guests not to smoke in your house. Cigars are the current rage. But if you don't like them, don't offer them.

If you are a guest and you see the host light up, feel free to smoke. Otherwise, if you are dying for a smoke, continue to die. Do not ask your nonsmoking hosts or friends if they mind if you smoke. Polite people will say they don't mind. They are lying.

A host can accommodate both smokers and nonsmokers by turning an outside porch or patio into a smoking lounge for those who want to indulge. If you don't have an available outside area and you don't mind smoking in your house, you can invite smokers to puff away on their cigars and cigarettes around the table and lead the nonsmokers to another room for coffee and drinks.

In business situations, be especially careful about smoking. Smokers stand out, and smoking can be damaging to your image. If you are dining with your boss at his house or in a restaurant and he is smoking, then it's okay for you to smoke. But if other nonsmoking business associates are present, you are wise to refrain.

Pits from olives, apricots, plums, or cherries can pose a problem. Remove pits from your mouth with your fingertips and put them on your plate. You may do the same with gristle from meat. However, removing pits or chewed up gristle from your mouth can look indelicate. You can remove it more discreetly by bringing your napkin up to your mouth with one hand and using the other hand (behind the napkin) to remove the gristle or pit and either placing it on the plate or in the napkin.

How you actually eat the food is only a part of good table etiquette. We promise not to overload you with do's and don'ts, but a few good table manners never hurt anybody. Following are some general guidelines that can help you survive any meal:

- ✔ Wait for the host to tell you to sit down before seating yourself.

- ✔ Put your napkin on your lap. Keep it there until you are ready to leave the table at the end of the meal, at which time you should fold it loosely and lay it on the table to the left of your plate. (If you must leave the table during the meal, leave your napkin on the seat of your chair, not on the table or the back of the chair where others will have to look at it.)

✔ Use flatware from the outside in. If you make a mistake and take the wrong utensil, just continue eating. Chances are, no one will notice. Never put the dirty utensil back on the table.

✔ Take small portions of food to start. You can always get seconds, and the host will be highly complimented when you ask for more. Taking small portions also ensures that all guests will have a serving. Avoid a situation like what occurred on an episode of the old *Mary Tyler Moore* show. Her boss, Lou Grant, helped himself to a double portion and then had to put one back because there wasn't enough to go around!

✔ Begin eating when the host or hostess begins unless otherwise directed. If the host implores you to start because there are so many people still waiting to be served or because the soufflé will fall or soup will get cold, then start eating.

✔ If you drop a utensil in a restaurant, a waiter will bring you a replacement. If you are in someone's home, you should lean over, pick it up (wipe it off with your napkin, if you like), and continue using it.

✔ Dip your spoon away from you — from the front to the back of your soup bowl. After you're finished, leave the spoon on the underplate, not in the bowl.

Questions and answers

Q. What should you do if you drop your food on the floor?

A. If you are in a restaurant, the waiter will take care of it. If you are in someone's home, you should first wipe up any mess you made. If the food is something solid, put it back on your plate and continue eating. (If you drop a bite of food, you may set it on the side of your plate and leave it uneaten. But if it's the whole entree, go ahead and eat it.)

Q. What should you do if you are served something you do not like or cannot eat?

A. You can shuffle it around on the plate to make it appear that you ate some, or you can force a few bites and then claim to be full. If you are allergic to some item on the plate, simply skip over it and eat everything else. Don't call attention to yourself. You can eat on the way home.

Q. What should you do if you have food stuck in your teeth?

A. Try discreetly swishing some water in your mouth to dislodge it. If that doesn't work, go to the bathroom and work it out.

Q. What should you do if someone else has food in his or her teeth?

A. Discreetly tell the person. Wouldn't you want to know?

Q. What should you do if you accidentally burp?

A. Depending on the crowd, either say "Excuse me," or make light of it to alleviate your own embarrassment and everyone else's. We once heard a man say he was making room for more!

✔ Don't talk with food in your mouth.

✔ Don't reach across the table or in front of people.

✔ Don't lick your fingers.

✔ The first time a woman leaves or returns to the table, men should rise from their chairs.

✔ Women may keep their hats on while at the table. Men should always remove their hats indoors.

✔ When you finish your meal, place the fork and knife at an angle on the right side of the plate (in the 4:20 position, as shown in Figure 12-1) to signal that you are finished.

✔ Keep your elbows off the table until after the last course. Then you can lean your elbows on the table.

Figure 12-1:
The host or the server will know that you are finished eating when you place your utensils in the 4:20 position.

Utensils are placed at the 4:20 position, signaling that the guest is finished.

Making Conversation

If you are hosting a party, the best way to ensure success is to invite people who are good conversationalists. If you're having a sit-down dinner, plan your seating arrangement so that the conversationalists are scattered among the tables.

When you are a guest at someone else's party, it is your duty to circulate and talk to others. Although one particular person may interest you most, try not to monopolize him or her. Make an effort to meet and talk to a few people.

Good conversationalists are essential to unforgettable parties. To be a good conversationalist, you must be comfortable with yourself. Only then will you be able to connect with others and make them feel comfortable. The good news is, you don't have to be a walking encyclopedia to make good conversation. In fact, you don't have to know the first thing about the topic on the table. When you listen carefully, ask questions, and appear interested, you are contributing as much to the conversation as the person who introduced the subject or is leading the discussion.

Small talk

Almost all parties start with casual conversations and move on to meatier, more substantial talk. What seems like small talk actually puts people at ease — it's not just chitchat about nothing. Small talk is a way of breaking the ice and getting to know someone. A talent for small talk is handy not only at cocktail parties, but in almost every kind of social situation — from a first date to a job interview.

People who are not comfortable initiating conversations are often seen as rude or are mistaken for snobs. To avoid such perceptions, you can learn the simple skill of making small talk.

If you are shy, take a few deep breaths. Repeat a mantra to yourself: "I am attractive; I am smart; I am interesting," and so on. If you find you don't know very many of the other guests, make it a point to approach at least three strangers. Introduce yourself. Most people will be flattered that you approached them and will be more than glad to talk to you.

There is no graceful way to break into a tightly clustered group of people. Rather than interrupt their conversation, wait until they have finished the discussion, or better yet, approach a lone guest or one or two people talking.

People will welcome your company if you are more interested in what they have to say than in what you want to tell. When you are genuinely interested in others, you will be perceived as an interesting person.

If you are uncomfortable starting conversations, try thinking of some topics before you give or go to a party.

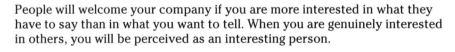

- ✔ Ask people about themselves (their jobs, hobbies, families, pets, and so on). Most people love to talk about themselves.

- ✔ Compliment a person.

✔ Talk about what's going on in your neighborhood, town, state, country, or the world. Current events are always good conversation openers.

✔ Discuss a play, movie, or art exhibit you have seen recently.

✔ Tell a funny story about something that really happened to you.

After you break the ice, chances are that you will find common ground and the conversation will continue. If not, you can always say, "I enjoyed talking to you," and move on to the next person.

Here are a few tips for carrying on conversations:

✔ **Learn to tell a story.** A good story has a beginning, an end, and a clear point of view.

✔ **Make eye contact.** Slowly and deliberately, look at each individual long enough for him to feel you are talking directly to him.

✔ **Look interested.** Even when you are not talking, you are communicating. Arrange your face so that it appears interested.

Never approach professionals (doctors, lawyers, stock brokers, architects, carpenters, auto mechanics, and so on) for advice at a party. At social events, they are away from their jobs. Save your questions and make an appointment to see them during working hours. Don't expect a free consultation.

On an opposite note, don't use a social situation to drum up business by handing out your business cards to all the guests. In the course of conversation, if someone asks how they can get in touch with you later, you can give that person a business card.

Before or after dinner, or at a cocktail party, if you find yourself involved in a conversation that doesn't interest you or if the topic is uncomfortable or offensive to you, excuse yourself and find a new group or another person to talk to. You can say, "That's an interesting idea. Would you excuse me? I need to go refresh my drink."

If you are in a one-on-one conversation and an offensive topic comes up or a discussion threatens to turn into an argument, interrupt to introduce the person with whom you are talking to another guest who is standing nearby. If you can get the two of them talking, you can make a graceful exit.

If one person is monopolizing you or you are stuck with a bore, you can always say, "Please excuse me. I must say hello to . . . ."

Questions and answers

Q. What should I do if someone calls me by the wrong name or introduces me incorrectly?

A. Gently correct that person right away before it goes any further.

Q. What should I do if I forget someone else's name?

A. You can try waiting for someone else to come along and address the person by name, or you can be honest and say, "I'm sorry, but I've forgotten your name." Most people will not be offended. However, if you are a notorious name forgetter, don't ask more than twice. Try to avoid using a person's name until you can discreetly ask the host or another guest who knows the person's name.

Dinner conversations

Long ago, dinner conversations followed a strict protocol. Guests took their cues from the hostess. If she began talking with the guest on her right, every other guest would turn to the person on their right. During the second course, people would switch partners and talk to the person on the other side, and on and on. Conversations appeared orchestrated, almost like watching a tennis exhibition.

Today's conversations are more relaxed to include the people all around you — the guests on both sides and across the table. Group conversations at a dinner table are not only acceptable but can be more fun than one-on-one exchanges.

If you do get into a lengthy conversation with one person, others may feel that you are monopolizing that person and ignoring everyone else. After a long conversation, turn to the person on the other side and start a new topic, or introduce a topic that can involve several people.

Whether you are engaged in a conversation with two people or the entire table, the greatest compliment you can pay others is to really listen to what they are saying and respond appropriately. If you are playing with your silverware and your eyes are wandering about the room, your obvious lack of interest won't go unnoticed.

If someone is droning on endlessly about her political views, her vacation, or her grandchildren, however, you may find it necessary to change the subject. The host or hostess is responsible for butting in before the rest of the guests nod off for a nap. But even a guest can save the situation; changing the subject can be as simple as redirecting it. Try these steps:

Getting more out of a party than a couple of drinks

You can get more enjoyment out of a party by making a point to talk to almost everyone at the party. Even at a large party, you can "work the room" (get around to talking to many people) in an hour, if you approach the party with a plan.

Go straight to the host or hostess when you arrive at a party and when you leave. Don't hang around with your spouse or date all evening or confine your conversations to people you already know well or see all the time.

After you have greeted the host and hostess, get away from the front door. The front door is a trap. So are the food table and the bar. If you start talking to the person standing by the door, milling around the food table, or hanging over the bar, you get stuck in that spot and remain on the fringe of the party. Instead, go right to the middle of the party. You can circulate more easily from the center of the action.

Start by talking to the person you like the least. You can finish that conversation and move on to other guests whom you enjoy more. By starting with the person you least want to talk to, you may catch her totally off-guard and, as a result, have a surprisingly pleasant discussion.

Next, move on to a person or people you don't know or someone standing alone. Who knows? The person standing by himself may be the next Bill Gates.

Remember not to dominate any one person's time. A party is not the place for a long heart-to-heart talk with a friend or neighbor or the time for spilling your whole life's history to a new acquaintance. Keep moving by politely breaking off conversations. You can excuse yourself by saying, "I'd love to talk to you more later. I need to speak to so and so."

1. Listen for a subtopic that you can glean from the monologue. Look for a chance when the person pauses or takes a breath. Ask a question or inject a comment that allows the conversation to spin off in a new direction.

2. If the person doesn't take the hint (cuts back in and continues), open the floor for another guest by saying, "Let's see what Caroline thinks about that." Or ask another guest what he thinks about the future of cloning or what he knows about the mating habits of whales — anything to start a new topic.

3. When all else fails, break up a boring conversation by suggesting a move. If the dinner you are hosting is over, you can have guests move to another room for coffee, dessert, or after-dinner drinks. If dessert has already been served, you can invite guests to tour your home or to view some special object in another room.

It's My Party and I'll Cry if I Want To

You are the host. You burned the main course. A guest just broke one of your antique plates. The guest of honor just slipped and fell on your hardwood floor. Are you on the verge of a nervous breakdown? Or do you have enough wit, imagination, and common sense to rise above the situation and figure out what to do?

Mistakes are human. Accidents happen. If you make a big deal out of an accident or mistake, it will become the focus of the party and make everyone uncomfortable. If you call attention to what embarrasses you, others will be embarrassed, too. On the other hand, if you can remain calm, handle the problem, and put it behind you, your positive outlook will give other people permission to act just like you — to get over the mishap and get on with the party.

Sometimes a mishap can actually turn a party around, add a little excitement, and allow people to take a deep breath and relax. With a small change of attitude, you can gain a whole new perspective on disasters, mistakes, and embarrassing situations. With a positive attitude and an open mind, you will find many more solutions than potential problems. Guests don't care. Secretly, they are thrilled that it's happening to you and not them.

When minor things go wrong (the toilet overflows, the cat leaps on the table, or the cork breaks off in the wine), your best plan of action is to make light of it or laugh it off. Sometimes you can even get away with ignoring it or pretending it was planned.

If your party is an outdoor event, *always* have a Plan B. This may mean moving the party inside your house, making arrangements with a local bowling center, or reserving a tent, just in case. Know exactly what you will do in a sudden downpour.

Once, but rarely twice, you may have a major disaster, such as burning the main course or dropping it smack in the middle of the kitchen floor. Even though the mistake is not a health hazard, you must take action to save your party. You can serve the part of the dinner that survived or quickly prepare something else. You can call for take-out or round up your guests and go to a restaurant. If nobody's really hungry, you can forget about the food altogether. Whichever solution you choose will be fun for the guests as long as you appear comfortable.

Even if the kitchen is ablaze and you have to evacuate and call the fire department, try to think of it as an adventure — an inconvenience, at worst. Look on the bright side: Guests will surely remember your party.

Tale of two parties

Story #1 — Huntsville, Alabama — 1890

An eighty-year-old grand dame asked a few friends to dinner. They arrived on the right evening, dressed and ready to dine. The hostess had forgotten about the party. However, she graciously welcomed the guests and conferred with the servants.

After a lengthy cocktail hour, the double doors of her dining room opened. The scene was magnificent: gleaming candles, beautiful china, silver appointments — a formal setting. The guests were seated and served the first course: a clear consommé with the correct wine.

She had no other food in the house, so the hostess ignored the food problem. For the rest of the courses, empty plates were brought out, each with the appropriate wine for the food that wasn't there. She rose above the occasion, using her wit and imagination, by deciding to open her magnificent cases of French Bordeaux, fine champagne, and Spanish Madeira. Everyone had such a marvelous time, they didn't care about the food. The party became a legend.

Story #2 — Canada

A Canadian woman who was an excellent cook invited guests for a black tie party in her home. She ordered a whole salmon from British Columbia. On the day of her party, she poached it and set it aside and took a short nap. She awakened to find her cat nibbling on the corner of the salmon.

She threw the cat out the door, and then cut off the end of the salmon and covered the rest.

The party was elegant and a raging success. Afterward, while she was cleaning, she found the cat dead on the back doorstep. Certain that the salmon was the problem and uncertain what to do, she called the doctor. She had to call all the guests and confess that she knew the cat had eaten the salmon but had served it to them anyway. She also had to advise them to go to the emergency room to get their stomachs pumped at 2 a.m.

The next day, a neighbor, who was not invited to the party, dropped by with the sad news, "I saw all the cars in your driveway last night and didn't want to disturb you. I ran over your cat and left it by your back door."

If you were this hostess, what would you do?

A. Kill the neighbor.

B. Move out of the country and change your identity.

C. Relax.

If you chose C, you deserve a medal of honor. The hostess of this party could console herself with the fact that her party would never be forgotten. It would be the talk of the town and the topic of discussion for generations to come.

Coping with breaks and spills

Sometimes the mistake or accident is not your fault, but a guest's. The key to coping is to be mentally prepared. For example, if a guest leans back in a chair and breaks it, you must concern yourself with the guest and not the object. Try not to look upset. Tell the person you were thinking of getting another chair anyway. The point is to make sure that the guest is all right and to smooth over his embarrassment. You can worry about the chair the next day.

The same applies to spills. The guest who created the mess is already feeling terrible. For her sake, remain calm. Perfect manners come from thoughtfulness. Say, "This has happened before, and it's not a problem." Clean up quickly and get on with the party. Be prepared by knowing what you can and cannot do. For example, if a guest spills red wine on your tablecloth, you cannot move your guests and reset the table. What you can do is dab the stain with club soda and put a big platter over it so people are not staring at it all night.

If you have something that is extremely valuable, irreplaceable, or highly sentimental, think twice before using it at a party. Unless you can act like it doesn't matter that the priceless bowl you inherited from your grandmother just got smashed, you should put it away during parties.

The same goes for borrowing other people's things. If you use your friend's china or linens and they get broken or ruined, you will be responsible. You are better off to buy or rent the extra items you need than to take the chance of someone else's property being damaged at your party.

Coping with accidents and emergencies

From the time guests arrive in your driveway until they leave your property, you are responsible for their comfort and well-being. If a guest has an accident or health problem, be prepared to act quickly. Medical situations can be as simple as bandaging a cut finger or as complicated as calling the rescue squad. For purposes beyond parties, it's a smart idea to learn first aid, CPR, and the Heimlich maneuver. Your quick action can save someone's life.

But worrying about your guests' potential heart attacks should not prevent you from having parties. Even if you entertain frequently, facing a major medical emergency is rare. Minor mishaps are more common, and you should be prepared.

If a guest falls, cuts himself, is bitten by your dog, or has any other kind of physical problem, take control of the situation immediately. Focus on the individual, not the blood on your floor or the fact that the dinner is getting cold. Do everything you can to make the guest comfortable. If medical attention is needed but the situation isn't serious, have someone drive the person to the local emergency room or clinic. If you are uncertain of the extent of the injury and think that it may be serious, call 911 for assistance in transporting the guest to the nearest medical facility. After the party is over, don't ignore what happened. Even if the guest seems fine and insists it was nothing, follow-up by calling or taking the person a gift.

Coping when you are a guest

If you are the guest who dropped your whole plate of food, broke the host's best china, stained the tablecloth and the rug, and ruined the clothes of the guest sitting next to you, you would probably prefer to crawl in a hole and disappear from society forever. Because that is not an option, you must do your best to rectify the situation with your own good manners.

The first thing you should do is help the host clean up the immediate mess. Apologize once and get on with the evening. When the party's over, kick into action. Offer to get the table cloth in the sink to soak. Tell the host or hostess that you will pick it up the next day and take it to the dry cleaner of choice. Offer to replace the broken dish or have it repaired. Arrange for a professional cleaning service to clean the rug or carpet, and make sure that the bill is sent to you. If someone's clothes were splattered, insist on paying the dry cleaning bill.

If you are having a health problem, act now and apologize later. For example, if you are a diabetic and know you need a shot, excuse yourself and do it. If you've already waited too long and you have to do it in front of everyone, that's better than falling in the soup and having the host call an ambulance.

One woman's disaster

This is the true story of a guest who made a party unforgettable because of her clever use of a triple pun.

At a United Nations dinner in the 1950s, many ambassadors were seated at a long table. At one end sat a voluptuous woman wearing a dress with no visible means of support (it was strapless). On either side of her were the Archbishop of Canterbury and the Canadian Ambassador to the United Nations.

She was telling a story to the two men when, halfway through, her dress fell down. No one knew what to do. No one dared look. No one dared look away.

But the woman knew exactly what to do. Without a moment's hesitation, she went right on with her story. When she was finished, she reached for the shawl on the back of her chair. In one swoop, she whipped it around her, hoisted up her dress, held out both arms and asked: "How did you like *that?*"

The triple pun:

✔ How did you like my story?

✔ How did you like what you saw?

✔ How did you like the way I recovered?

Part IV
Occasional Opportunities

The 5th Wave   By Rich Tennant

"Oh, will you take that thing off before you embarrass someone!"

In this part . . .

Need a reason to plan a party? This part is filled with opportunities for entertaining, from your child's tuba recital to your boss's retirement and everything in between. We help you plan special family meals, survive the holidays, host the big one, amuse your children, and entertain your business associates.

Chapter 13

Everyday Celebrations

· ·

· ·

*E*ntertaining isn't all about big parties or fancy festivities. In fact, entertaining doesn't have to be about parties at all. Entertaining can also be about celebrating the everyday and about cooking for and eating with people as a way of showing love or giving comfort.

We all look forward to major life events such as milestone birthdays, anniversaries, holidays, and other special occasions. However, because the expectations surrounding these events are so high, disappointments are likely. That's what makes everyday entertaining so much fun — most people have the best time when they least expect it.

You can find something worth celebrating almost every day — find the holy in the ordinary. When a friend, a spouse, or a child does something special that makes you feel proud or thrilled, think of that action as an opportunity to celebrate. You don't have to go to a lot of trouble to entertain the ones you love — just share a simple meal or a cup of tea.

In this chapter, we show you how you can make everyday meals (even leftovers) special. We offer some menu suggestions and tips for hosting meals for your family and friends, including pizza parties, potlucks, picnics, and teas. We even show you how to stock a friend's freezer in a time of need, and how to dine well by yourself.

What's for Dinner?

Along with the certainty of death and taxes is the certainty that you must eat. And of all the daily chores you do, such as taking out trash, doing laundry, paying bills, and cooking, just a few have the potential to turn into something magnificent, fine, and life-changing. Balancing your crazy, over-worked life with relaxing meals shared with people you love changes your life for the better. With just a little planning and patience, mealtimes can turn into a brief hiatus from the trauma and tediousness of daily living.

If mealtime at your house is mostly a matter of throwing together whatever happens to be in the refrigerator, or if your family eats in shifts, then you are a candidate for a mealtime makeover. Once a week or once a month, consider getting everyone together for a special meal. It doesn't have to be a grand production. You are not trying to paint the Mona Lisa or win the Nobel Peace Prize, you just want to put a simple meal on the table.

Where can you find the time?

In real life, when you are frazzled (your tax return is overdue, your toddler is searching for her toy, you missed a deadline at work, your teenager missed his ride to soccer practice, the dry cleaner lost all your clothes, your best friend is calling for advice, and you have a pounding headache), you probably aren't in the mood to celebrate anything. If you do manage to get a meal together, more than likely you want to get it over with and get the mess cleaned up so you can escape into a long hot bath or hide behind a newspaper. Your attitude toward fixing dinner doesn't have to be that way.

Successful everyday meals start with a simple idea and an easy trip. First, think of what you want to eat. Meal planning can occur in five-minute segments, whenever you can fit it in: as you drive to work, during your coffee break, or while on the treadmill. Look for recipes and menu ideas in magazines as you wait in the doctor's office, while getting your hair cut, or riding the subway.

Choose foods that you can cook ahead (earlier in the day or on the weekend), and food that is easily put together at the last minute — any food that can be served cold or at room temperature or that you can reheat without ruining its taste and texture. For example, most vegetables get mushy and lose their color and nutrients when reheated. Save enough time to cook them at the last minute. Fish and steaks do not reheat well, either. Plan to serve them on days when you have more time to cook.

After you decide what to eat, plan a quick trip to the grocery store. The key word is "plan." Don't waste time milling around trying to figure out what to cook. Shop with a list — on paper or in your head. If your schedule is flexible at all, save more time by shopping when the grocery store is least crowded, yet fully staffed. (Sometimes, when the store's least crowded, the check-out registers are understaffed, as well.) If you don't know the best times to shop, call the manager and ask. The ideal time to shop could be on your way to work. A cooler and a bag of ice keep perishables cool until you get home.

Fun things to do with leftovers

The wonderful thing about leftovers is that you can put together another meal in 15 minutes or less. It can be a repeat of the same meal (on clean plates, of course), a variation, or a whole new creation.

Everyone has leftovers. Even families with teenagers (aka eating machines) occasionally have a few morsels left. Other families eat so many leftovers, they never remember the original meal being prepared.

When you can find time to cook only once or twice a week, cooking extra is a smart move. Even if you have a small family, go ahead and purchase a turkey breast or whole turkey, an entire roast, the largest chicken, an extra pound of ground beef, pork, or veal. Plan additional meals around the leftovers.

- Use cold turkey and chicken to make sandwiches and salads, or use what's left to make potpies, casseroles, or hash.

- Boil carcasses and turn water into rich, flavorful stock for soups or other recipes. (Stocks can be frozen for months.)

- Reincarnate roast beef as shepherd's pie, or use it to make fajitas, a stir fry, or hot roast beef sandwiches with melted cheese.

- Shred leftover beef or pork and spice it up with your favorite barbecue sauce.

- Convert extra ground beef, veal, or pork into meat sauce for pasta. Add any leftover sauce to risotto, or serve over polenta. (Polenta is a wonderfully versatile Italian cornmeal mush that you can serve hot like grits. You can also chill, slice, and grill the polenta, and top it with sauce.)

- Freeze overripe fruit and use for sorbets and smoothies.

You can transform even tidbits of leftover food and the most ordinary ingredients into something satisfying:

- Use small amounts of leftover beef, chicken, or lamb in omelets, frittatas, burritos, or stir fries, or mix with a béchamel sauce to make fillings for crêpes.

- Save leftover vegetables to top a pizza, fill a frittata, or stuff a calzone.

- Turn day-old mashed potatoes into potato cakes or a potato soufflé, or use them to thicken a sauce.

- Make fried rice, rice stuffing, rice pudding, or miso soup from leftover rice. (Miso is a Japanese fermented soy paste. For miso soup, you need hot water, miso, scallions, and the rice.)

If you work long hours or if you often do your grocery shopping with children in tow, a once-a-week shopping trip may be most practical for you. If you are a weekly shopper as opposed to a more frequent shopper, buy all the basics at once for a few meals. Then you can whiz in and out of the bakery, the fish market, the butcher shop, or the vegetable stand to buy fresh bread, meat, and produce as needed.

After you have the food in your house, the work is half done. Prepare as much as possible in advance. Enlist some help. Your spouse can learn to chop onions, your child can learn to load the dishwasher, and the dog can learn to take out the trash. Well, that last one's a little doubtful. But you get the idea.

Then all you have left to do is sit everyone around a table, talk, and eat — even if it's only for half an hour. This is not only a cause for celebration, this is a miracle.

Prevent headaches by cleaning up as you prepare the meal. When the meal is over, remind everyone that the cook doesn't do the dishes — the eaters do.

If you lack the time or energy to prepare a meal from scratch, frozen food, packaged food, fast food, or leftovers can come to your rescue. Ask the people around you to pitch in and help. The point is to spend some uninterrupted time around a table sharing food with the people you care about. If that means serving something simple such as pasta with cheese, reheating leftovers, zapping a frozen entree in the microwave, going to a neighborhood restaurant to sit with your friends and family, then do it.

Elevate ordinary meals to extraordinary new heights

Whether you are serving T-bones or tacos, you can make the simplest meal seem more special. Think about the atmosphere you want to create. A few small changes can elevate your ordinary meal to extraordinary new heights:

- **Use candles instead of overhead light.** Transforms the atmosphere, soothes and relaxes.
- **Use cloth napkins instead of paper.** A tiny gesture that says, "This meal is special."
- **Turn off the television.** Makes way for real conversation.
- **Take the phone off the hook, or turn off the ringer.** Guarantees no interruptions.

✔ **Put away books, magazines, and newspapers.** Gives conversations a chance.

✔ **Have everyone sit down for the entire meal.** Fosters family unity: No one eats standing or leaves the table before the meal is over. Inevitably, someone (usually Mom) ends up jumping up and down during the meal to get this and that. For a change, let others take turns getting what is needed.

✔ **Seat family members in places different from where they normally sit at the table.** Breaks up a dull pattern. Gives family members a new view of each other.

✔ **Listen to and show interest in what others have to say during the meal.** Makes everyone feel important. They will want to do this again.

✔ **Expect children to use manners.** Helps them establish important social skills. If they don't know the meaning of manners, it's high time they learn. See Chapter 12 for lesson plans.

✔ **Enjoy the meal slowly.** Don't be in a rush to clean up. Makes mealtime more relaxing, not just another chore.

A Meal is a Terrible Thing to Waste

You don't need an excuse for a celebration. Opportunities surround you everyday to celebrate the people in your life. No need to wait for a birthday, a graduation, or a promotion. You don't need to celebrate anything except the feelings you have for a friend, the pride you feel in your child, or the love you have for your grandmother, spouse, or significant other. If you want a reason, pay attention to what's happening around you. When a child accomplishes a small task, when your mate does something nice for you, or when a friend goes out of his way to help you, it's an opportunity to pay some extra attention to that person. Sharing a meal is a perfect way to celebrate.

Making children feel special

Instead of waiting for your child to accomplish something big, like making the honor roll or being elected President of the United States, celebrate her individual character. When your child tries something new and different, cook a special meal. Reward her with a special dinner so she feels good about herself, not for how well she performed (the result), but for the fact that she made an effort.

While recognizing grades and sports accomplishments is fine, why emphasize an A in English, a touchdown, or being chosen homecoming queen
when teachers, coaches, and peers are already reinforcing these triumphs?
Make a dinner to honor your child for small, everyday successes:

- Riding a bike for the first time
- Acting in the school play
- Swimming across the pool
- Catching a fish
- Reading a book
- Playing in a band concert or recital
- Folding and putting away laundry (or any other chore) without being
  asked
- Passing algebra after a second try
- Sharing a toy or treat with a playmate
- Breaking a bad habit

After you begin to recognize these small accomplishments, you will find
frequent opportunities to celebrate. Acknowledging such efforts is an
excellent way to help children develop self-confidence and self-esteem.
Cooking your child's favorite meal is another way of saying, "I love you;
I am proud of you."

You can use meal preparations as a way to interact with your children.
Instead of sending them to a playroom or den to get them out of the way, let
them come into the kitchen and help with the preparations. Even if you're
exhausted and don't have much to say, you and the children can be doing
something together. Children of almost any age can participate. Toddlers
can wash vegetables or fruit. Young children can stir pots. Teenagers can
actually make part of the meal.

Open your children's minds even further by showing them how to select
ripe fruit or vegetables at the store. Then show them how to peel, chop, and
cook the produce. When children participate in the cooking process, they
are likely to taste foods they usually "hate" — even eggplant or mushrooms.
Tasting doesn't mean they will want the food again, but at least you will have
given them a chance to like it.

Beware of the hazards of having kids in the kitchen.

- Keep pot handles turned in from the stove so that children as well as
  adults don't bump them and knock them off.
- Keep sharp knives out of reach of young children.

✔ Wipe up any spills from the floor immediately so no one slips and slides.

✔ Warn very young children not to touch hot surfaces.

When kids cook, your kitchen is a little messier, and preparations and clean-up take longer. But the point is to spend time together.

Meals to make together

To get family and friends together without anyone going to a tremendous amount of trouble, plan to have a joint-effort meal. Try to choose foods that present opportunities to involve everyone in some capacity. Figures 13-1 and 13-2 show menus with which family members or friends can easily help.

Figure 13-1:
A dinner everyone loves to make and eat.

> *The Kids' Favorite (Ages 2–92)*
>
> *Macaroni and cheese*
>
> ❧
>
> *Brownies*

Figure 13-2:
Give everyone a part, and this menu will be a cinch.

> **Midweek Treat**
>
> *Grilled sirloin steaks*
>
> *Baked french fries*
>
> *Green beans*
>
> ❧
>
> *Milk shakes*

On weekends, hang out; stay in your pajamas, and make a big pancake breakfast together, as shown in Figure 13-3.

A Reason to Wake Up

Buttermilk pancakes

Scrambled eggs

Bacon

Blueberries and oranges

Coffee

Figure 13-3:
Your menu doesn't have to be fancy to be fun.

Once or twice a year, invite friends and their families to share in a Sunday meal. If the weather is freezing and everyone is dressed in church clothes, there is a good chance the children will be willing to sit still long enough to eat a meal in a civilized fashion. If you have fine china or linens, this is a good time to bring them out. Involve your children by teaching them to set and clear the table and/or help you serve. Use the meal as an opportunity to teach them how to use good table manners and how to converse with adults. Sample menus for finer family dining are shown in Figures 13-4 and 13-5.

In warmer months, invite another family to share a picnic. Involve children by letting them help choose the location for the picnic, prepare or select some of the food, pack the picnic basket, load and unload the car, and arrange stools or blankets. You may decide to use a menu like the one shown in Figure 13-6. (For more ideas and details about picnics, see the "Picnics" section later in this chapter.)

The Peanut-Butter Alternative

Lamb shanks

Turnips and carrots

Turnip greens

Buttermilk pecan biscuits

ᶻ▲

Boston and Bibb lettuce salad

ᶻ▲

Chocolate bars

Figure 13-4:
When it's cold outside, use this menu to show your kids that there's more to life than peanut butter and jelly.

Figure 13-5:
A fun and delicious warm-weather menu. Children will love putting their favorite condiments on the curry.

Everybody Loves Toppings

Chicken curry

Condiments (raisins, peanuts, green onions, shredded coconut, sliced bananas, chutney)

Rice

❧

Pineapple-Coconut cake

Picnic Spread

Fried chicken

Potato salad

Lentil and goat cheese salad

Green beans and red peppers

Biscuits

❧

Lemon bars

Pecan bars

Figure 13-6:
The whole family can help plan, prepare, and pack this picnic.

Spending time with friends

Inviting close friends for a meal is a relaxed form of entertaining. We're not talking about requesting the pleasure of their company at a party with fascinating guests, where the food is outstanding, the house is cleaned up and decorated, and the children are all put to bed. We're talking about inviting them to come over and have a bite to eat — to come as they are and share what you have.

Real friends don't judge you by your house or your food. What they really enjoy and will remember most is the chance to just hang out and shoot the breeze — share secrets, get the scoop, and have some fun without having to get dressed up, fight a crowd at some noisy bar, spend a fortune on a meal at a restaurant, or worry about which fork to use.

If you are a single parent entertaining your friends who don't have children, you have the added bonus of saving on baby-sitting services and assuring that you don't get left out while your friends go gallivanting around town.

If you like cooking, prepare a yummy meal for your friends. Chances are, many of them don't cook. They will be thankful for a home-cooked meal without having to visit relatives to get it. With friends, you can serve anything — simple food, messy food, your signature dish, or your latest experiment.

Friends don't expect anything fancy, especially if the invitation is spur-of-the-moment. Getting together informally with no planning, no house cleaning, and no figuring out the perfect guest list is precisely what makes meals with friends so memorable. You can add to the fun by having your friends get involved creating the meal. Serve risotto or polenta and let them take turns stirring; grill outdoors and give everybody a job; or have them create their own pizzas (see the next section, "Make your own pizza"). Take a look at Figures 13-7 and 13-8 for *friend-ly* menus.

Figure 13-7:
Pasta is perfect "friend food." It's slurpy, sloppy, and fun to eat.

> ### *Pasta for Friends*
>
> *Proscuitto, melon, and lime*
>
> *Spaghetti alla Carbonara*
>
> *Fennel, celery, and parsley salad*
>
> ❧
>
> *Biscotti*

Make pizzas

A fun way to please friends and get everyone involved is to make homemade pizzas. If you are feeling industrious, you can make your own pizza dough. Otherwise, save time and energy by purchasing small balls of pizza dough from your favorite pizzeria. (Most pizza establishments are happy to sell their dough, which is inexpensive and keeps well in the freezer.) On the day of the party, thaw, roll out, throw on some toppings, and presto! Make the pizzas yourself, or lay out the ingredients and let your friends do their thing. This is a great meal: It's fun, cheap, and really easy. Make the meal different from a trip to the local pizza parlor by offering unusual combinations of ingredients, as shown in Figure 13-9.

Figure 13-8:
A simple and delicious Italian meal to share with friends. *Mangia!*

> ### Polenta Dinner
>
> *Antipasto of assorted vegetables and salami*
>
> *Polenta with garlic, onion, and tomato sauce*
>
> *Fresh fruits and ripe cheeses*

Figure 13-9:
Instead of calling the pizzeria down the street for the third time this month, why not create your own pizza?

> ### Make Your Own Pizza
>
> *Fresh mozzarella, tomato, and basil*
>
> *Peppers, coriander, and andouille sausage*
>
> *Fresh and dried wild mushroom*
>
> *Shrimp, shallot, and tomato*
>
> ❧
>
> *Champagne (tastes great with pizza)*
>
> ❧
>
> *Grilled apples and bananas*

If all this sounds like too much trouble or if cooking is not your idea of fun, go ahead and invite friends over anyway. Find out what kinds of pizzas they like, and then call the best pizza place in town and order a variety.

Tacos are another "make it yourself" option. All you have to do is lay out the taco shells, fillings, and sauce, and let friends stuff their own.

Pack a picnic

Picnics are a great way to entertain friends as well as family. For a successful picnic, think: location, location, location. People usually associate picnics with the outdoors, where all the senses are stimulated. Picnickers can watch butterflies, throw Frisbees, catch fish, or just lie on blankets and enjoy the fresh air, the autumn leaves, the spring wildflowers, or a sunset.

Ideally, a picnic is near water — a lake, river, pond, stream, or the ocean. Mountaintops, forest clearings, and parks are also popular picnic spots. But you can actually enjoy a picnic anywhere — in planes, cars, trains, on a rooftop, or anywhere you prefer to take your own food. Often, a simple picnic of your favorite bread, cheese, and wine is more satisfying than restaurant fare.

Having an open bottle or can of alcohol is illegal in many places. Find out what's permissable before you pop the cork on public grounds.

Because you will not be at home or near a store, you must plan ahead to ensure that you have everything you need to comfortably enjoy the atmosphere and to serve and eat the food you have prepared. Following is a list of essentials:

- Paper or plastic plates (sturdy weight)
- Heavy-duty plastic utensils (forks, knives, spoons to eat with)
- Serving utensils (metal or plastic, as long as the plastic is sturdy)
- Paper or plastic cups
- Paper towels
- Sharp knife
- Insulated/thermal containers for hot or cold foods
- Cooler and ice
- Blankets (or something to sit on)
- Sun block
- First-aid kit
- Garbage bags
- Picnic umbrella (if you need shade)
- Insect repellent

If you are looking for a more pleasant alternative than bug spray, try citronella candles or plants or torches with citronella oil. If you live in a "buggy" area, use special insect repelling lotion. Other lotions protect against hazards such as poison ivy. Check your local drug store to see what's available for the kind of protection you need in your area.

Depending on what you are serving, you may need the following:

- ✔ Small, portable grill (plus charcoal, lighter fluid, and matches)
- ✔ Corkscrew
- ✔ Bottle or can opener
- ✔ Cutting board
- ✔ Bread knife

Add these extras to enhance the picnic atomsphere:

- ✔ Picnic basket (to carry non-perishables)
- ✔ Checked or chintz dishtowels (to line basket and use as napkins)
- ✔ Camera and film (to capture the moment)

Picnics can be a challenge because of the packing and transporting of the food and because of the unpredictability of Mother Nature. Preparation is key.

Follow this sage advice for any successful picnic:

- ✔ Use thermal containers to keep cold foods cold and hot foods hot. To avoid spoilage, chill any food containing dairy products (eggs, cheese, butter, mayonnaise, or milk) for a few hours at home before packing it into a cooler for transporting to your picnic. Keep food in the cooler until just before serving. Serve in the shade, if possible. Throw away any leftovers, especially salads.
- ✔ Always have a Plan B in case of rain or other inclement weather. (See Chapter 13 for alternative suggestions and disaster relief.)
- ✔ Never leave trash or garbage at the picnic site. In many states, you can be fined for littering. But who wants to be a litter bug, anyway?

Figures 13-10 through 13-12 may give you some ideas for what to bring to certain types of picnics.

Fall Picnic

Vegetable tart

Rotelle pasta with herbs

Assorted cheeses

French bread

Green plums

Red apples

Warm cider

Warm tea and coffee

Summer Picnic

Cold roasted chicken

Artichoke and feta salad

Olives

Cold rice salad with tomatoes and cucumbers

Blueberry muffins

Oranges and fresh strawberries

Fresh lemonade

Lover's Picnic

Fruit

Cheese

Bread

Champagne

Even if you don't have a Rolls Royce, you can have an elegant picnic. Pack the pickup with dinnerware, glasses, and an outdoor lantern. Fill your cooler with champagne, chilled shrimp, and cold cucumber salad. Or load your car with china, crystal, and a candelabra. Fill your hamper with champagne, smoked herring, and cold partridges.

Organize a potluck

Another way to get out of cooking is to host a potluck, having everyone contribute a dish. Potlucks were at the height of popularity in the United States during the 1950s and were a common form of entertainment for neighborhood gatherings, bridge clubs, and church groups. Guests brought their favorite salads, casseroles, breads, and desserts. These parties were great sources for recipe swaps among friends.

Today, potluck is still a terrific way to host a party, and it's a way to save time, money, and energy. If you organize the potluck just right, all you'll have to do is provide the place to gather. Guests can bring the rest.

A potluck can be a pig roast where 50 guests each bring food, or you can call a friend, telling her what you have and asking what she has, and suggesting you merge your menus. Figure 13-13 is a potluck menu for a couple of adults who are at the end of their ropes, don't have a babysitter, and need a break and a little adult conversation.

Figure 13-13:
Two friends can almost always combine the contents of their refrigerators to come up with a potluck meal.

In Luck with Potluck

For the kids:

Macaroni and cheese

Popsicles

Milk

For the adults:

Mixed lettuce

Ripe tomatoes

Homemade croutons

Delicious red wine

In most cases, potluck parties are organized so that each guest brings a dish of his choosing. So what if you end up with two salads and four desserts with no meat or vegetables? It's potluck!

If the element of surprise bothers you and you want a little more control over the meal, suggest what you want guests to bring, or make up the menu and give each guest a recipe to prepare for the party.

If a meal is not what you have in mind, why not invite all your friends to bring a dessert? You can provide the coffee and drinks for a sweet retreat they're sure to remember.

Tea parties

Tea parties are a wonderful alternative to full meals and a perfect way to celebrate friends and loved ones. Whether it's tea for two or for a dozen of your nearest and dearest, people associate tea parties with relaxation and contentment. Tea parties are cozy, chatty affairs. They are personal and intimate. Consider a tea party as a special way of entertaining when

- ✔ **You want to invite friends that you may not necessarily invite for dinner.** Maybe you don't particularly care for their spouses or you just prefer to share time with them alone.

- ✔ **You want to include many generations.** For example, invite mothers, daughters, and grandmothers.

- ✔ **You want to catch up with your very best friend.** The private setting is perfect for sharing personal information.

- ✔ **You want to invite the person you are deeply and madly in love with.** Cozy up with your spouse or lover.

If loose tea and strainers make you nervous, or if you want to offer guests a variety of teas, you can use individual tea bags instead. True tea purists may turn up their noses, but the fact is, tea bags are a fine substitute for loose tea. The water must be boiling hot. The tea must be delicious. Provide a small waste plate or bowl where guests can discard the used tea bags.

The best way to select delicious tea is to experiment before you have a tea party. You can find good tea bags at the grocery store, in specialty stores, or in gift shops. Look for herbal tea, fruit tea, Chinese tea, or English tea. Try different teas to find the ones that appeal to you. You can choose to serve one kind of tea at your party, or offer guests a choice.

Some people take their tea plain. But be sure to provide sugar, lemon, and milk for those who may like to add them.

How to prepare tea

You need a teakettle for boiling water on the stove and a teapot for brewing (or steeping) and serving the tea.

✔ Start with enough cold water for the number of cups of tea you are serving.

✔ Bring water to a boil in a teakettle on your stove.

✔ Just before the water boils, swirl your hottest tap water in the teapot to warm it.

✔ Pour out tap water and add loose tea to the teapot. Use one teaspoon of tea per person plus one more for the pot. (If you are serving six, use seven teaspoons of loose tea).

✔ As soon as water boils, pour it into the teapot. Do not bring the water to a vigorous, rolling boil, which boils away the oxygen in the water and leaves the tea tasting flat.

✔ Steep the tea for 3–5 minutes.

✔ Pour tea through a small strainer into the cups.

If you use loose tea, a strainer is a must; otherwise you end up with a mess of leaves in the cups. Strainers are inexpensive, and you need only one. Set the strainer on top of each cup to collect the leaves while pouring the tea.

Remember: As the tea leaves continue to steep, the tea in the pot becomes very strong. You need to keep the teakettle filled with hot water so guests can dilute subsequent cups to the desired strength.

A tea party can be as easy as mugs and cookies, or as complicated as silver tea pots, porcelain cups, lace cloths, fancy finger sandwiches, and petit fours.

Consider the menus in Figures 13-14 through 13-17 for a broad range of ideas.

Figure 13-14: A simple tea menu to share with a friend.

Tea for Two

Cucumber sandwiches

Scotch shortbread

Fresh figs

Earl Grey tea

Figure 13-15:
Even the
Mad Hatter
would love
to be invited
to this tea
party.

> ### Tea for Dozens
>
> Assorted finger sandwiches
> (cucumber, watercress, salmon, tomato)
>
> Cream cheese on date nut raisin bread
>
> Scones
>
> Macaroons
>
> Seed cake
>
> Frosted grapes
>
> A variety of teas

Figure 13-16:
Steal away
for the
afternoon
and enjoy
tea with a
lover.

> ### Courtship Tea
>
> Raisin scones
>
> Whipped heavy cream
>
> Strawberry jam
>
> Blackberry tea

Figure 13-17:
A fun tea
party to
make with
your
children
and a few
of their
friends.

> ### Children's Tea
>
> Jelly sandwiches
>
> Cinnamon toast
>
> Gingerbread cookies

Filling a friend's freezer

When you want to be an angel, be remembered for life, and save someone's day, fill that person's freezer. If someone you care about is sick, has a new baby, has a very sick child or spouse, or is grieving for a lost loved one, go immediately to your kitchen. Don't ask what you can do to help. Stand in front of your stove and start cooking.

For occasions when people need one less thing to worry about, stocking their freezers with meals they can thaw, heat, and eat is one of the most helpful things you can do. (See "Time-Saving Do-Aheads" in Chapter 8 for a list of foods that freeze well.) Maybe you don't think of this as entertaining in the strictest sense of the word, but it is. It just happens to be in their house, not yours; and it's when they need a little vacation the most.

Consider these tips when providing meals to others:

✔ If you are temporarily staying with the person, cook extra for the freezer everyday so that the family has food after you leave.

✔ If you live far away, cook several items. Pack the food in coolers; drive to the person's house; stock the freezer.

✔ If a neighbor or friend needs help, double your recipes every time you cook. Pack the extra food in a cooler; go to the person's house; fill the freezer and quietly leave.

✔ Package food in disposable containers so that the person doesn't have to worry about washing and returning dishes.

✔ Label containers with the contents, date, and directions for defrosting and reheating. If the person doesn't know you well, you may want to put your name on the package.

In the confusion of dealing with newborns, illnesses, or deaths, people may forget who brought the food and they may not remember to thank you. In their hearts, they will thank you forever.

Dining Alone

Entertaining doesn't always have to include other people. Every now and then, think about entertaining yourself.

Treat yourself to the foods you love. If cooking is relaxing and fun for you, there's no reason why you shouldn't prepare a five-course feast for yourself. Many people associate dining alone with loneliness. Eating can be lonely if you do it standing up by the refrigerator or microwave or in front of the TV, and not paying attention to what you are putting in your mouth.

You may think there is no need to prepare anything special for yourself. But dining alone can be a great opportunity to eat well and enjoy solitude. You may find you are your own best companion.

Dining alone has many advantages:

✔ You can eat your favorite foods without worrying about pleasing anyone else.

✔ You can be a glutton — eat as much as you want of anything.

✔ You can quietly savor each morsel.

✔ You have the chance to enjoy your own company instead of eating with a television or newspaper or in a crowded restaurant.

If you're not in the mood to cook or clean up, plan something simple (see Figure 13-18). You don't have to cook elaborately to eat a delicious, healthful meal. Set a table for yourself. Light a candle. Enjoy one of the most peaceful, nostalgic times known to anyone.

Figure 13-18:
Dining
alone can
be pure
bliss.

Simple Menu for One
Large bowl of soup
A few slices of fine cheese
A ripe pear
Sourdough bread
Celery sticks
Glass of wine

Chapter 14

Holiday Entertaining

• •

• •

*E*ven if you don't entertain any other time of the year, you may just have the urge during the holidays. This may come as a surprise, but you don't have to be a super achiever who accomplishes everything and then collapses. You don't have to overdecorate, serve fancy food, invite the entire town, or do anything else that requires a month's recuperation. By taking a new approach, you can make sure that holidays remain centered on what they really symbolize and not what our commercial society has turned them into.

You can apply many of the same principles to all your holiday entertaining, whether it's Valentine's Day, Easter, or the Fourth of July. Because celebrations are so individual, we won't attempt to cover the entire range of possibilities for each one. As each holiday approaches, look to your local magazine stand for thousands of fresh, inspiring ideas.

The main focus of this chapter is to take you through the major holiday season in the United States (Thanksgiving to New Year's) with a different approach. Instead of offering you three-day marathon menus and ten-step decorating tips, we concentrate on helping you get organized and prepared. You get some tips on guests, food, and decorations. We also help you evaluate expectations (yours and everybody else's), carry on old traditions, create new ones, and survive to do it all again next year.

What Do You Expect?

At most parties, all anyone really expects is a few hours of fun. But when the holidays roll around, expectations fill the air about food, drink, dress, decorations, behavior, and more. For this reason, holidays are a considerable source of anguish.

The difference in what works and what doesn't, what comforts or causes exhaustion, what astonishes or disappoints is all in the expectations. Start with your own. Do you expect to prepare holiday dinners for your family plus have a holiday party for your friends? Do you really expect to grow your own pumpkins, bake from scratch, chop down the Christmas tree, make the decorations, and shop for the gifts, all while looking glamorous and being pleasant? Pleeeeze! Give yourself a break. Most people feel highly accomplished if they just get the presents wrapped, much less prepare meals for their families and entertain everyone else, too.

The first step toward an enjoyable holiday season is to figure out what is most important to you. Do you have time and energy for a special family gathering, a big lavish party, and a private celebration with a friend? Can you handle it all, or do you need to make choices? Is it more important to make the pumpkin pie from scratch, or would one from the bakery give you more time to spend with your family? Is it more important for your tree to be perfect or for your children to have fun decorating it?

Many things are beyond our control during the holidays. The one thing you can control, however, is yourself — your attitude, how you spend your time, and with whom you spend it. Once a year, we have this marvelous chance to take a trip back in time, to revisit people and places of the past. We also have the opportunity to create new memories for ourselves, our families, and friends.

Instead of being bound by expectations (yours and everyone else's), turn your holiday entertaining into one great big opportunity. Use it to

- ✔ Discover your family history.
- ✔ Explore old traditions and create new ones.
- ✔ Spend time with the people who matter to you the most.

Family Gatherings

A big part of the holiday madness revolves around the expectations of different generations. Every family has its own set of annual rituals or traditions. You can either kill yourself trying to do it the way it's always been done, revolt and go on a major guilt trip, or find a way to compromise so that everyone gets what he or she wants and needs. The trick is to figure out exactly which traditions are worth the trouble to preserve and which ones you can alter or eliminate.

Sometimes a problem begins when you need to blend different sets of traditions. Today's expanded families often combine different cultures, religions, and ethnic backgrounds. Find out which traditions mean the most to your loved ones, and try to include some of everyone's favorites.

While you are busy blending, banishing, and/or preserving the old, you may want to create a few traditions of your own. Incorporate a family activity or a favorite food — something to make your celebration unique and to pass on to the next generation.

If you are going to break a tradition of always cooking the holiday dinners at your house, tell your relatives months in advance. Suggest that everyone go out to a restaurant together or offer to help with the planning and cooking if someone else wants to play host.

Making menu choices

The food you choose sets holiday gatherings apart from everyday meals. At holiday meals, families want and expect traditional food, even if the menu hasn't changed for the past 25 years.

Does that mean you are doomed to the same menu for the next quarter of a century? Not necessarily. If you are itching for a change, add a new dimension to the traditional holiday meal. Play around but stick to the range of flavors that go with the holiday by moving "must have" foods to different courses. For example, at Thanksgiving, instead of having cranberries as a condiment and pumpkin or sweet potato pie for dessert, serve pumpkin soup, sweet potato rolls, a cranberry apple pie or cranberry tart, cheesecake, or mousse. All the expected foods are there — you've just juggled them around.

If your family is accustomed to having a 20-pound turkey for Christmas, don't suddenly spring a surprise like a standing rib roast. Make changes gradually. Cook a smaller or different bird (such as goose, pheasant, capon, or a few quail) for family members who attach meaning to the tradition, and add the beef. The same applies to Hanukkah fare. Just because your family always has a brisket doesn't mean you can't serve something new. Keep the traditional potato latkes and applesauce or sour cream and change another course. People are more inclined to accept the new when you balance it with the old.

Other ways to change the menu and please everybody:

- ✔ If you have invited friends or distant relatives, ask them about their holiday favorites and incorporate some of them into your traditional menu.
- ✔ Add an ethnic dish to celebrate your family heritage.
- ✔ Serve a new version of an old standby.
- ✔ Introduce a new first course, side dish, salad, or dessert.

For Christmas, think about adding a cheese course at the end of the meal. This course encourages guests to sip wine and enjoy each other's company a little longer. Children can open small presents, play with their toys, or watch Christmas videos while the adults linger.

In addition to the traditional holiday meals, think about other ways to entertain your family during the holidays. See Figures 14-1 to 14-3 for a few menu suggestions.

Creating a festive look

Go all out for your family by presenting a meal in a fashion ordinarily reserved for company. If you have these items, holidays are definitely the time to bring out the good china, polish the silver, shake the dust out of your grandmother's lace tablecloth, and dare to use your finest crystal.

Use symbols of the holiday for decorating. Choose the ones that have the most meaning to you and your loved ones. All families have holiday decorations that they unpack year after year. Familiar decorations contribute to the holiday nostalgia. As the festive season comes around, add something new

Figure 14-1:
Children can make cookies, decorate them, eat them, hang them on the tree or windows, or make a gingerbread house together.

Children's Gingerbread Party

Gingerbread cookies
Icing and candies to decorate cookies

Apple cider

Figure 14-2:
Indulge
your family
with these
mouth-
watering
favorites
and give
everyone a
part in the
holiday
decorating.

Tree Trimming Party

Eggnog with honey and vanilla

Hot mulled wine

Hot tea spiced with orange peel
and cloves

Christmas ale

🐚

Honey glazed ham

Ultra rich macaroni and cheese

Crisp green salad

Parker house rolls

🐚

Apple cobbler

Christmas cookies

Figure 14-3:
Celebrate
Hanukkah
with this
traditional
family meal.

Hanukkah Dinner

Red beet borscht

Potato latkes with sour cream
and homemade applesauce

Green salad with tuna, cheese, celery,
and pignolias sunflower seeds

🐚

Sufganiyot (Jelly doughnuts)

---

to the old pleasures. During Hanukkah, combine heirloom menorahs and
dreidels with children's handmade versions to link the generations. Discover
new ways to incorporate symbols into your holiday decorating by buying
seasonal magazines; visiting friends' houses or walking around your neighborhood; noticing the decorations at beautiful stores; and visiting historic
homes.

Holiday Parties

As the holidays draw near, chances are you've already cleaned up the house and decorated, so you may as well have some people over to see it. In your quest for success, go back to the basics: special guests, a festive menu, and an enticing atmosphere. After these elements are taken care of, you can figure out a manageable time schedule and a plan of attack.

The holidays are an opportune time to have a big party for a broad range of friends and acquaintances. Make your holiday guest list special by inviting all generations, from the eldest matriarch to the tiniest infant and everyone in between. Invite people you love and people you want to love. Invite a single person or someone who doesn't have family nearby. (See Chapter 3 for more help making your guest list and Chapter 15 for big party plans.)

Holidays are also a perfect opportunity to draw close — to connect and reconnect — with family and friends. For a more intimate holiday celebration, the optimal party size is the number of people who can fit around your table. But if that seems too limiting for the number of family and friends you want to entertain, rent additional small tables and put them wherever you have space.

Indulging guests with special foods

Holidays are not the time to serve skimpy, low-fat foods. You are supposed to be counting your blessings, not your fat grams. The food should reflect abundance and luxury. Parties are the time to open up and serve those food gifts you've received instead of letting them collect dust in the pantry. Order whole tenderloins, fresh turkeys, the finest hams, and sides of salmon. These foods may cost a little more, but the extra expense is worth it for the time you save. All they need is a few minutes of preparation work and some roasting time.

Figures 14-4 to14-7 give you menu ideas for holiday gatherings. For foods that are not available in your local market, see Appendix C for mail order sources.

Creating a festive atmosphere

Luxurious foods are only a part of the holiday picture. Holiday parties just don't seem festive if your house is not decorated. Decorations distinguish the party as a special event — not just any old party. But decorations don't have to be overdone or elaborate to add festivity. Little touches make people excited and get them in the mood.

Mother, Daughter, and
Granddaughter Tea

Smoked salmon sandwiches

Watercress sandwiches

Cucumber sandwiches

Marmalade and cream
cheese sandwiches

ॐ

Lemon tarts

Scotch shortbread

Macaroons

Pecan balls

ॐ

Tea

Champagne punch

Figure 14-4:
All
generations
of women
enjoy
sharing
tea and
conversation.
Include
female
friends and
their
families.

Elegant Seated Dinner

Oyster stew served in silver cups

ॐ

Buffalo tenderloin or roasted capon

Sautéed wild mushrooms and potatoes

Glazed brussels sprouts

ॐ

Stilton cheese, grapes, nuts

ॐ

Flaming Christmas pudding

Assorted cookies

Coffee

Figure 14-5:
A beautiful
presentation
makes this
menu a
perfect
choice for
an exquisite
holiday
dinner.

Christmas Buffet for a Crowd

Smoked seafood and cocktails

❧

Cassoulet

Virginia ham

Breads, biscuits, mustards

Endive, beet, and, mixed green salad

❧

Bûche de Noël

Poached fruits

Assorted cookies

Figure 14-6: A fun, festive, and delicious way to serve a crowd.

Kwanzaa Feast

Fruit salad

❧

Baked ham

Fried chicken or roast chicken

❧

Black-eyed peas and rice

Collard greens

Baked sweet potatoes

❧

Apple bread pudding

Figure 14-7: Traditional Kwanzaa foods are combined in one meal, called *karamu,* held on the night of December 31.

For Christmas, Hanukkah, and Kwanzaa, candles are important accessories. Besides being significant holiday symbols, candles make the atmosphere of your party. (See Chapter 6 for more detail on the importance of lighting and the magic of candlelight).

For holiday parties, use the best of everything you own: tablecloths, china, silver, crystal. It doesn't matter if everything doesn't match. If you don't own anything like that, you can still have a beautifully decorated holiday table. Borrow what you need or buy holiday paper goods for serving and setting the table. (For more ways to make your table attractive, flip to Chapter 10.)

Decorate yourself, too. Taking the time to look different, better, and more glamorous than at any other time of the year gets you in the holiday spirit. The extra effort makes guests feel special, too.

Adding some action

Holiday parties are a good time to plan a special activity, use entertainment, or ask something of your guests. Your objective is to grab guests' attention and get them into the spirit of the holiday.

The following are a few examples of activities to heighten your guests' joy:

- **Thanksgiving:** If the weather permits, do something outdoors. Instead of having half the people slaving in the kitchen and the other half sitting in front of the TV, organize walks, touch football, or feeding the local ducks.

- **Christmas:** Hire singers with beautiful voices to dress up in costume and become Dickens-era carolers. Have them sing as guests are arriving. Or ask someone to lead guests in carols around the piano. You can also invite Santa Claus to make an appearance and pass out small gifts.

- **Hanukkah:** Bring families together to celebrate. Children can play dreidel games and exchange Hanukkah gelt (chocolate "coins" wrapped in gold foil) or make menorahs out of nuts and bolts. (Use nuts for candleholders.)

- **Kwanzaa:** Ask guests to dress in traditional African attire. Arrange Kwanzaa symbols and decorations, conduct a candle lighting ceremony, sing the Kwanzaa song, and provide children with materials for making homemade gifts to exchange.

- **New Year's Eve:** Ask guests to wear hats for a Mad Hatter's party. Besides the fun of looking outrageous, guests can win prizes for their efforts and steal kisses under their hat brims. Or engage guests' imaginations. Give a New Year's Eve Century party. Request each person to dress in the fashion of one of the decades in the past century.

Staying Alive from Thanksgiving to the New Year

Planning a holiday party or meal is much like any other, but with a double dose of added stress. (Those expectations, again!) But you can turn harum-scarum holidays into joyful experiences. The key to survival is commitment, time, and planning.

Rule No. 1: Start way ahead.

Preparing for the eating, drinking, entertaining, and decorating just a day or two before the holiday is impossible. Besides putting yourself under immense stress, a rushed schedule doesn't allow you to take care of the details that can make the holiday stand out.

You don't have to tackle all the details. Choose the one that gives you pleasure. Whether it's your holiday baking, your artful decorating, your handmade ornaments, or your spectacular package wrapping, these are the details that stay in people's memories. All these things can be done weeks in advance.

Coping with relatives

Holiday alert: Your relatives know where you live. If you can't run away, you may as well get prepared. Some people welcome visits with relatives as a chance to strengthen family ties. Others dread them because of the stress they feel after a few days of forced togetherness. If you find family visits just slightly more agreeable than a rush hour traffic jam, you can do more than just grin and bear it.

One solution is to keep everyone busy and productive so that there's less time to get on each other's nerves. Take advantage of their presence by letting them do some of your work. Think of different jobs for different personalities. Ask a quiet or shy person to shell peas, polish silver, or iron linens. Solicit energetic or hyperactive guests to play with the children outside. Send the most obnoxious person to the grocery store and to do the daily errands.

Cooking for a house full of relatives can be difficult if too many well-meaning helpers overrun your kitchen. For best results, do the thinking part ahead of time. Make lists, measure out ingredients, and set timers so that you don't wind up ruining the food and your mood.

If you have a visiting relative who is difficult to be around, find a polite way to keep that person out of the kitchen when you are cooking. Build a fire in the fireplace or suggest an activity that creates a focal point other than under your feet.

Guide to Thanksgiving

Thanksgiving is one of the best holidays. The holiday is not affiliated with any religion and can encompass anyone and everyone. The celebration can be a small family affair or a huge meal for tons of people. Either way, this meal is an enormous undertaking. But if you work it right, you can have a relaxing Thanksgiving meal at home without feeling like a wrung-out rag by the end of the day. Here's how:

2nd week in October: Make and refrigerate cranberry relish and pear chutney.

3rd week in October: Make breads and rolls and freeze them.

4th week in October: Make pie crusts and freeze them.

1st week in November: Order turkey, buy wines, and polish silver.

2nd week in November: Make cakes or other desserts that you can freeze.

3rd week in November: Finish your menu with side dishes that you can prepare in advance and refrigerate. Save only a few final cooking chores for the day of the meal.

Thanksgiving is the one holiday when it is permissible and advisable to take all the help you can get. Besides taking a load off you, it gives everybody a chance to get involved. Your guests will enjoy and appreciate the holiday more when they participate.

Give everyone a job. Figure out the special talent of each person and organize your help force.

Children can

 ✔ Set tables and make centerpieces.

 ✔ Draw place cards.

 ✔ Organize games for younger children or produce a skit.

Adults can

- ✔ Make a favorite food and contribute to the meal.
- ✔ Bring wine.
- ✔ Organize a ball game for older children and willing adults.
- ✔ Help finish cooking.
- ✔ Carve the turkey.

Cleaning up after the meal can even be a group activity that brings people together and allows more time for reminiscing and sharing family history and gossip.

An organized adult can be in charge of cleanup. Energetic people can scrape dishes. Lazier ones can dry the dishes. Exhausted people can lounge in front of the fire or television.

Rule No. 2: Keep things in perspective

When you begin to feel the squeeze of too much to do and not enough time, step back and think about what the holiday is really about. Take the time to do the things that mean something to you and to others. Fancy food and elaborate decorations pale in the light of the true holiday spirit.

- ✔ Spend a little extra time with special friends. Make cookies or truffles together to give away as gifts.
- ✔ Involve your children in holiday meal preparations. The afternoon you spend teaching a child to cook or make an ornament is a gift that keeps on giving.
- ✔ Be observant and sensitive. Is there someone you know who is going through a difficult time, is lonely, or needs a little extra tender loving care? Invite that person to share a meal.

Rule No. 3: Take care of yourself.

Your family and friends cannot enjoy the holidays if you end up exhausted and sick. As much as you want to make everyone happy, be brutally honest with yourself. Know your limitations. Learn to ask for and accept the help you need. You do not have to cook an elaborate meal for Christmas Eve, Christmas breakfast, and Christmas dinner. Choose one, and make the rest extremely simple.

Make a list of things you hate to do so that if people ask what they can bring or how they can help, you are prepared to tell them.

Keep the following points in mind as you gear up for the holidays:

- ✔ **Don't be a martyr.** There is no reason to work yourself to a frazzle while others loll around your living room. You can delegate duties, chores, errands, and food preparation to others. You can buy the entire meal from a restaurant or caterer.

- ✔ **Don't be monotonous.** Giving the same holiday party every year becomes boring. The process becomes a chore for you, and the festivities become less exciting for everyone else.

- ✔ **Don't balloon up.** You can get through the holidays without a double-digit weight gain. Major-league calories are everywhere. But you can eat moderately. Enjoy everything but limit your portions.

Countdown to the big day

Whether you celebrate Christmas, Hanukkah, Kwanzaa, or a combination of these holidays, your entertaining can be more successful if you get a head start.

- ✔ Plan your holiday menus weeks in advance. Plan realistically for your time frame. If necessary, you can buy or delegate parts of the meal.

- ✔ Draw up a time line. The work seems more manageable when divided into small segments.

- ✔ Share projects with someone else. Cook and create with a child or a friend. Divide the work and double the joy.

If you are planning a large party or family gathering, get started in early November. Begin making some of the foods and storing them in the freezer — soups, appetizers, breads, pies, cakes, and cookies freeze well. (See Chapter 8 for more information on foods you can freeze and how and when to defrost them.)

Make small molded puddings and cakes to be give away as presents. If you start in November, you have plenty of weeks to douse them with brandy for a luxurious homemade gift.

Celebrating New Year's Eve: The last hurrah

If you've made it through Christmas, Hanukkah, and/or Kwanzaa, ringing in the new year should be icing on the cake, unless, of course, you are in charge of the party! People think it is their duty and obligation to have more fun on New Year's Eve than any other night of the year. To satisfy such high expectations, a host must possess an abundance of self-confidence, daring, and nerve.

If you possess the drive, energy, and ambition to be in charge of everyone's fun, go for it. Pull out all the stops. Invite enough people to fill your space and then some. Create such a buzz that people are dying to be at your wingding.

New Year's Eve essentials:

- ✔ Music to make people dance
- ✔ A small, crowded dance floor
- ✔ Plenty of champagne
- ✔ For nondrinkers: sparkling cider, non-alcoholic champagne, spiced hot tea

Decorate with flowers, gleaming silver, candles, clocks, mirrors, and mistletoe. Don't start the party too early lest it fizzle before midnight. Serve heavy hors d'oeuvres at 9:00 and dessert and champagne at 11:30. After the midnight hoopla and the toasting of the new year, most people are ready to go home or on to other parties. If you want the party to go on, serve breakfast at 12:30.

If you prefer to stay home and usher in the new year quietly, one alternative is to ignore the whole New Year's Eve spectacle and plan a dinner for two. Invite your spouse, lover, or friend for an unforgettable evening. All you need is an intimate setting, simple but luxurious food, and a sumptuous bottle of champagne. The menu in Figure 14-8 makes a private celebration worth remembering.

Figure 14-8:
Ring in the
New Year
with a
special
menu for
that special
someone.

> ### New Year's Eve for Two
>
> *Oysters*
> *Blanc de blancs champagne*
>
> ❧
>
> *Pasta with king crab*
> *Vintage champagne*
>
> ❧
>
> *Raspberries and chocolate truffles*
> *Demi-sec champagne*

Chapter 15

Big Parties

. . . .

. . . .

*A*re you a person who likes to create a buzz? Shake things up? Make your mark? Keep the town talking? Once a year, or once in five, consider having a big bash. You can get all your entertaining done in one swoop. Having one big party can be easier than having lots of little parties throughout the year. You can invite all the people you love and include everyone to whom you owe a reciprocal invitation.

Of course, big parties mean a bigger guest list and more food. But they also entail more planning, more organization, more work, and more time. Yes, big parties can cause big headaches. But with thorough planning, they also have the potential to reap big rewards.

Is perspiration breaking out on your forehead already? If you are thinking of a big party as something that involves a trained staff, a band, and a five-star chef, no wonder you're in a panic. You definitely need some help to make your big party successful, but getting the help you need doesn't have to cost you an arm and a leg.

In this chapter, we show you how to host a big party that is neither back-breaking nor bankrupting — a party that feels like a big accomplishment when it's over. We help you decide what kind of party to plan. We suggest the number of guests to invite so you can cope, and the amount of help to hire so you can manage. We also help you figure out how much work you can reasonably expect to accomplish yourself and what that work should be. The result? Guests will remember your party for years, and others will wish they had been there. This chapter is not only a "how to," but a "why not?"

How Big Is Big?

Perhaps ten people sounds like a big party to you. If so, you may want to skip over this chapter for now and concentrate on small dinner parties, luncheons, picnics, or teas. Gain some confidence hosting small affairs before attempting the big one.

When we say *big party*, we're talking about more people than you can fit around your dining-room table. That kind of party can be for 15 or 50, or more. What constitutes big is always a matter of perspective.

A professional chef at a major hotel chain recalls his first day on the job. As he looked at the enormous stack of paper on his desk, he asked if this was his work for the week. He nearly panicked when he found out it was his work for the day. A few weeks later, this same chef had finished preparing a banquet for 1,200 and was calmly working on a party to be held two days later while his staff was serving a roomful of guests in the restaurant.

The point is that someone else's definition of big is not important. What's important is that your party is a size you can handle. For some people, a party for 20 people may seem huge. For others, a black-tie dinner for 75 is no big deal. (If that's you, you probably are reading this book strictly for amusement.) Adjust the size of your party to fit your own definition of big.

Unless you are a politician, a celebrity, or a caterer, it's most likely that you'll host only a few big parties over the course of your lifetime. That's why giving them can be intimidating. Giving large parties is not something most people practice or do everyday.

When planning a big party, remember: You aren't competing with the catering staff of a luxury hotel or the Queen of England's party-planning committee. You don't have to go a step too far. Just being yourself is enough. Rely on your own impulse, inspiration, and sense of theater.

What Kind of Party Can It Be?

When you decide to throw a big event, one of the first things to consider is what kind of party it will be. There are as many kinds of big parties as small ones, but some may be better suited to your circumstances, your budget, your time, and your crowd:

Cocktail parties are one way to entertain lots of people at once in a short amount of time. If you want to serve a meal, but don't want to worry about how you're going to keep the food the right temperature while you get it on the plates, then think about serving buffet style. On the other hand, if you have the money to hire plenty of help, you may want to serve an elegant seated meal. (Don't try this alone for a big crowd.) If space is your problem, you can always rent a place or have the party outdoors or under a tent. The type of big party you give relates directly to how much time and effort you want to exert, how much and what kind of food you want to serve, and how much money you have to spend. Following are some tips for successful big parties, no matter which route you choose.

Cocktail parties

While cocktail parties can be small (one or two hors d'oeuvres for six to eight people before going to a restaurant or the theater), they can also be enormous (the equivalent of dinner for 50 or more). Most cocktail parties have a starting point and an ending point such as 6 to 8 p.m. (Cocktail buffets usually have a starting point, but no specified ending.) Habits are different in different parts of the world. In the southern United states, for example, people tend to stay from beginning to end. In the northern United States, guests tend to come and go. In Los Angeles, it all depends on the traffic.

Cocktail parties have a few distinct advantages:

- ✔ You can prepare almost everything in advance.
- ✔ You need little equipment (just glasses, trays, and napkins).
- ✔ You can pay back a lot of invitations at once. (Just be sure to invite other guests besides your paybacks.)
- ✔ You can keep the party short and invite anyone (a diverse group).
- ✔ You can allow flexibility in arrival and departure times. Guests are not trapped. They can come and go as they want.

People who have gone to many parties in their lifetime sometimes complain about cocktail parties. They don't particularly enjoy going to them, much less giving them. They don't really expect to have fun or to have interesting conversations, just chitchat about nothing. (Often the room is too noisy to hear anything anyway). But cocktail parties can be marvelous parties to host or attend. If you are planning a large cocktail party, you can make yours a success.

Start by inviting enough guests to fill your space, but not so many that people feel trapped. A roomful of people is more fun than a few. You want it crowded, but not smothering. For more tips on how much space you need and how to use it, see Chapter 5.

When guests show up, you don't want them to walk in and stand in one spot. People have a tendency to crowd around the bar or stand around the buffet table or in a doorway. To prevent bottlenecks, have your party in one big room or in two or more rooms with large openings between them. Make guests want to explore by serving drinks and hors d'oeuvres in different rooms, but don't set the food table or bar too close to the door. Create different moods with lighting, decorations, food, and drink. (See Chapter 5 for more suggestions on moving people through space.)

Cocktail parties feature a variety of hors d'oeuvres. When deciding what and how many to serve, consider the size of the party. Following is a general guideline to help you figure out how many different kinds of food you need:

- ✔ **8 to 12 people:** Serve four kinds of hors d'oeuvres.
- ✔ **12 to 16 people:** Serve five to six kinds.
- ✔ **16 or more:** Serve seven or eight kinds of hors d'oeuvres.

Choose one of each of four categories: fish or shellfish, cheese, vegetable, meat. Guests will eat more when there is more variety. The principles of balance apply. Variations of color and texture are important visually. Variations of temperature are important for the ease of the host. Choose some foods that can be served cold or at room temperature so that you aren't overstressed trying to keep everything hot at once. Vary substantial hors d'oeuvres with lighter ones. Alternate color, texture, temperature, and taste.

At large stand-up parties where guests are spread out and have to go to the food table, they don't eat as much. No one wants to be the first one or the only one eating. In addition to the food table, it's a good idea to pass food at stand-up parties. You can ask your children or a teenage neighbor to help, or hire professional waiters. People who have gotten involved in conversations appreciate the circulating food. Plan on six to eight pieces per person per hour of passed hors d'oeuvres, more if you are serving shrimp.

Another smart move is to place small trays or plates of food in different rooms or different areas. (Be sure to lock up your pets so they don't discover the treats before your guests get there.) Have someone whizzing around to remove and replenish platters. Put out bowls of nuts and other snacks that can be refilled periodically throughout the party. Pay attention to the food table, too. After the first ten people have been through the dishes on the table, it may not look so enticing. Replenish often so the food doesn't look like it's been through a feeding frenzy in a fish tank.

Along with the food, place an ice bucket, a bottle of wine or two, and a tray of glasses in an out of the way room or space so that guests can help themselves instead of having to return to a crowded bar. Or, have a waiter wander around taking drink orders and passing wine.

Beware of serving foods that give people bad breath: anchovies, sardines, strong cheeses, and so on. This is especially important at a cocktail party where people are in close quarters. Be careful not to serve foods that are difficult to eat standing up. Little key lime pies may look charming and taste delicious, but if guests need a fork to eat them or can't eat them in one or two bites, they are not a good choice for a cocktail party or any other party where guests are standing.

Buffets

If you plan to serve more food than is typical of a two-hour cocktail party, consider a buffet. Buffets are one of the most manageable ways of serving large numbers of people. Other advantages of buffets:

- ✔ The overall impression is sheer abundance.
- ✔ The look can be casual or elegant, depending on the occasion.
- ✔ People can eat as much or as little as they please.
- ✔ Guests can choose the foods they like and skip the rest.
- ✔ At most large buffet style parties, guests are allowed to choose their own seating, making them more spontaneous than sit-down dinners.

Buffets are usually set up on a dining room table. If you don't have a dining room table or if you need extra room, for a smaller group, you can set up a buffet table next to a wall. Guests can move in a single line from one end to the other. For a larger crowd, speed the buffet line by keeping the buffet table in the middle of the room so that guests can go down both sides. (Be sure to provide two sets of serving utensils.) Or, if money and space are not a problem, you can set up two separate buffet tables with the same food.

A good buffet doesn't have to overwhelm with food choices. You don't need to make the buffet look like Sunday brunch at the Ritz. You don't need to go overboard with variety. Whether you make one dish or five doesn't matter. What matters is that the food is delicious and there's plenty of it.

Display foods beautifully by choosing serving pieces of different shapes and heights. Arrange items on the table in the order guests will pass: plates, salads, main dishes, starch, vegetables, and bread. Place napkins and utensils at the end of the line so that guests don't have to juggle them while serving themselves.

Keep your eye on the buffet table. Remove platters that are half empty and replace them with full platters from your kitchen. Also, beware of decorating the buffet table with anything large or showy that would interfere with guests reaching the food.

Choose foods that are easy to handle. Unless you have room for every guest to have a place at the table, do not serve anything that requires cutting with a knife. Guests need only one utensil: a fork.

Thin pastas are not a great choice for a big crowd because in large quantities, they are difficult to prepare, serve, and keep hot. If you are planning a pasta-based dish, choose larger noodles such as lasagna or large stuffed shells. Stay away from runny sauces that can easily slop off the plate when guests are eating from their laps.

Select foods you can prepare in advance and don't need a lot of last-minute attention. Make sure the foods are sturdy enough to sit for an hour or so. For a big party, think of foods you can reheat and foods that retain heat well. Most egg dishes with heat under them wind up overcooked. Without the heat, the egg dish turns cold. Better choices are: meats, stews, gumbos, paella, lasagna, chili, risotto, mashed potatoes, and so on. You can make these dishes and many others ahead of time. Some of them can be frozen.

Following are a few more tips for a successful buffet meal:

- ✔ Provide plenty of comfortable places to sit.
- ✔ Use hot trays to keep foods hot. (We don't recommend chafing dishes, because the temperature can't be regulated and the food continues to cook all evening).
- ✔ Supply large plates so guests can take everything without having to juggle more than one plate.
- ✔ Supply large napkins to cover laps.

✔ Have someone circulating with wine and other beverages after guests are seated so they don't have to leave the table for refills. If you don't have help to serve drinks, set up a separate table for drinks, ice, and glasses so that guests can refill their drinks without breaking through the buffet line.

✔ Use a separate table or sideboard for desserts and coffee. Better yet, serve the dessert so guests don't have to get up again.

Seated dinners

Seated dinner parties are about dinner and conversation. Guests expect to relax, talk, and meet fascinating people. Guests can wander in the beginning while you greet them, make introductions, and serve cocktails. When you're ready to serve the meal, make sure to seat each guest next to someone you think he or she will enjoy being with for an hour.

After guests are seated, get on with the dinner. If guests are sitting too long, conversation may run out and fannies go numb. Don't dilly dally. The key is to serve at a good pace. A large seated dinner is not the time or place to serve multiple courses: Three courses is plenty. Save time by having the first course on the table before guests are seated. That eliminates a hot soup. But a cold salad is easy to have on the table in advance and looks beautiful, too. After the main course is cleared, get guests up and moving again by serving a dessert buffet or serving dessert and coffee in another room so people can rearrange themselves.

You have three serving options for large seated dinners:

✔ Plate the food in the kitchen.

✔ Have servers pass food to each person (French service).

✔ Serve casual/family style.

Regardless of the method you choose, for large seated dinner, you need help. When plating food in the kitchen, you need one or two people putting food on plates and one or two others delivering it to the tables.

You may want to arrange one plate exactly as you want it and ask the help to plate the rest of the food in the same way. However, if you've paid for professional catering services, leave it in their hands. They know what to do and that's one less detail you don't have to worry about.

Usually, the servers work together to serve one table at a time. This approach helps with the flow of the party. Later, the servers can pass more bread, offer second helpings, touch up wine, and clear plates. The servers are the timers and pacers. They can stagger the service so the kitchen catches up with the eaters or vice versa.

An alternative to plating the food in the kitchen is to have servers pass platters of food to seated guests. (This is called French service.) Ideally, you have two servers per table of 6 to 12 guests. If you don't want that much help, three servers can easily handle 14 people at two tables; one can pass meat, one can pass a vegetable, and the third can pass bread and pour wine.

When servers pass platters of food to seated guests, the servers should bring the platters back to the kitchen to replenish before serving the next table. Refilling the platters not only assures an attractive presentation, but guests at the next table won't be served hot foods that got cold.

A good way to keep food hot until it's served is to heat it in throw-away aluminum foil baking pans. In most home ovens, you can fit two pans to a shelf. (If you have more food to heat, buy an extra oven rack to add a third shelf.) Cover the baking squares with tin foil and rotate the pans while heating.

Be careful not to turn the temperature of the oven so hot that the food gets over-cooked. Most foods can be kept warm in an oven set at 200° to 250° F (93° to 121° C). Some foods such as soufflés cannot be kept warm in the oven. Check your recipes for reheating and warming instructions.

A practical, economical, and more casual way to feed a large crowd is to serve family style. Put bowls and platters of food on the table. Guests can pass the food around and help themselves. Get help to refill platters and bowls, refresh drinks, clear plates, and clean up.

Outdoor parties

Outside parties can be casual, relaxed, and more fun than anyone can imagine. Even a fancy party outdoors has an easy-going feel.

What makes big outdoor parties different from big indoor parties is that they don't need extra elements to make them outstanding. If your party is outdoors, the main thing you need is a beautiful day. (Add a keg of beer and a bucket of oysters or a grill full of burgers and bratwurst, and you've got a sensational party.) Besides an adequate place, all you really need is food, drink, and possibly music. You don't need to worry about decorations, themes, or special effects unless you particularly want to add extras. Even if you have too many guests (100 or more), somehow everything comes together outdoors.

You can also have some fun with the food. Outdoor parties lend themselves to foods that may not be as easily enjoyed indoors. For example, watermelon is messy and no fun to eat with a fork. If the party's outdoors, guests can eat it with their hands and discard the seeds without feeling self-conscious. Watermelon is the one food you can eat, drink, and wash your face in at the same time.

Outdoor parties are also perfect opportunities to serve simple foods. Even at the fanciest party, hot dogs and hamburgers are appropriate and taste special when they're cooked outdoors. They are familiar and make people feel comfortable.

Perhaps the very best part about outdoor party food is that you don't have to worry about plating it or having help to pass it unless the party is fancy or formal. Otherwise, you can just lay it all out, and people will come.

The trouble with planning a big party outdoors lies in the question of weather. When you are planning weeks in advance, there is no way to second-guess Mother Nature. Don't let a cold front, a windstorm, or a little rain spoil your party. Instead of worrying, have a backup plan. You have two options:

1. **Specify an alternate date.**

   This option may not be practical if you've already made large amounts of food in advance.

2. **Secure an alternative location.**

   A secondary site can be your house, a friend's house, a clubhouse, a restaurant, or a last-minute tent rental. Make arrangements in advance just in case.

The best alternate location is near the original outdoor site. It's much easier and less confusing to guests if you can move the party from your backyard into your house or from the picnic grounds into a nearby pavilion.

If you have to move the party indoors, start relocating as soon as you're sure outdoors is out. Don't worry if the indoor site becomes a little crowded. People will rally around and make the best of it.

Be sure to specify your "Plan B" on the invitations. Early on the day of the party, check the weather. If you see that the weather is not cooperating, call the guests to remind them of the alternative plan. Start by calling any out-of-town guests, then locals who have the furthest to come. If your guest list is enormous, solicit some help from another guest (or guests) to make some of the calls.

Following are a few more tips for successful outdoor parties:

> ✔ **Insect control.** If bugs are a problem in your area, provide cans of bug repellent for guests' use. You can keep a can in the restroom and one behind the bar. To keep annoying bugs away from the food, use citronella candles or torches or electric bug zappers.

✔ **Wind.** Even a slight breeze can blow napkins and other lightweight items right off the table. Place napkins under the plates or forks. Place cards can go under the glasses. Wait until the last minute to set out centerpieces so they aren't wind-whipped. Tie down the corners of your tablecloth with corner clips or beautiful ribbons and/or lean the backs of the chairs against the table to prevent the tablecloth from blowing until guests are seated.

✔ **Shade.** When the weather is hot and the sun's bearing down, guests need a shady reprieve. Think about providing shade when you choose the location for your party. If there are no big trees in the area, consider a tent or tables with umbrellas.

✔ **Food safety.** Fill barrels with ice and use thermal containers to keep foods and beverages at the desired temperature and to prevent spoilage.

✔ **Personal safety**. If your party is near water, keep any electrical equipment as far away from it as possible. Warn children not to go near any sound, lighting, or other electrical equipment, especially if they are wet from swimming. For a large party involving children, you can hire a baby-sitter to come to the party and keep a close eye on all the children. You are responsible for the safety of all your guests. Be cautious when combining alcohol with swimming. If an electrical storm approaches, move the party inside.

Developing a Central Theme

After you decide what kind of party to have, you need to begin thinking about the structure of the party. What a large party needs that a small party does not is a central theme, a handle, a form, or a concept. Although large parties come with various names and in various sizes, the successful ones have the same basic structure. Think of the cohesive elements as the bones of the party: invitations, entertainment, guests, and food are bound together by some common theme. You need something to build on and something to tie it all together.

The theme serves two purposes:

1. **To organize your party.**

2. **To get guests involved.**

A theme does not have to be a fully developed, overdone concept. A home party does not need a full-blown theme as with a big charity event or a black tie ball. For example, you don't have to stage a Hawaiian luau complete with hula dancers, fire-eaters, and poi. You can have a tropical theme without carrying out the details that far.

A theme can start from the simplest idea. It can be as subtle as the season or as flamboyant as a masquerade. For a starting point, think about:

- ✔ **The season.** How about a fall oyster roast, a winter ski party with warm drinks around a fire, a spring picnic, or a summer cookout?

- ✔ **An event.** Think of holidays, anniversaries, birthdays. Any upcoming event can suggest a theme for your party.

- ✔ **A reason.** Are you building a new home? Have a cocktail party in your half-built house. Is your best friend moving? Have a good-bye party.

- ✔ **A longing, a secret desire, or a whim.** Do you feel like dancing the night away, performing karaoke, dressing up in costumes? Host a party that fits your mood of the moment.

The point of having a theme is to create a mood. People respond to parties where they can get involved. Parties with themes often give guests permission to cut loose and let another side of their personalities emerge for a few hours.

For the event to be a success, you must be comfortable with the overall theme. If you love country music, plan a party around that. Or maybe you prefer hosting elegant seated dinners with blazing conversations. Whether you are more comfortable giving fancy cocktail parties, clambakes, or large family reunions, pick your kind of party, and go with it.

After you have figured out what you want the theme to be, concentrate on the elements that can flesh it out. A theme can begin with any one element (the invitations, the table settings, the menu, the decorations, or the entertainment) and extend to all others.

Big-Party Pizzazz

Huge parties need outstanding things:

- ✔ A few fabulous guests
- ✔ An eccentric, exclusive, or unique space
- ✔ Enormous or abundant decorations
- ✔ Incredible lighting
- ✔ Knock-out entertainment
- ✔ Simple food, but plenty of it

One of these elements alone is not enough to elevate your party to the stratosphere. What your party needs is joy, and everyone has a different idea of what makes a joyful occasion. Because guests' interests vary, you need to use everything you can get your hands on to tantalize, titillate, and lure them in. (See Chapter 6 for ways to target the senses.) A big party bursts with attention-grabbers, like a treasure trove of surprises.

But the number of elements alone will not improve your party. Using many mediocre elements only adds up to a mediocre party. If nothing sparkles, excites, or raises the blood pressure, your party may not generate enough joy. You've probably been to at least one party with lousy jug wine poured into plastic cups, nondescript food, glaring overhead lights, blaring music, and a bunch of bores besieging you.

For your party to rise above mediocrity, put a little extra effort into the things that matter the most to you. You can focus on the food, music, drinks, decorations, entertainment, or any combination of elements. You don't have to spend a fortune or try to do them all. Choose a few and have fun making those elements stand out.

The crucial step of any successful party is to infuse it with your personality. The simple way to do this is to figure out what you are good at and put your energy there. Whether it's cooking, decorating, socializing, or mixing drinks, do what you do best and what you enjoy the most. You don't have to be an expert on everything. Use whatever talent you have. (Later in this chapter, we tell you how to delegate the rest.)

Big-party guests

Parties are about participation, not observation. Guests can go to the theater to observe a performance. But when they come to your party, they are the performance. When selecting guests for a big party, the guests should be at least subtly endowed with the gift of being remembered. If too many guests are infinitely forgettable, you've got big trouble.

In Chapter 5, you figure out how to make a guest list for any party. The same principles apply to a big party, but on a grander scale. A big party is your opportunity to invite a dazzling convergence of strangers. It's your chance to include a few oddballs of every sort. Like moonshine whiskey, a varied guest list can pack quite a wallop. The effect can be exhilarating. Big parties can handle a bizarre mix of people that may not click at a smaller affair.

Do invite people

- ✔ Whom you are curious to meet or want to get to know better
- ✔ Who are not in your immediate social circle
- ✔ Who have moved out of your present life

✔ Who are fascinating and can carry on lively conversations

✔ Whom other guests will want to meet

✔ Who are willing to expend the energy to have a good time and not just take up space

Do not invite people solely to pay back invitations and no one else. It may be too obvious that's what you are doing, and it can be a dull mix. Go ahead and invite the paybacks, but include some new faces to liven up the group.

If you have too many guests you want to include and can't handle them all at once, think about having two parties, back-to-back. If you have the strength and energy and enough help, have the parties on consecutive nights instead of a week apart. Back-to-back parties can actually save you time and trouble because everything will already be in place.

When making up your guest lists for back-to-back parties, don't separate them into categories like one for your office and one for your friends. Go ahead and have two parties, but mix the two lists. Everyone has a better time if you mix up your coworkers and your nearest, dearest, and weirdest friends.

Big-party invitations

The invitation is a good place to begin your party's theme or concept. The invitation is primary. It sets the stage. Big parties need to start with an air of, "This will be something special. This is not to be missed." The invitation can help create a buzz. Your goal is to cut through all the guests' potential objections:

"I'll be too tired."

"It's too far away."

"It's too much effort."

"I've been there and done that . . . ."

To present an opportunity that reeks of excitement and the anticipation of pleasure, you need a hook. Grab guests' attention and reel them in. If you are calling people to invite them or to follow up your written invitation, tell them about someone special you want them to meet, the exciting entertainment, the fabulous music — something they can look forward to at your party.

If you are sending invitations by mail, get the message across with words, pictures, or both. If it's a dance, come right out and tell them so. Arouse curiosity about the music by simply drawing a few musical notes on the invitation. Look at Chapter 4 for more help with invitations or at Chapter 20 for some ideas for invitations to go along with specific themes.

Big-party food

Feeding a large crowd is not the same as feeding four friends your favorite chicken recipe. If you are the cook, keeping the food simple is imperative. Trying something new on a large number of people is risky. Stick with the tried and true, whether the event is a buffet or a sit-down dinner. Choose foods that you can be make ahead so you don't have to cook and host all at once. Forget complicated recipes. Not only can you make yourself crazy, but when the volume increases, so do your chances for error.

Instead of doubling, tripling, and quadrupling all your recipes, why not go for one delicious, flavorful, knock-their-socks-off dish? Decide what you want to call attention to, and put your time and energy into that one course. Showcase the dish by making everything else plain and simple. You end up with anything but a plain meal. The menu in Figure 15-1 is a perfect example.

Figure 15-1:
One knock-their-socks-off dish stands out when everything else is plain and simple.

> ### *Menu for Large Buffet or Seated Meal*
>
> *Shrimp Creole*
>
> *Rice*
>
> *Green salad*
>
> *French bread*
>
> *Beer/Wine*
>
> ❧
>
> *Sorbets and pralines*

This meal makes a statement. People love it because it's spicy, delicious, and luxurious. The shrimp Creole is the star. Everything else is simply there to enhance it. What makes the dish even more perfect is that you can make the sauce ahead of time and freeze it. On the day of the party, all you have to do is thaw out the sauce, heat it up, and add the shrimp.

Even when you aren't doing the cooking (because you've hired a caterer), keep the food simple. You may be surprised how much more people enjoy the food when they know what they are eating. Exotic or fancy food is more appropriate for small parties. If you are dying to serve something exotic, prepare it as an hors d'oeuvre. Guests can experiment with just one bite. If they don't like it, they won't be stuck with a whole plateful.

If you find it difficult to estimate how much food to prepare for a crowd, you aren't alone. See Chapter 8 for help in balancing menus, and don't forget to use your common sense. Always overestimate a bit. You are better off having a little food leftover than running out of something that guests are devouring. (Leftovers are never a waste. You can always freeze them or eat them the next day, or send a plate home with guests.)

Big-party atmosphere

Big parties become famous for a number of reasons. Usually, it's not the food that stands out. Few people remember what they have eaten at a large party. Even fewer care. (This doesn't mean the food is unimportant — it should be delicious, but simple.)

The setting of a party makes an impression, but don't worry if the setting isn't spectacular. The overall atmosphere is the most important. For big-party atmosphere, you want a high-spirited mood and unexpected twists so guests can be amused and delighted.

One of the best and easiest ways to affect the senses is with the lighting. At a big party, go crazy! Put your dollars in this detail. Hundreds of 15-watt bulbs can transform a large room. Masses of candles can create magic, as will dozens of flickering oil lamps. Even if the party's outside, you can surround the entire area with votives. Use kerosene lamps for a barbecue. (If you have hired party professionals, let them take care of providing extra electrical outlets, candle holders, lamps, and so on.) If professional help is beyond your budget, look for ways to adapt under "Don't Blow Your Budget," in this chapter.

To make a big party pop, you need some form of entertainment. A regular old party is not a regular old party if you add entertainment. But having entertainment doesn't mean you have to spend a fortune. In fact, if you have a theme, the entertainment doesn't have to cost you a nickel. The theme can be the entertainment. For example, at a costume party, the guests' attire is the entertainment. At a dance, people are entertained by the movement of their own bodies and by watching others. Consider a hat party for a ladies luncheon or a 1920s flapper party. These parties encourage creativity and individuality and keep guests entertained for hours.

The setting can also be a part of the entertainment: At a picnic, the great outdoors may be all the entertainment you need. If you've hired a barbecue chef (even if it's your Great-uncle Louis), he becomes a part of the entertainment.

Music is also an essential part of the entertainment. The tunes set the tone. Music brings people together and gives energy to the event. Play upbeat music. Rent a jukebox or play your favorite CDs. Balance your sound systems. Adjust the volume so it doesn't drown out conversations. If you want your party to be voted "Party of the Year," consider live music. Hire a band, a fiddler, a piano player, or a folk singer.

Just rent it

If you give big parties frequently and have plenty of storage space, you may decide to invest in dozens of glasses, plates, folding tables, and chairs. But if you're like most people, you don't have everything on hand for a big party.

Take heart. You can rent almost any party item you can think of. Following is a partial list of items you may want or need for a big party:

- Glasses
- Plates
- Flatware
- Serving pieces
- Linens
- Tables (different sizes and shapes)
- Chairs (folding, ballroom, and chair covers)
- Coat rack
- Decorations
- Candelabras
- Plants
- Sound systems
- Dance floors
- Trellises
- Gazebos
- Tents

If you plan to hire a caterer, let him take care of all the rentals. Otherwise, prepare a complete list of the items you need.

Before you call or visit your local rental company, know exactly what you want. (Don't necessarily rely on their advice. Often, they will try to rent you the biggest and the most of everything they offer.)

If you are renting tables, insist on the sizes and shapes you want. (See Chapter 5 for help in choosing tables.) If you are renting items such as glasses, plates, flatware, or linens, don't mix them in with your own. Rent enough to service the entire party so that there is no confusion about what belongs to whom. (The great advantage of renting dishes and linens is that you don't have to wash them. The rental company picks them up and does all the dirty work.)

After you find the items you need to rent, get a net price for everything, including rental fees, delivery, setup, and pickup. Next, schedule delivery and pickup. Some companies deliver the day before the party, which is convenient because it allows you to get everything set up ahead of time. Others prefer to deliver the day of the party. Make sure the date, time, and location are clearly understood.

See Chapter 6 for more information on creating the atmosphere. See Chapter 11 for more entertainment options.

You Need Help

You may know what kind of party to have and whom to invite, but how many guests can you handle? The answer depends to a large degree upon how much help you have.

Unless you frequently entertain on a large scale, you may not realize how much time and effort is involved. You may find it difficult to estimate how much time everything takes. Trust us: If you are plating dinner for 25 people, it takes you forever to do it alone. By the time you serve the main course at the last table, the first table is waiting for dessert. Professionals can whip out the plates in no time so that all the guests eat at approximately the same time.

Even if you think you can handle the food service, you can always use an extra pair of hands. For example, if you borrowed extra china from your neighbor and at the last minute you realize it needs to be washed, a helper can do that. You can enjoy the event much more when you have sufficient help.

The following is a rough guideline you can use to decide how much help you need for the number of people you want to invite and the kind of party you are planning. You may find you need more or less help, depending on your own expertise, what you are serving, and who your guests are. Remember, there are no magic numbers; this is a *guesstimate*.

- ✔ **8 to 14:** Although not really a "big party," this is a great size for cock-tails before going to a restaurant or for a seated dinner in your home. You may be able to entertain this number of guests without hiring outside help. However, spouses, children, or friends can still lend a hand. Feel free to delegate or to accept any offers.

- ✔ **15 to 24:** This is a lovely size for a stand up cocktail party. One helper is all you need. If you are planning a seated meal for this number, you may need 2 to 4 extra sets of hands to help serve and to take care of piles of dishes and masses of glasses.

- ✔ **25 to 50:** This a great size for a big party because you can have a few extended conversations in addition to being everywhere at once. This number is good for cocktail buffets, dinners, outside events, and large tea parties. For a cocktail buffet or stand-up event, in addition to a table of food, use one helper to pass food and another as a bartender. For a seated meal, the number of service people you need depends on the serving style you have chosen. (See the section "Seated dinners," earlier in this chapter.)

Working with caterers

The first few times you give a big party, don't try to do it yourself. Hire a caterer. The idea is to tell that person what you want and let her handle everything: the food, the bar, the rentals, and even the flowers. Talk to several catering services and get proposals.

For a large party, most caterers suggest an on-site visit. To help you with the menu and to determine the feasibility of getting everything ready, they will need to evaluate the size and location of the kitchen, oven space, and room arrangement.

Tell them what you want, and listen to their suggestions as well. Now is the time to discuss your vision of the tables. Ask what kind of serving pieces and napkins are available. If the caterer doesn't have what you want, you may prefer to use yours. For a party other than a picnic or barbecue, have it understood that condiments such as mayonnaise or ketchup are not to be placed on the table in their original containers. (Most caterers would never do this, but it has happened.)

Ask about the per-person cost and any additional service charges. Get a net price for the whole job. It is the caterer's responsibility to work within your budget. She can help you make adjustments to your plan without sacrificing overall quality.

The largest cost, other than the food, is the service staff. You can pay one bill to the caterer, inclusive of service. To save money, you can pay the caterer's service staff directly. Some caterers don't mind, if you are a frequent customer, and will provide names so you can write the checks in advance. By paying the service staff directly, you avoid any added service fees from the catering company.

Service people usually work for an hourly wage. Some will only work if you guarantee a minimum number of hours of work. Be sure to ask, and don't forget to add an appropriate tip. You can add it onto the check or offer the tip in cash.

✔ **50 to 75:** This usually is the maximum for most home parties. This number of guests is most suitable for cocktail parties, dances, and outdoor events. For this size cocktail party, hire one bartender, two passers, and one kitchen person. For sit-down dinners of this size, you need many people helping. (See the section "Seated dinners," earlier in this chapter.) If it's an outdoor event, consider hiring a bartender and possibly someone to cook — a professional oyster shucker, clam baker, barbecue chef, or pig roaster. At informal outside events, guests will enjoy serving themselves. For more formal events, hire servers and passers.

✔ **100 or more:** Hardly any house can comfortably handle this many people. Even if your house can, you may never get around to talking to 100 people unless you are a superb politician. If you decide to have a party of this enormity, you must have good traffic flow, two bars, and beautiful buffet tables. You need plenty of waiters and a caterer to oversee the entire operation.

Professional caterers, bartenders, and service people are a godsend for big parties. They know what to do and how to do it and will follow your instructions. To find them, ask your friends who entertain, or hire outstanding bartenders and servers from restaurants you frequent. Another option is to ask for recommendations from local hotels or check under "Caterers" in the Yellow Pages.

If you have a nanny and/or cleaning person who works in your house, ask them if they want to work late or work at your party. Even if you have a catering staff, your regular help can come in handy by showing them where things are.

If professional help is beyond your budget, you may consider hiring a neighborhood teenager or your own child. Be realistic and pay them a fair wage. Otherwise, they may decide to disappear when they get hungry, thirsty, or bored. If you don't have children or don't trust the neighborhood teens, consider calling local high schools, colleges, or temporary agencies to get names, or ask your friends if they know a good, reliable, person who may want the job.

Regardless of who the help is, treat them well. Provide food for them and be sure to tip them fairly. For good service, offer whatever tip is standard in your area of the country for restaurant servers. For exceptional service, add a little extra. You may want to hire this person again.

Don't Blow Your Budget

By now, you probably think we have forgotten all about your budget. The good news is, you can have a big party without spending a fortune. A party's success doesn't depend on big bucks. Far more important than the number of dollars you spend is the amount of imagination you invest. Go ahead and think big — big food, big decorations, big entertainment. . . . The key is to think more but spend less.

When developing your budget, think about invitations, liquor, food, rentals, service, entertainment, flowers, and decoration. Figure out how much you can reasonably afford to spend on each category, and then figure out where you can trim back to stay within your budget.

If your plan doesn't exactly fit your pocketbook, a little creativity can go a long way toward creating the illusion that you had a big budget. Following are some ways you can cut corners without sacrificing quality. Use any money you save to hire extra help. Hiring help is worth every penny!

✔ Handwrite invitations instead of spending money on custom printing.

✔ Serve one or two choices of alcoholic drinks instead of having an open bar. Remember: A good punch is better than bad champagne.

✔ Make smart food choices. For example, buffalo tenderloin is lovely, but it's five times more expensive than beef. Few people will realize (or care) they are eating such a delicacy. Go with the beef.

✔ Give recipes to friends who like to cook and ask them to prepare the recipes for the party. (Be sure they're invited to your party!)

✔ Invest in candles for luxurious lighting at a minimal cost. (If you don't have enough candleholders, float votives in bowls or drip a little wax on any small plates and stick the candles in the warm wax.)

✔ Rent a jukebox instead of a band. Jukeboxes are relatively inexpensive, but guests' enjoyment is enormous.

✔ Make your own arrangements of flowers, weeds, twigs, fruits, or vegetables. If you are not comfortable with your artistic ability, go ahead and spend a little extra having someone help with flowers and decorations.

Make a Plan and Stick to It

You don't just wake up one morning and decide to have 30 people over for a party. You start planning a few weeks in advance. The success of a big party is 80 percent organizational. No matter how much help you have, it's up to you to follow-up and follow through.

Organizing a big party is much like organizing a small party in that you need lists, lists, lists. Take a look at Chapter 3 for tips on what lists to make and how to use them. The major difference in organizing a big party is that your lists will be more extensive. Create a long-term planning guide to keep track of everything you need to do prior to the party.

Following is a sample planning guide for a big party in your home. Use it as a guide and adjust according to your individual time constraints:

6 to 12 weeks prior (or longer)

✔ Decide to throw a big party for whatever reason.

✔ Think about what kind of party it should be: Cocktails? Dance? Buffet? Midnight supper?

✔ Pick a date and time.

✔ Figure out where to have the party. (If it's not your house, reserve the space.)

✔ Start a guest list.

✔ Determine a theme.

✔ Establish your budget.

✔ Figure out how much help you need. Arrange for it now. Meet the person in charge of providing the help.

✔ Choose and hire entertainment.

6 to 8 weeks prior

✔ Send out invitations.

✔ Make a list of any special needs (china, coffee urn, glassware, and so on).

✔ Arrange for any rentals. Ask about delivery, pick-up, cleaning, and so on. Leave no question unasked and nothing to chance. The caterer, if you have one, can handle those services.

✔ If your yard looks like a trash pile, get thee to the dumpster. While you're at it, schedule the window cleaner and rug cleaner to come to your house the week before the party. (If you wait until you want them, they may not be available.)

4 weeks prior

✔ Start cooking food and freezing it.

✔ Take inventory of the liquor cabinet, and restock.

2 weeks prior

✔ Continue cooking and freezing.

✔ Order flowers.

✔ Check your stereo or sound system to make sure it's working.

✔ Figure out where guests will put their coats and umbrellas. (Don't create a traffic jam by putting them next to the door. A guest bedroom, back porch, or other out of the way place is a better choice. Depending on the number of guests and time of year, you may need to rent a coat rack.)

1 week prior

✔ Call the help you've hired and confirm the date and time they are due to arrive.

✔ Make follow-up calls to any unconfirmed guests to find out if they are coming.

✔ Spiff up your house.

✔ Mow the lawn.

✔ Keep cooking.

1 day prior

✔ Begin decorating and setting tables.

✔ Receive deliveries of any furniture, tableware, or other rentals. (Or day of party.)

✔ Receive flowers.

Early — Day of

✔ Write checks for help and get cash for tips.

✔ Finish decorating and setting tables.

✔ Defrost food.

✔ Remain calm.

Later — Day of

✔ Greet, and give last-minute directions to help.

✔ Dress.

✔ Reheat food.

✔ Lay out desserts.

✔ Relax.

In addition to your planning guide, make a master checklist that includes everything, right down to the last detail. The master checklist is your party at a glance. (We'll call it your "dummy list," because everybody gets a little crazy as party time draws near.) This list is your best insurance against forgetfulness. Fill in all the information and check off each item as it is completed.

Dummy List

- ❏ Date
- ❏ Guest list
- ❏ Location
- ❏ Theme
- ❏ Invitations
- ❏ Menu
- ❏ Drinks
- ❏ Caterers/Hired help
- ❏ Rentals
- ❏ Entertainment (book, contract, arrival time)
- ❏ Decorations
- ❏ Air conditioning/heating
- ❏ Lighting
- ❏ Parking/valet
- ❏ Weather
- ❏ Umbrellas
- ❏ Coat rack
- ❏ Photographer
- ❏ Seating chart
- ❏ Menu and place cards
- ❏ Bathroom accessories (toilet paper, soap, hand towels, toiletries)
- ❏ Payments and tips

Party Time

The party begins as soon as the doorbell starts ringing. What you do in the first ten minutes affects the tone of the entire evening. You want guests to walk in your door, take a deep breath, and say, "Ahhh . . . ." Make this happen by doing everything possible to assure instant comfort.

✔ Personally greet and welcome guests as they arrive.

✔ Have help (or your child) take guests' coats.

✔ Have someone circulating with trays of drinks.

✔ Inform guests where to find the bar.

✔ Introduce guests to one another.

Your role as a host evolves with the progress of the party. While you should be aware of what's going on, if you have done your homework and instructed your help, the party will flow naturally. You will be able to relax and enjoy yourself.

After the guests arrive, your mission is to circulate, observe, and enjoy. With the eyes in the back of your head, you may need to watch over your mate, your children, or anyone else who needs a gentle reminder or a swift kick in the pants.

Watch to make sure food is being passed. Circulate among guests, make introductions and start conversations, and then move on. If you want to make sure you have a chance to talk with everyone, help pass the food or refill drinks. This way, you can make your way around to more guests and have an excuse to keep moving.

By midpoint, your party should take on a life of its own. If the party is a success, you will detect an air of excitement — a tempo — a heat and a beat not found in small parties. Planning and organization make that hum happen. You may wish the party would never end.

Eventually, it will, one way or another. If people stay a long time, you know you've got a hit on your hands. If everyone marches out right on time, it doesn't necessarily mean failure. (Better that way than a slow fizzle.) On-time departures may mean that they all have to go to work the next morning or they are self-conscious about staying too late or being the last to leave. Sometimes one person leaving signals the beginning of the end and others simply follow like sheep. But you will know if they had a good time: If guests crawl out high on conversation, food, and laughter, you can pat yourself on the back. You know how to give a party for a crowd.

Chapter 16

Tots to Teens: Planning Parties for Children

*W*elcome to a whole new world of entertaining. Even if you don't have children or if your children are grown, you may be asked to help plan or supervise a children's party at some point.

There is a magic formula for success, and we give it to you in this chapter. We take you from the guest list and invitations to the food and activities. With a little knowledge and a lot of planning, you can save your sanity, have some fun, and create a lasting memory for your child.

Making Your Child's Day

Whether you currently have toddlers, tykes, or teens at home, at least one day out of every year each child deserves his or her very own party. In a child's world, his birthday is the most important day of the year. Children measure everything by their special day.

"I'm 7¹/₂ years old."

"School starts after my birthday."

"It's 63 days, 4 hours, and 17 minutes till my birthday."

"I want a _____ for my birthday."

"I get my driver's license on my birthday."

Nobody can do things better for your child than you. If you are too overwhelmed to plan a party (your child's birthday is on Christmas or you are working 14-hour shifts), have a family celebration instead. Plan a special meal, even if it's take-out. Let the child choose the menu. And whatever you do, don't forget the birthday cake and candles.

You don't have to plan a party to show your child how important he is. You can make the whole day special from beginning to end. Start with breakfast in bed, no school, no chores. Let the child dictate all the day's meals, choose the television stations, ride shotgun in the car, and have a special privilege, such as a late bedtime.

Planning Your Child's Party

In some ways, children's parties are just like any other party you may give. Parties for children don't have to be perfect, but they do need careful planning and orchestration. You can apply many of the same party-planning principles we cover in this book to children's parties. But some important differences can occur in the way you plan the guest list, the menu, and the activities. However, keep in mind that, regardless of their ages, guests just want to have fun.

Special considerations

As with any party, you need a complete plan with lists of all the things you need to buy and do. If you need help getting organized, look for some hints in Chapter 3. For a children's party, give yourself ample planning time. We suggest allowing yourself two to four weeks. The following are some other thoughts to consider when planning a children's party:

 ✔ **A time limit for the party.** Whether the time limit is an hour and a half or half a day is up to you and what you think you can handle. (Two hours is average.) The goal is to give yourself enough time to feed and entertain the guests with no time left over for idle hands to get into trouble.

✔ **Photography.** Don't trust your memories to your memory. Photographs are important, not only for your own memory book, but to send to relatives and other parents. You may want to take some photos yourself. But because you'll be busy running the show, ask someone else to take candid shots throughout the event. Even if you plan to videotape the party, take still pictures as well. Chances are, you'll look at your photo album more often than the video.

✔ **Discipline.** No matter how well you plan your party, sometimes a child gets out of hand. Don't let that child ruin the party for everyone else, but be careful how you discipline someone else's child. You can try to divert the child's attention or channel his energy somewhere else. You can invite her to help you in the kitchen, ask her to put candles on the cake, or ask another adult helper to take him to another room or do something else with him. Most children listen to adults who are not their parents. If you know a child is particularly difficult to handle, invite that child's parent to help you chaperone the party.

✔ **Breaks and spills.** Before hosting a children's party, put away any valuables you don't want handled or possibly broken. If a child breaks or spills something during the party and it is purely accidental, chalk it up to experience and forget about it. If the item is valuable and the cause of the accident is unruly behavior, whether or not you approach the child's parents is entirely up to you. You can tell the parents and hope that they offer to replace or pay for the object or, in the case of a spill, pay for the cleaning. Or, you can absorb the cost and say nothing.

The following are a few more facts about children's parties:

✔ Surprise parties don't always work for little ones. For them, the anticipation and build up of excitement is half the fun. You may want to save the surprises for ages 10 and up.

✔ If you are planning a slumber party, don't expect anyone to slumber, including you.

✔ If you don't believe in Murphy's Law, just wait until you plan an outdoor party for 25 kids. It's bound to be pouring rain that day. Inside the house is no safer; the day of your child's birthday party will be the day the electricity goes off. Be prepared for the unexpected. Always have a Plan B ready — a rain date, an alternative place, or an optional activity.

Themes and schemes

You need a definite theme when planning a party for a child. But not just any old theme will do — it must be of interest to the child. Think beyond what you want or what you think your child wants. For example, you may be dreaming of a tea party for your daughter. Maybe she would rather play cowboys and Indians than dress up and eat petit fours. The key is to know your child's favorite things. Plan the party around the child's age and interests. Make suggestions and get your child's response. Clearing the theme with your child is very important. Then, you can coordinate everything from the invitations to the activities around that central idea.

Finding a theme is as simple as watching what your child and his friends do everyday. What television show, video, or movie is the current rage with them? Who are their favorite action figures and superheroes? What characters do they pretend to be? If media figures don't suggest an appropriate theme, think about toys and activities that interest your child. For example, have an art party for a child who loves to color, draw, or paint. Plan a trip to the fire department for a child who enjoys playing with toy fire trucks.

If you have trouble thinking of a theme, take your child to a card shop or other party supply store. Browse the party favor section and see what attracts the child. If she goes bonkers over Barbie or Superman, you have found a theme. Expand the theme by suggesting that children come dressed as related characters and/or by providing props for role play.

Middle school and high school age children may enjoy a back-to-school party, scavenger hunt, sock hop, disco dance, or jukebox party.

One way to simplify your party planning is to use the services offered at many public facilities. Some fast food restaurants, miniature golf courses, bowling centers, and ice cream parlors arrange complete parties for a flat fee. Look in the Yellow Pages of your telephone directory or ask at local facilities. Find out what kinds of food and drink they provide and if a cake is included. (Some will let you bring your own cake if you prefer.) Most provide all the decorations and activities. Some offer extra help with supervision. Kids of all ages love these parties. Best of all, you don't have to clean up the mess.

Guest Lists and Invitations

If your child is between the ages of 1 and 3, limit the guest list to family only, or invite whomever you want. The child may not remember it, but you will make some important memories of your own and perhaps enjoy some adult conversation with your fellow chaperones.

By age 4, many children want to be involved in determining whom to invite. One way to decide how many guests to have is to invite the same number of children as your child's age: If the child is 4, invite four guests of the child's choosing.

If your children are in elementary school, consider inviting the whole class to your child's party. Otherwise, you risk deeply hurting those who are left out. Even if your child does not like one of her classmates, this is a good opportunity to teach tolerance and compassion. If you need to pare down the list because of space or budget limitations, consider inviting all the boys or all the girls.

When children reach their teens, you probably know who their friends are. If the party's a surprise, you can make out the guest list or enlist help from one of your teen's best friends. If your teen is aware that you are planning a party, ask him to participate in the planning by making the guest list and helping with the invitations.

Written invitations are a must for children's parties. Otherwise, parents may not get the message about your child's party or important details, such as the time and date, may be miscommunicated. Because most schools are not allowed to give out information about students, finding the guests' addresses may take some sleuthing. You can find most of the addresses in the telephone directory unless you are unsure of the parents' names and/or the last name is extremely common. For addresses you can't find in the phone book, ask friends or neighbors. Or if your child is old enough, give her the responsibility of getting the addresses for you. (If she wants the party badly enough, she'll come through with the list.)

Some children like to take invitations to school to distribute. That's okay. But you need to follow-up with a phone call to the parents. Most of the time, you are better off putting the invitations in the mail.

The purpose of the invitation is twofold: to inform the parents and to excite the guests. Use the chosen party theme to create an invitation that immediately evokes excitement and anticipation.

Here are some examples of creative invitations for children's parties:

- ✔ **Magic party:** Purchase Crayola changeable markers. Use the white one to write the invitation on white paper. (The words will be invisible.) Include a colored changeable marker in the envelope with instructions to color the entire invitation. The words appear like magic! Plan to have a magician or fortune-teller at the party. This invitation can also work for a Halloween party with a ghost theme.

- ✔ **Costume party:** Write the invitation on masks. You can ask guests to wear the masks to the party, have them create their own masks and costumes, or have them come dressed as the host. (Use an enlarged picture of your child's face on a stick to create a life-like mask.)

Help!

For safety and sanity, don't give a children's party by yourself. No matter what the ages of the children, you need at least two extra pairs of adult eyes and hands. If a parent asks if you need help, just say, "Yes." If no one offers, hire a couple of responsible high school students.

Small children need hands-on help with everything from tying their shoes to going to the bathroom. After age 4, children don't want adults to do things for them. Sometimes it's better if guests' parents aren't at the party, unless it is that exceptional parent who has a wonderful way with kids.

Chaperoning escalates as children get older. At teenage parties, adults don't have to be eavesdropping spies. Using the eyes in the backs of their heads, parents can be in the background, grilling hamburgers, making milk shakes, or chatting among themselves.

✔ **Bike race or parade:** Write the invitation on a checkered flag. (For the Fourth of July, use red, white, and blue flags.) Tell each child to bring his bicycle or tricycle to the party. Let the children know that you will provide materials for decorating the bikes: streamers, stickers, brightly colored cards to click in the spokes, plastic horns, and so on. Children can race or parade down a sidewalk, a long driveway, a beach, or a path in your yard. Send each child home with a safety flag for a party favor.

Kid-Friendly Food

Most children don't care what the food is as long as they know what it is, there's plenty of it, and it's not too good for them. You don't need to be elaborate. Kids don't care if the peanut-butter sandwiches are cut in the shape of stars or simply cut in half. Teens won't notice if the pizza is served on a silver platter, a paper plate, or straight out of the box.

Choose age-appropriate food. Most children under the age of 16 are not excited over anything green unless it's jelly beans, limeade, or pistachio ice cream. Don't worry about the balance or nutritional value of the menu. A birthday splurge is once a year, not everyday!

Very young children (ages 2 to 4) don't have highly developed motor skills yet, so they need finger food. Here are a few more points to keep in mind as you entertain these wee ones:

✔ No forks or spoons to accidentally jab in an eye

✔ No hot dogs, grapes, or hard candy to choke on

- No messy food to get all over their clothes and your floor

- No spicy food to burn tongues or upset stomachs

- No colored beverages unless the party's outside or you don't care if you have to look at that color for the next ten years. Better choices: ginger-ale, lemon-lime soda, lemonade, or clear sports drinks.

Remember to feed the adults who are helping. You can plan a kid menu and an adult menu. The grown ups' menu doesn't have to be anything elaborate, but offer something besides gummy bears and fruit punch. (Cold beer never hurts. Serve sparkling water for the nondrinkers.)

Older children may like to be involved in preparing the food. As a part of the entertainment, let them:

- Make their own banana splits.

- Build their own tacos.

- Top their own pizzas.

- Share a long submarine sandwich.

Activities and Entertainment

When it comes to entertainment, children's parties pose a different challenge from adult parties. Unlike an adult party, you cannot expect a group of children to go with the flow and make their own fun. For a child's party to be a success, each child must be interested and active.

Rarely does everyone show up for a party at exactly the same time. Plan an activity for the arrival time so that the first guests who show up have something to do while waiting for the others.

- Ask everyone to sign a big birthday card with crayons or markers.

- Provide materials for drawing or coloring.

- Have someone with a video camera greet and interview each arriving child. (You can show the video later.)

- Designate one of your adult helpers as photographer and have each child pose for a picture.

Depending on the age group, you may need a few or many planned activities.

Party favors

Give each guest a small gift or party favor to take home. Give something suitable to the gender, age, and interests of the guests, not something that can break in 15 minutes. If your party has a specific theme, think of something that goes along with it. Or, make up goody bags. Include items such as bottles of bubbles, jump ropes, coloring books, markers, candy, gum, and so on.

For young children (ages 10 and under), plan two different kinds of activities. The trick is to balance active activities with calming activities so that children don't get too wound up. You may want to offer both kinds simultaneously. Some children would never play on a water slide (see activity list) but would be perfectly content at a face-painting station.

Plan the activities in a logical order. For example, start with a series of active (or physical) activities: games, relays, contests, and so on. Then move to calming activities: sitting down drawing or making something. Serve the food next, and then open presents and give out party favors.

Planning extra activities is crucial. The game you think will consume an hour may actually take 15 minutes. If you allow half an hour for opening gifts, they will be ripped open in 5 minutes flat. You need a bevy of back-up options that you can tap into without hesitation.

Having a long list of activities doesn't mean you need to do each one. If children are enjoying a particular activity, don't interrupt to start another one. You will know when it's time to move on.

Part of your plan can be some unstructured time for children to play on their own — children often enjoy the unplanned time the most. If children lose interest or appear bored with the planned activities or if they become too competetive, some free play time may be your best alternative. Otherwise, suggest free play whenever it seems most appropriate to you. In other words, play it by ear.

Fun for all ages

The following is a list of activities, group games, and contests suitable for children's parties of all sizes and adaptable for age groups 2 to 12. Children can do some activities indoors or out, and most are appropriate for both sexes. Most of the games and contests make use of simple items you are likely to have around the house or items you can easily buy at discount stores, toy stores, and department stores. You can hold the activities separately, one at a time, or simultaneously, having children rotate from one activity to the next.

Activities:

- ✔ **Sidewalk chalk.** For drawing on the sidewalk and playing hopscotch.

- ✔ **Buckets of bubbles and big wands.** The most fun ever with soap and water.

- ✔ **Crayon rubbings.** Put paper over found objects; rub crayon over surface to make texture pictures.

- ✔ **Straw painting.** Put a thin layer of paint on paper. Children blow through straws to create designs.

- ✔ **Make-up.** Use samples and castoffs of eyeshadow, blusher, lipsticks, nail polish, and so on. Avoid eyeliner and mascara that could spread germs or get poked in an eye. Provide cotton squares and giant cotton swabs so everyone has her own applicators. Give each child a mirror to use at the party and to take home afterward.

- ✔ **Face painting.** Buy washable paints. Let older children paint younger children's faces, or let children take turns painting each other.

- ✔ **Water slide (such as Super Crocodile Mile or Zig, Zag, Zoom).** A commercial outdoor sliding surface (available in toy stores) used with a hose pipe.

- ✔ **Penny/candy hunt.** Get a bale of hay and put it in a plastic swimming pool to contain any debris. Stick in pennies, wrapped candy, or small toys from the dollar store. Put a blindfold on children. Let each child have two minutes to get all he or she can. As an alternative, spread the goodies on a lawn. Leave off the blindfolds, and give each child a small paper bag to collect as many prizes as possible in the time allotted.

- ✔ **Pass the orange.** Players stand in a circle with hands behind their backs. They must pass an orange from chin to chin without dropping it. (Teenagers especially love this one.)

- ✔ **Make banana splits.** Provide each child with his own bowl. Spread out all the fixings and let children concoct their own ooey-gooey desserts.

- ✔ **Piñata.** Purchase a piñata and fill it with candy and small prizes. Hang it from a tree branch or some other apparatus that allows the piñata to swing freely. Lead blindfolded children to the piñata one at a time to take turns hitting it with a stick or baseball bat until it bursts. When the candy falls out, children scramble for it and keep what they can gather.

- ✔ **Costume party.** Dressing up is fun for children of all ages. Young children enjoy the fantasy and role play. Older children may enjoy a costume contest with prizes for various categories: scariest, prettiest, most original, brightest, coolest, and so on. Have enough categories for everyone to win a prize.

Games:

- ✔ **Giggle belly.** Children lie on the floor. Each rests his head on the next child's stomach. The first player says "Ha," the second, "Ha, ha," the third "Ha, ha, ha," and so on until everyone is convulsed in laughter.

- ✔ **Telephone game.** Everyone sits in a circle. The first child whispers a sentence or two to the next person. It is repeated around the circle. At the end, it's fun to see how much the message has changed.

- ✔ **Musical chairs.** You need a circle of chairs and music (one less chair than the number of players). Everybody moves around until the music stops, and then scrambles for the nearest chair. The person who doesn't have a chair is out and removes another chair. The last child out is the winner.

- ✔ **Pretzel.** One person leaves the room. The others join hands in a circle. Without letting go, they twist themselves up every which way, until they resemble a tight knot. The child that's out tries to unravel the human pretzel without loosening the other player's hands. This can be a competitive race between two teams.

- ✔ **Twister.** A board game requiring players to twist their bodies into awkward positions.

- ✔ **Cake walk.** The prizes don't have to be cakes — you can offer pumpkins, an inexpensive portable radio, a T-shirt, or anything else the age group may like. Mark numbers on squares of paper on the floor, or hide numbers underneath chairs. Make a set of corresponding numbers to draw out of a hat or bowl. Have children walk from square to square or chair to chair while playing music. When the music stops, each child stops at the nearest square or chair. Draw a number, and give the winner the cake or other appropriate prize. Continue until all the prizes are gone.

Contests:

- ✔ **Speed shaving.** (with tongue depressors). Players divide into teams of two. On signal, one player covers the bottom part of his partner's face with shaving cream and shaves it clean with the tongue depressor. Then they switch places. The first team finished is declared the winner. (For an all-girl party, let them "shave" their legs.)

- ✔ **Bobbing for apples.** Fill a huge tub with water and apples. Players are timed to see who can get a floating apple out of the water fastest without using hands.

- ✔ **Balloon-blowing.** Each player receives a deflated balloon. The winner is the player who makes his balloon biggest in two minutes. Any child who breaks a balloon is out of the contest. Continue until only one player is left.

✔ **Coat and hat relay.** Divide players into equal teams. Give each team one hat and one coat (preferably the same kind of coat with plenty of buttons, zippers, and hook and loop tape). On signal, the first player must put on the hat and the coat, and fasten the coat completely. She must then take them off and pass them to the next player. The first team to finish is the winner.

✔ **Shoe hunt.** Children take off their shoes and place them in a large box. (Make sure that the box is big enough for all the children to fit around and that the height of the box is appropriate for the size of the children.) You mix up the shoes. On signal, everyone runs forward to find his own shoes. The first person with his shoes on wins.

✔ **Pin the tail on the donkey (or dinosaur or Winnie the Pooh).** Each child takes a turn putting on a blindfold. She spins around a few times and tries to pin the tail on the right spot. The child who gets closest wins.

✔ **Egg or Ping-Pong ball hunt.** For Easter, dye hard-boiled eggs to hide, or hide the candy ones. Children keep what they find. As an alternative any time of the year, hide Ping-Pong balls. Give a prize to the child who finds the most.

✔ **Pie-eating contest.** Children kneel on the floor with hands behind their backs. Each child has a quarter of a pie on a paper plate in front of him. On signal, they lean forward and eat the pie. The first one to eat all the pie and pick up the empty paper plate with his teeth is the winner. (Blueberry and cherry are great for color, and kids love slurping them up. Spread newspapers on the surrounding floor and give players old T-shirts to wear or towels to cover their clothes.)

✔ **Obstacle course.** Set up a series of activities for the children to perform in order. You can incorporate sports, stunts, and relay activities. Children can compete individually or in teams to see who can get through the series fastest.

✔ **Scavenger hunt.** Issue a list of items to each child or each team to find within set boundaries and a set time limit. Whichever team finds the most items from the list is the winner.

If you need more help with ideas, details, and directions for activities, we suggest that you go to the library or buy a book on children's games. Use the games book like a cookbook. Mix and match activities that suit your child's age, interests, and the theme of the party.

One of the best ways to decide what to do is to use your theme and choose activities to go with it. If the theme revolves around one central activity such as pony rides, plan other simultaneous activities in which children can participate while waiting their turn. For example, while waiting for the pony ride, some can enjoy the penny/candy hunt while others have their faces painted. Every child can participate in all three activities without a long idle wait.

Here are two more examples of theme parties that incorporate some of the preceding activities:

Picasso Party

- ✔ **Invitation.** Guests come dressed as artists with smocks and berets.

- ✔ **Party favor.** Sketch pad and washable markers.

- ✔ **Food.** Cupcakes with an assortment of frostings, candies, and sprinkles. Each child decorates her own.

- ✔ **Activities.** Sidewalk chalk, crayon rubbings, straw painting, face painting.

Junior Olympics

- ✔ **Invitation.** Write the information on construction paper cut in the shape of medals or blue ribbons.

- ✔ **Party favor.** Give each child a hoop, jump rope, or ball, and so on.

- ✔ **Food.** Make your own Olympic size banana splits.

- ✔ **Activities.** Obstacle course. Have each child compete individually, or divide the group into teams. You can use a series of standard athletic events, combine them with a few of the activities listed previously, or make up some of your own.

While waiting in line for the obstacle course, others can attempt to set world records with a jump rope, hula hoop, or pogo stick.

There may be times when you want to hire entertainment for your child's party. Look in the Yellow Pages under "Entertainment" or "Entertainment Bureaus" to find professional services. Contact local high schools or nearby colleges for aspiring amateurs who would love the chance to perform for a group of children.

See the entertainer in action before the party so that neither you nor the children are disappointed. Arrange to observe someone else's party or ask the entertainer for videotapes of past performances. If you cannot see the performance, rely on word of mouth (from parents and especially from children) or ask the performer for a few references.

Some types of performers you may want to hire include:

- ✔ Juggler
- ✔ Magician
- ✔ Clown
- ✔ Storyteller

Opening the gifts

Children like to open gifts in front of their friends. Guests love seeing all the gifts and especially enjoy having their gifts opened. Before the party, discuss with your child how to receive gifts graciously. Explain that the size or expense of the present is not what's impor-tant. Explain the importance of saying "Thank you," even if she doesn't like the present or already has one just like it. Have an adult write down who gave what so that you can teach your child how to write a thank-you note afterward.

- ✔ Puppeteer
- ✔ Face-painting artist
- ✔ Balloon sculptor
- ✔ Mascot from the local sports team

Entertaining teens

Teenagers need activities, too. However, most teens are not enthusiastic about planned parties and planned activities. Given the kinds of food and music they like and a little free space, teens often can entertain themselves. But if they think that you are watching too closely, they may take off to do something else.

Getting teenagers to a party is half the battle. Your best hope is to surprise them with something they can enjoy without too much parental interfer-ence. After they are at the party, most teens enjoy games like charades and activities such as hay rides or scavenger hunts.

Here are a few more suggestions for a teenage party:

- ✔ Stage a murder mystery for them to solve.
- ✔ Let them produce a movie.
- ✔ Organize kite making and flying.
- ✔ Hire a disc jockey, fortune-teller, or line-dance instructor.
- ✔ Take them bowling, skating, skiing, or river rafting. (Get someone younger and cooler than you to help supervise.)
- ✔ Take them some place where they can just hang out, such as their favorite pizza parlor or hamburger joint.

Providing alcoholic beverages to teenagers is dangerous and illegal. Don't do it. If a teen shows up at your party with alcohol in his possession, ask him to leave.

If public displays of affection are a problem at your party, ask the lovebirds to knock it off. You can tell them that hugging and kissing have their time and place, but that your party is not the time or the place. You can explain to them that their behavior makes other people uncomfortable.

Chapter 17

Business Entertaining

*W*hether you are the big cheese, low man on the totem pole, or somewhere in-between, you've probably discovered that entertaining is a part of doing business. It is a way for clients, coworkers, or the boss to get to know you and see you in a different light. It makes them feel positive about you. It breaks the ice and helps take the stiffness out of the relationship. It helps you get business accomplished and helps you get ahead. If you sit alone in the back room and eat your salami sandwich every day, you're probably not going anywhere.

When you entertain for business, you must approach the event differently than the way you would if it were strictly social. Even though the event itself may be "casual," there is nothing casual about business entertaining. Think of this type of entertaining as an extension of the office.

In this chapter, we help you examine your goals and establish your purpose for business entertaining so that you can get along better with coworkers, gain trust from clients and customers, increase productivity, get the edge on your competition, and advance your career. We guide you through the basics of entertaining business associates (coworkers, clients, and customers) in your home or in a restaurant, give you some tips on when and how to entertain the boss, point the way for entertaining government officials and foreigners, and help you organize a charity function for your office.

Keep in mind that business relationships are highly individual, and there are always exceptions to the rules. Use the information in this book along with your intelligence and common sense to best suit your own circumstances.

You Need a Purpose

All business entertaining is entertaining done for a purpose. Whether you are hosting or attending a business affair, your primary purpose is not eating a great meal, sipping a superb wine, or having fun. If you do happen to enjoy yourself, consider it a side benefit.

When you entertain business associates, the purpose is not to discuss business (except in specified situations), nor is it to suck up to the boss or try to make a sale. Whatever your purpose, you want to make a favorable impression. This is one goal you can best achieve by being yourself.

Don't put on airs or pretend to be something you're not. You will only come across as fake and not confident. If your natural personality is more like Jim Carrey, don't try to pretend you're Pierce Brosnan.

One or more of the following may be your purpose for business entertaining:

- ✔ **To establish a personal relationship with a potential client, customer, boss, or coworker.** Trust is the key. You want people to be comfortable doing business with you. Use entertaining to establish common ground, relax, and let business associates see the personal side of you.

- ✔ **To disarm people.** If you have a jealous coworker or a client who thinks you are always after something for yourself at work, improve the relationship by entertaining that person. If you invite the person and she still responds negatively or seems jealous of you, the situation is out of your control. You've done all you can to include her and make her feel more comfortable with you.

- ✔ **To increase productivity.** Entertaining existing clients can be one of the best sources of new clients. You're likely to get referrals from happy customers. Another way to increase productivity is by entertaining potential clients or customers.

- ✔ **To show appreciation.** When you're willing to take the time, go to the trouble, and exert the energy to entertain employees, clients, or bosses, you show your appreciation for them in a personal way.

- ✔ **To get your spouse involved.** When you include your spouse, not only will he or she gain a better understanding of your work, but your business associates will see what a great family you have and that you and your spouse are a team.

✔ **To set yourself apart from the crowd.** By making the effort to entertain your business associates, you are going a step beyond what is expected. Your entertaining efforts can be a vehicle to achieving your business goals by allowing you to demonstrate personal skills (organization, communication, family values, and stress management) which are obvious assets at the office.

Hosting a Business Party at Home

Restaurants, country clubs, and golf courses are popular and appropriate venues for business entertaining, but inviting business associates into your home has its own distinct advantages.

One of the greatest advantages of entertaining in the home is the opportunity to relax. People will often discuss topics and tell stories they wouldn't mention in a restaurant for fear of being overheard. Most people feel more comfortable and free to be themselves in a private home as opposed to a public setting.

The big benefit for the host is that you are in control and can use your surroundings to reflect well on you. If your spouse is charming, your children are well-behaved, your house is in order, and the meal is well-organized, business guests will see a side of you that may not be apparent at the office.

Use your entertaining as a subtle means of displaying your

- ✔ Management/organizational abilities
- ✔ People skills
- ✔ Attention to details
- ✔ Family values
- ✔ Special talents
- ✔ Confidence
- ✔ Sense of humor
- ✔ Overall character

Boost your career in a natural way by showing your business associates what kind of person you are. Do not use the occasion to obviously promote yourself. Do nothing for effect. A fussy, overdone, elaborate party distracts from you. Keep food and decorations simple and understated so that your personality comes through. If you are serving duck bon-bons, foie gras, and flaming flamingos, surrounded by four dozen flower arrangements and burning incense, you are way off the mark.

Whatever you do, remember to mind your manners. Whether hosting or attending a business function, you are on trial. Like it or not, you are judged by your behavior. This is not the time to wear an outrageous outfit, tell all your best jokes, stage a chugging contest, or demonstrate your favorite dance steps. Make it a point *not* to be the life of the party.

Of course, basic table manners apply to all shared meals. Forget which fork to use? Got some gristle between your gums? Dying for a smoke? Read Chapter 12 for the answers and more on manners.

If you are entertaining a business associate for the first time, consider inviting him to a restaurant instead of your home. Restaurants are less personal and there is less pressure for him to accept the invitation.

You can also be fairly assured that things will go well. (At least it won't be you who burns the entree or drops the plate). With no outside distractions like pet hair or unwieldy children, you can concentrate on making that all important first impression. For more tips, see the section, "Entertaining in Restaurants."

To successfully host a business party, remember:

✔ There is no such thing as a minor detail. It's the minor details that make the major impression.

✔ Business loves stability, not upsets or surprises. Be conservative in everything from the invitations and the food you serve to the clothes you wear and the topics you discuss.

The first step: Getting people to show up

Before you go too far with your party plans, take a minute to figure out how you will get your guests to show up. Choosing the right day of the week can be an important factor. Don't have a business-related party on the weekend (Friday–Sunday) when most people prefer to socialize with friends and family. Monday is usually a hectic day at the office and may not be the best night for your party. That leaves Tuesday, Wednesday, and Thursday. Try to plan your party for one of those evenings.

Your invitations can also play a role in determining people's responses. Written invitations are a must, unless you are planning a lunch where you will discuss or conduct business. In such a case, a phone call or face-to-face invitation is acceptable. For any other kind of business party, written invitations are more appropriate because they give everyone a chance to respond without being put on the spot.

Written invitations should be visually attractive, but not overdone. Avoid themes or anything else that may seem unbusinesslike or tacky. Stay away from anything frilly or silly. Do not put confetti in the envelope. You can never go wrong with ecru or white invitations with black or blue ink. No matter what your profession, this conservative and traditional approach is always in good taste and projects a solid business image. Figure 17-1 shows a sample fill-in-the-blank invitation.

Charles Pollak

Editor, Newsgeek

requests the pleasure of your company

at *dinner*

on *Wednesday, March 3rd*

at *7:30 P.M.*

The Willard Hotel

Washington, D.C.

R.S.V.P

000-0000

000-0000

Figure 17-1:
A simple
and safe
fill-in-the-
blank
invitation.

In the response line of your invitation (RSVP), be sure to give a telephone number that is connected to voice mail or an answering service. The last thing you want to do is irritate your business guests when they are trying to respond to your invitation.

If you intend to have a guest of honor, it is gracious to invite that person before issuing any invitations. When you call or write the intended honoree, tell the guest that you would like to honor her at a dinner and mention who the other potential guests are. Ask if the date you have chosen is convenient. *Do not* call the person's assistant to get her schedule or put the guest on the spot by asking her to choose a date. It is up to you to choose a date so that the guest you intend to honor can accept or decline.

If the guest accepts, follow up with a letter reiterating the date, time, and place, thanking the person for accepting, and telling her how much you are looking forward to the event. Figure 17-2 shows a sample follow-up letter.

Figure 17-2:
If the guest of honor accepts your invitation, follow up with a letter.

> Dear Mr. and Mrs. VIP:
>
> My wife and I are delighted that you have accepted the invitation to be our honored guest. We look forward to seeing you at our house (1698 Woodberry Ave.) on Thursday, January 16th, at 7:30 p.m.
>
> Sincerely,
>
> Sam Subordinate
> Sam Subordinate

Food for thought

At a business party, food should not be the focus. People and conversations should stand out beyond what you serve.

When you make your menu, choose foods that are simple, delicious, and easy to handle. Avoid huge hunks of meat that require major surgical skill to dissect or dishes with the potential to drip all over a guest's blouse or tie. Serve a meal that is easy to eat.

Inviting the boss

You should not invite your boss for dinner unless you know him very well or unless he has previously asked you. Even if you know the boss well, you should not invite him for a one-to-one dinner, or even a dinner that includes the two of you plus your spouses or companions. Keep in mind that business relationships are highly individual, and use your common sense. If you and your boss have a close relationship, you may consider inviting him to a small dinner party with six or more guests. Otherwise, you are better off inviting him to a large dinner party or cocktail party so that he feels less obligated or pressured to attend.

After the boss accepts your invitation, call his assistant. Ask these questions:

✔ What do your boss and his spouse (if your boss is married) like to eat and drink? Any special preferences?

✔ Which fellow guests would your boss most likely enjoy sitting next to?

This extra effort is what will make the points. The boss will notice that you have gone to the trouble to find out what pleases him.

You don't need to go out and borrow silver or other finery. The boss doesn't come over to be impressed by what you have. By accepting the invitation, your boss has already shown recognition and respect for you. Your graciousness and good manners will leave the most lasting impression.

For your guests' sake and your own, beware of foods such as:

✔ Spaghetti or French onion soup, which are easily worn down the front of your shirt

✔ Fried chicken, corn on the cob, spare ribs, and other foods that must be picked up with the hands and can end up all over your face

✔ Lobster, crab claws, or anything that must be dislodged from its shell

✔ Whole artichokes, quail, or other foods that require undivided attention

✔ Cherry tomatoes or other foods that may squirt or fly off the plate when cut

✔ Parsley and other herbs that are roughly chopped instead of finely minced, which can cause the pieces to cling to your teeth like a vine or stick out like a branch

✔ Blueberries, which can turn your teeth purple

A business party is not the time to experiment with new recipes or to serve exotic or unusual food. You want guests to be able to identify what they are eating without having to scrutinize or ask.

Finding out a business guest's likes and dislikes is also smart strategy, especially if the party is small. Serving the guest of honor something she has hated since childhood, or even worse, something that breaks her out in hives, is terribly embarrassing. You would be wise to consider any religious prohibitions, as well. You can ask directly or do a little subtle sleuthing through her assistant, spouse, or friends.

Choose a menu that is elegant but not beyond your means. Serve foods that you can prepare ahead or that don't require too much last-minute attention. You can't make a good impression on your business associates if you are toiling in the kitchen all night.

If you are making the menu shown in Figure 17-3, for example, you can make the soup and mousse a day ahead. Roast the tenderloin an hour before dinner. Prepare the potatoes and vegetables in the afternoon and roast them along with the tenderloin. The only thing left to do at the last minute is slice the meat and plate the food.

Figure 17-3:
Choose a
menu that is
elegant but
not beyond
your means.

All-Purpose Business Menu

Soup

෨

Roasted beef tenderloin
Roasted vegetables
Roasted potatoes

෨

Chocolate mousse

Mixing beverages with business

For many people, choosing wine for a party generates the most anxiety. If you are uncomfortable making a choice, go to your local wine merchant. Give the wine merchant your menu and ask for advice. The wine merchant can suggest a selection of wines within your budget that complements the food you are serving.

Whatever you are offering in the way of cocktails or wine, make sure that you also offer nonalcoholic drinks and plenty of water. This approach applies to all parties but is especially important for a business gathering. No one wants to over-imbibe in front of the people he or she has to face at the office the next day. Your business guests will appreciate the choice.

Seating arrangements

What works at a social dinner is not necessarily appropriate for business. Squeezing a group of friends into every nook and cranny of your home may be okay, but when you are entertaining for business, allow a little more elbow room.

Seat business guests according to their rank within the company without regard to gender. Make an attempt to seat the sexes alternately, but don't fret if there is an uneven number of men and women.

Do not make the mistake of seating guests randomly or allowing them to seat themselves. Senior-ranking officials most likely will notice. For a small party (eight people or fewer), you may be able to direct guests to their seats. Never try to do this for a larger party. Avoid confusion and give yourself one less thing to worry about by distributing place cards on the table in advance. (Place cards include first and last names. Titles are unnecessary unless you are entertaining the President of the United States or royalty.) Place cards are appropriate for any size party.

The following sections can help you create your seating plan.

Dressing for the occasion

Many companies have dress-down Fridays or allow relaxed clothing every day. Casual dress codes do not translate to business entertaining. This doesn't necessarily mean you have to wear a business suit at your party, but you are wise to select something conservative.

For women, the rule for dressing is to ask yourself how you want to be remembered — for your earrings or your ideas? For your cleavage or your intelligence? When you get dressed, find a full-length mirror. As you walk away, notice if anything stands out about your appearance that shouldn't (dress too clingy, slip hanging out, makeup too heavy, hair overdone, and so on).

No matter what the business occasion, it is never appropriate to wear sexy clothes. You send out inappropriate signals to men and alienate other women. Sexy clothes get attention, but not the kind to further a career.

If you are not the host but an invited guest, your best bet is to research what to wear. If the invitation says "formal," find out exactly what that means. Depending on the area of the country, formal can mean anything from white tails to a T-shirt advertising tobacco products. If there is no one to ask or if you are still unsure, it's best to err on the side of being overdressed. You stand out more if you are underdressed — if you show up in a pullover and everyone else is wearing a dark suit.

Ranking your guests

To create a seating chart for a business party, start by ranking your guests. (Number them as a point of reference, but don't leave the list lying around for guests to happen upon.) If the ranked business guest is accompanied by a mate or date, that person assumes the same rank as the person he or she is with and should also be seated in a place of honor.

Numbering your business guests by rank of importance may sometimes be easy and obvious. However, if you are unsure about the positions of any of your business guests, do some research. Call the company or the guests' assistants to find out their official positions and titles.

At other times, strict business ranking may not be your only criterion. You may have to make your own judgment call and decide whose rank rates highest or whom you choose to honor.

Any of the following may qualify for a seat of honor:

- The senior ranking official within a company
- An elected official (such as a senator, the mayor, or the school superintendent)
- People of prominence within the community (such as a priest, the president of a university, or the chairman of a local board or charity)
- A visitor from another country
- A person celebrating retirement or promotion
- Someone who formerly held a high ranking position

If you have many guests with similar or equal professional ranking, consider seating them by personality. For tips on mixing and matching guests, see Chapter 2.

Creating a seating chart

After you determine the ranking order of your business guests, figuring out where to seat them is easy. When you are working with one table, the host and hostess sit at opposite ends, or, in the case of a round table, directly across from one another.

- **Guest No. 1:** If the highest ranking guest is male, he sits to the right of the hostess. If female, she sits to the right of the host.
- **Guest No. 2:** The person accompanying Guest No. 1 sits to the right of the host or hostess who is seated at the opposite end of the table.
- **Guest No. 3:** The second-highest ranking person sits to the left of the host or hostess (depending on the ranked person's gender).

▙ ✔ **Guest No. 4:** The person accompanying Guest No. 3 sits to the left of the host or hostess who is seated at the opposite end of the table.

Continue alternating the honored guests and their spouses in order toward the center of the table, as shown in Figure 17-4.

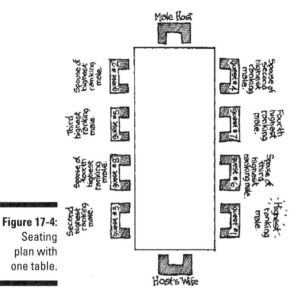

Figure 17-4:
Seating
plan with
one table.

If you use more than one table, treat the group of tables as one big table, as shown in Figure 17-5. The hostess should sit at table No. 1, the host at the opposite end of the table farthest from it. All guests should be seated in between the host and hostess. At additional tables, ask someone to be the host of each table.

Seat the first four people by rank order. The highest ranking person should sit to the right of the host or hostess (depending on gender) at the first table. The person accompanying the ranked guest sits to the right of the host or hostess at the far table. The second-highest ranking person sits to the left of the appropriate person (host/hostess, depending on gender) with the person accompanying him to the left of the host or hostess at the far table.

Don't let the matter of gender throw you off. While alternating the sexes is desirable, when same sex couples or unaccompanied guests attend your seated dinner, follow the same seating protocol. If you've done you home-work ahead of time (requested an RSVP), you know exactly who is attending with whom and can plan your seating chart accordingly.

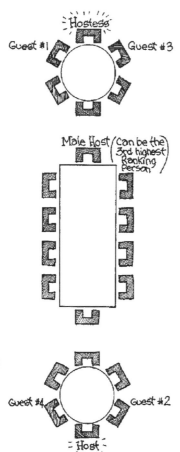

Figure 17-5:
Seating
plan with
three
tables.

You may consider asking the third-highest-ranking person to be the host of the third table. From that point, don't fret over rank. Distribute the remaining guests so that you have a good mix of personalities at each table.

Setting up and serving

When setting your table for a business dinner, do not use masses of candles or an abundance of highly fragrant flowers. Keep the table setting plain and simple. Don't make the mistake of using a huge centerpiece that people cannot see over.

If you prefer one centerpiece, make sure that the arrangement is very low (below eye level) or so airy that butterflies can fly through it. Guests should be able to see the faces of those opposite them.

As an alternative to one big centerpiece, consider a few small flower arrangements down the center of the table with space in between or bowls of fruit.

When choosing a serving style, consider what is appropriate for business. If the event is a casual company picnic, you may be able to get away with having guests serve and seat themselves. If you are entertaining in your home, whether you're hosting a plated dinner or a buffet, don't expect business guests to stand or eat from plates on their laps.

When guests are busy juggling their food, they can't notice anything else, which defeats your purpose for the party.

If you are serving a sit-down dinner, don't try to do everything yourself.

- ✔ For a party of six or more, hire a server to help you.
- ✔ For a party of ten or more, hire a bartender and a server.

Hiring a server or a bartender doesn't cost that much; it's impressive, and it keeps you out of the kitchen.

For more information on serving styles, see Chapter 10.

Entertaining in Restaurants

Sometimes, entertaining somewhere other than in your home is simply more convenient. Restaurant entertaining has its own special advantage for the host: By having someone else tend to the cooking and serving, you can relax and concentrate on the business at hand. However, successfully hosting a meal at a restaurant means you need to be socially savvy. For example, how do you make sure that you get the bill? Is it okay to have a one-on-one lunch with the boss? Where is the best place in a restaurant to have a business meal?

Selecting an appropriate place

The restaurant you choose says a lot about you. Don't invite business associates to a loud and smoky place. Unless you know your guests' food preferences, don't choose a restaurant that specializes in exotic food or a particular ethnic cuisine. To be safe, stick with a restaurant that offers broad menu selections.

Tips for singles

It is totally appropriate for a single man or woman to invite people for a business dinner in his or her home. A single person may consider hosting a business party for the same reasons a married person does: to establish better relationships with business associates and clients, to increase productivity, and to get ahead of the pack.

But if you are single, you must be a little more careful about who, how, when, and where you entertain. Whether you entertain in your home or in a restaurant, at noon or after five, inviting one person is not a good idea, especially if the business guest is of the opposite sex. Even in today's more open business environment, you don't want to take the chance of your intentions being misinterpreted or open yourself up to the possibility of gossip or innuendo. (for exceptions see warning on next page.)

If you host a business party that includes spouses, do not feel that you have to have a date or a cohost unless you know someone who would add something to your party.

If you need help, ask a guest or a good friend to assist with drinks or serving. Hiring someone to take care of all the details so that you can be with your guests is an even better idea.

To ensure that your choice pleases a particular business guest, ask the guest to recommend his or her favorite restaurant. If the guest is a regular there, make sure that the waiter knows that you are the host and that you will be paying the bill.

Restaurants with private rooms are a good choice for business entertaining. For a large party, you may also want to consider a limited menu. Offer three choices: red meat, seafood, and pasta. Offering a limited menu saves time and makes the meal flow more smoothly, simplifying matters for the guests and the restaurant.

Following are a few more tips for successful restaurant entertaining:

- ✔ Frequent one or two restaurants so that the staff gets to know you. If you develop a congenial relationship with the maître d' and wait staff, you improve your chances of getting a good table and exceptional service. If you are not normally an elegant diner, but you want to make an impression, buy a restaurant guide for your area. (The best are published by Zagat, which rates restaurants by food, service, decor, and price.) If you don't have a restaurant guide, ask various people you know. Choose the restaurant that most people recommend.

- ✔ Remember to call the restaurant in advance to make sure that the restaurant is open and to make a reservation, if needed.

- ✔ Request a table that is conducive to conversation — out of the mainstream of traffic, away from the kitchen, restroom, or telephones.

✔ Inform your guests how to find the restaurant and the best place to park. Provide a map for out-of-town guests or anyone who may be unfamiliar with the area.

✔ Arrive early so that you can check the table, arrange for hat and coat check, and make arrangements to pay the check and take care of tips.

✔ If the party is large, distribute place cards or provide the maître d' with a seating chart.

✔ Do not start eating bread, drinking (except water), or ordering before your guests arrive.

✔ Be a gracious host. Make sure that guests have what they need in terms of food and drink. Don't grill them with so many questions that they never get a chance to eat.

A one-on-one lunch at a restaurant with someone of the opposite sex and who works in the same company or office is not a good idea. Such a meeting can be entirely innocent, but may be judged in a social context. This judgment is unfair, but men and women should carefully consider other people's perceptions. Lunching *à deux* in the employee cafeteria is fine. Going to a restaurant may be misinterpreted. People will wonder why. They'll think, "Is their lunch confidential? Personal?"

Whatever you may accomplish in the meeting is not worth the questions it raises. You are better off to have one-on-one discussions or meetings at the office.

This warning does not apply to male/female lunches between parties from different companies. Such meetings are perfectly acceptable and should raise no eyebrows.

Lunch with the boss

Unless your boss happens to be your best friend, the only reason to invite her to lunch is if you have a business agenda and you want to accommodate her schedule. Be careful not to put the boss on the spot. Give her the option:

✔ "Would you like to talk over lunch?"

✔ "Would it be more convenient to meet in your office?"

If your boss has an "open door" policy, you may be able to ask her in person. Otherwise, a telephone call or e-mail message may be more appropriate. Use the preferred method of communication within your office.

If you do have lunch with your boss, remember that lunch is not the objective. Do not waste time with small talk. Get directly to the business.

Uncle Sam to the rescue

You may be able to deduct up to 50 percent of all your business entertaining expenses on your tax return. To do so, you must keep accurate records, including whom you entertained and for what specific business purpose. These records are essential.

Tax rules vary depending on the nature of your business and your position within the company. For more information on how to deduct entertaining expenses, call the United States Internal Revenue Service at 800 (829)-1040 and ask for publication 463 "Travel, Entertainment, and Gift Expenses," or ask your accountant or tax preparer to explain what is deductible in your individual circumstance.

Who coughs up the cash?

Paying for a meal in a restaurant can be awkward, especially in a business situation. Regardless of who is obligated or who offers, paying the bill should never result in an argument.

If you are the host (the person doing the inviting) you should arrange to pay the bill. Avoid all confusion by telling the waiter in advance that you will be paying and by giving him your credit card when you arrive at the restaurant.

When a meal is mutually arranged between two business associates within the same company, both parties should offer to pay. If you are the senior person, invited to lunch by a subordinate, you should offer to pay.

If you are the subordinate and did the inviting, you are obligated to pick up the check. You don't want the senior person to think you're after a free lunch! This is where it can be a little awkward for the senior person. If you're the senior person and the subordinate insists on paying, say a gracious "thank you" and drop the issue.

When several people of different ranks within the company are at lunch, it is customary for the senior person to pay, regardless of who did the inviting.

Never attempt to split the bill by deciding who ate what. If a group of business peers agree to split the bill, it should be divided evenly. One person should put it on his credit card and let the others settle with him in cash.

Making Your Conversations Count

Whether hosting or attending a business event, you will be involved in conversations with people who can influence your career.

The best way to be remembered as a great conversationalist is to do a lot more listening than talking. This tactic applies to all parties but is particularly crucial in business situations.

Often, the most effective way to sell yourself is to show interest in other people. Feed egos by asking questions about their background, hobbies, interests, families, and work. Ask superiors for their opinions on general topics.

Don't be a bore and dominate the conversation. You are not there to talk about yourself or tell the boss how wonderful you are. Because most people are interested in themselves, keep your own answers brief. As soon as graciously possible, turn the conversation back to the other individual.

Sometimes what you don't say is more important than what you say:

- ✔ Let nothing negative enter your conversation, particularly if there has been bad news within the company (like disastrous third-quarter earnings).
- ✔ Never gossip about the boss's spouse, or anyone else, for that matter.
- ✔ Don't bring up any subject that can be controversial.
- ✔ Stay away from the forbidden topics of sex, religion, and politics.

Entertaining Government Officials and International Business Representatives

Definite rules come into play when you entertain government officials and international business representatives, including regulations on gifts and limits to what you can spend.

In the United States, entertaining an elected official can be considered a campaign contribution that needs to be reported. The rules vary for federal, state, and local officials. Check with the personnel or human resource office in your company, or call the government official's office to ask what is correct. For additional information regarding protocol, contact the United States State Department at 202-647-1735. Ask for the Ceremonial Office of the Protocol Office.

The State Department is also an excellent resource for information regarding entertaining visitors from other countries. Call 202-512-1800. Ask for the desk of your guest's country to get information about any rules and regulations that apply.

You may also want to purchase background notes available through the State Department or government bookstore. The notes come in a large pamphlet that includes current issues and customs of each country.

A smart gesture is to duplicate the background notes for other guests. Before the party, send the notes along with a biography of the foreign guest so that everyone is knowledgeable about the guest's background and country and knows what is expected.

Planning a Charity Affair

Whether the event is a church picnic, the annual spaghetti supper at your child's school, or a gala ball for a national cause, the charity affair has an enormous potential to be a crashing bore. People have already donated their money. The last thing they want to do is sit with strangers, listen to long-winded speakers and eat food that is overcooked, cold, or two hours late. The following sections help you make the event worthwhile and enjoyable.

Find a new and different place

Long after the event is over, people will remember a unique setting. Even if they don't know anybody at the party, the setting will have a strong impact on their comfort and enjoyment. So choose a wonderful place — not a hotel room, which is automatic and dull. The minute people receive the invitation and discover the party is to be at a hotel, the word is out: "This party has a big possibility of being 'underwhelming.'"

Instead, take the time to do something different. Find an exciting space — near the water, in a beautiful park, or in the new "hot" restaurant. Most public places rent their facilities for a nominal charge. Lobbies of public buildings, beautiful boardrooms, zoos, aquariums, historic homes, and museums are other possibilities.

Visit your chosen setting at the same time of day the party will be held so that you can check out the lighting. From the entrance to the rest rooms, make arrangements for lighting to be adjusted. You don't want guests to feel as if they are still at the office. Softer lights transform the atmosphere and help people relax. See Chapter 6 for more tips on lighting.

Pick the right day

When choosing a date for a charity event, you should consider every angle toward achieving maximum attendance.

Check the community calendar to verify that you are not competing with another big event in town. As with all business parties, Tuesday, Wednesday, and Thursday nights are best for charity functions. Avoid weekends (Friday–Sunday) when most people would rather be with their families or just relax. Forget Monday, which is usually a long, hectic day for working people. Consider breaking this rule only if there is a good enough reason to motivate people to go on one of those days.

For example, the University of Virginia (UVA) recently held a highly successful fund-raiser on a Sunday. The setting was the High Museum in Atlanta, Georgia. A new Monet exhibit had just been installed and was not yet open to the public. By scheduling the fund-raiser on Sunday, guests had the unique opportunity to get the first look at the artwork without the crowds. That's motivation!

Seat people where they want to sit

Imagine walking in to a huge charity event and sitting at a table all night with people you don't know. How much fun is that? To increase guests' enjoyment, you may want to consider selling tickets in lots by table in addition to individual tickets so that guests have the option of getting up a group of friends and sitting with people they know.

 When making arrangements for tables, if possible, avoid the standard, round 72-inch diameter tables, which party organizers often use for large crowds. The large size limits conversations. By renting or requesting smaller tables, you give the guests an opportunity to communicate with more people than those to their immediate left and right.

Make the dress code easy

Don't leave guests guessing what to wear. Invitations should indicate the expected dress. Avoid vague terms such as "semiformal," "casual," or "festive." No one knows what they mean. To make things clear, you have two basic options: formal or business.

Think twice before specifying formal attire, which can be expensive and is often an imposition. Formal dress should be reserved for the most special events, such as the 100th anniversary of a college, an inauguration, the opening of a new arts center or theatre, or an annual event for which formal attire is a firm tradition. You may consider formal dress for an event centering on a holiday, such as Christmas or New Year's Eve when people traditionally wear more festive attire. Otherwise, in today's world, most events do not qualify for black-tie dress.

No type of charity event has to be black-tie. Your best guideline is to consider who's coming. An older crowd may be more accustomed to formal attire and may like it. For most young people who are working, not having to wear fancy dress is easier.

At a recent fund-raiser in New York where 10 million dollars was raised for AIDS research, a well-known celebrity who was a part of the program thanked the hosts for not making it a black-tie event. His comment received a standing ovation from the audience.

If the event is not formal, you will get the best response by suggesting "business attire." For men, this means a dark suit, dress shirt, and tie. For women a suit, dress, or pants suit is appropriate. Guests have the option of going directly from work instead of dashing home to change.

Serve plain, good food

When you choose a menu for your charity function, budget is a prime factor. Keep in mind that the purpose of the evening is to raise money. The food and wine should be delicious because you are asking for something. But if it is so fancy it represents two-thirds of the cost of the ticket, the evening is wasted.

Don't serve fancy hors d'oeuvres or expensive cuts of meat unless they are donated. The guests won't be expecting smoked salmon and filet mignon at a charity event. Chicken is a better choice than pheasant or quail. (Even if the price is the same, it sounds less expensive.) The first course should be a simple salad that looks pretty or a soup.

People do not attend charity events to eat gourmet food or drink a $100 bottle of wine. Find a caterer who understands simple, practical, and delicious.

Note that the IRS allows tax deductions for expenses directly related to a charity event. The cost of the meal is not deductible and must be subtracted from the total amount submitted, however.

The entertainment

Music helps the evening flow and creates excitement. Good music does not have to be live, but it should inspire shoulders to go down and feet to start tapping.

When choosing the music, know your guests. Think about their ages and interests. Do they listen to pop radio? Get a golden oldies tape or hire a local band that plays popular music. An older crowd may enjoy a selection from classic entertainers such as Frank Sinatra or Ella Fitzgerald.

You don't have to have music during dinner, but it can help with the flow of the meal if guests have the option of dancing or watching others dance between courses.

If you have guest speakers, schedule them at the front of the program. Get all the business out of the way at the beginning.

Leave nothing to chance. Tell each speaker how much time is allotted. If you want her to talk ten minutes, tell her she has five. We once heard a speaker say, "I just have a few things to say . . . ." Twenty minutes later, she was still yakking away.

Make an exception (don't give a time limit) only if the speaker is very well-known or someone who is unusually entertaining.

Part V
The Part of Tens

Khatchaturian's "The Sabre Dance" is appropriate music to play during a juggling or a plate-spinning act, but NOT during a soup course.

In this part . . .

This is the fun part. We offer lots more menus, a few cooking tips, some creative party ideas, and the answers to those questions that may still be bugging you.

Chapter 18

Ten Times Five = Fifty More Menus

. . . .

In This Chapter

▶ Giving in to the ultimate splurge

▶ Coming up with quick, inexpensive, and healthful meals

▶ Having some fun with food

▶ Serving the unexpected

▶ Cooking for your nearest and dearest

▶ Feeding a crowd

▶ Taking a seasonal approach

. . . .

*W*e may not be able to count, but we sure can multiply. This chapter is a conglomeration of menus for parties of all sizes. You find meals for every reason and every season. The menus are not meant to be absolute or confining. Use the menus as they are or use them to spark your own ideas. Have some fun!

Indulging Your Food Fantasies

If you want to indulge your guests or defy your diet, look no further. We devised a few divinely decadent menus for your party.

**Indulgence for Two
(A Tango for the Taste Buds)**

*Roasted summer peppers and
Turkish olives*

Grilled sourdough bread

Spaghetti with lobsters

Peach Melba

A Knock Your Socks Off Dinner

Salad of leeks, beets, and avocado

*Whole fish flamed with
gin and herbs*

*Grand Marnier soufflé with
creme anglaise*

The Whole Point of Being An Adult

Caviar

Oysters

Martinis

Pepper steaks

Sautéed spinach

Baked onions

Bordeaux

Passion fruit mousse

Cognac truffles

Champagne

A Menu to Make a Big Impression

Mussel soup

Roasted leg of lamb

Potatoes sautéed in goose fat

Green beans

Chocolate mousse

Madeleines

Midnight Supper

Cold ham

Large shrimp

Thick asparagus

Biscuits

Sorbets

Godiva chocolates

Champagne punch

No Point Being Prudent

Brie and butter on
baby croissants

Roast beef

Mashed potatoes made with
real butter and cream

Carrots and snow peas

Parker House rolls

Cheesecake

Cappuccino with whipped cream
and ground cinnamon

Fumbling Toward Ecstasy

Poached oysters

Artichokes

Pan sautéed quail

Chocolate eclairs

Luxurious Ladies' Luncheon

Lobster bacon club sandwiches on
grilled Sally Lunn bread

Individual chocolate puddings

A Menu Fit for a King

Oysters Rockefeller

Baron of beef with demi glaze

Duchess potatoes

Lady Baltimore Cake

Earl Grey Tea

Suiting Your Lifestyle

Just because you are watching your waistline, pinching pennies, running short on time, or joining the growing ranks of vegetarians doesn't mean that you can't find fabulous menus for entertaining. We put together a few heart smart menus, shoestring and time-shortage solutions, and vegetarian combinations.

Menus to keep your heart healthy

You and your guests can enjoy these healthy combinations without the slightest twinge of guilt.

A Menu to Keep Cool

Chilled cucumber and
non-fat yogurt soup

Skinless grilled chicken with
lime and ginger glaze

Jasmine rice

Sugar snap peas

Angel food cake with
raspberry sorbet

Warmth and Nourishment

Roasted onioin soup

Roasted turkey breast

Roasted sweet potatoes

Green beans

Non-fat frozen vanilla yogurt with
spiced pear sauce

Menus that cost two cents and take three seconds

Entertaining doesn't have to be expensive or time consuming. Prepare these menus in a flash without breaking your bank account.

Simple Satisfaction

Seared tuna
Red cabbage and apples
tossed in olive oil

Dried fruits

Quick and Easy Pasta

Linguine with garlic and olive oil

Amaretto cookies

Peeled orange segments

Light and Luscious "Quickie"

Stir-fried chicken

Cucumber salad in rice wine vinegar

Peaches and blueberries tossed
with brown sugar and topped with
a dollop of sour cream

Menus without meat

Guests won't miss the meat when you serve these satisfying combinations.

The Vegetable Kingdom

Artichoke and olive salad

Grilled asparagus

Creamy gratin of potatoes

Ratatouille

Goat cheese toasts

Carrot cake

Vegan Stir Fry

Asparagus, tofu, mushrooms,
and cashews

Szechwan green beans

Curried carrots and tofu salad

Spinach with garlic

Grilled polenta

Strawberries marinated in
Balsamic vinegar

Indian Summer

Corn, pepper, and tomato casserole
with olives and cheese

Flour tortillas

Cabbage salad with peanuts

Apple crumble

Eclectic Cosmopolitan Cuisine

Stir fry

Risotto

Saybayon

Clearly Having Fun

When is food more than just food? When you're having fun! Play around with these menus for a guaranteed good time.

Mexican Celebration

Shots of tequila with lime and salt

Sparkling limeade

Tortillas

Guacamole

Stuffed ancho chilis

Skinny sweet potato fries

Chili-glazed pork loin

Mango sorbet

Lime tart

Beer, Dogs, and Banjos

Keg of beer

All types of dogs and sausages

Many mustards: sweet, spicy, hot, coarse

Condiments: pickles, relishes, onions, ketchup, sauerkraut

Homemade potato chips with malt vinegar

Boston baked beans

Corn on the cob

Ice cream sandwiches

Cowboy Dinner

Ribeyes

Grilled vegetables

Potatoes cooked in the grill ashes

Fruit cobbler

Fresh churned ice cream

Roundhouse coffee

Porky's Last Day on Earth

Beer

Sweetened iced tea

Roast pig (the whole hog)

Hamburger rolls

Pickles, mustards, vinegars, hot sauce

Cole slaw

Potato salad

Baked beans

Banana pudding

Brownies

A Camping Breakfast

Fresh trout with bacon

Blueberry griddle cakes

Coffee

Escape to the Tropics

Rum drinks

Fried plantains

Coconut shrimp

Curried pork stew

Chutneys

Rice

Grilled pineapple and sorbet

Iced cappuccino

Spring or Summer Cookout

Grilled hamburgers

Sun dried tomato bread

Olive bread

Roasted corn on the cob

Sliced tomatoes

Asparagus and snow pea salad

Root beer floats

Butterscotch cookies

Adding an unusual touch

Throw your guests a culinary curve ball. These menus are full of surprises.

Pairing Sweet and Sour

Vegetable spring rolls

Sweet and sour soup

Ginger chicken

Mango compote with orange juice, honey, and red pepper sauce

Coffee meringues

A Banquet of Flowers

Clear soup with floating rose petals

Stuffed squash blossoms

Pasta with flowering herbs

Dandelion salad

Lemon tarts decorated with candied violets

A Fragrant Meal

Roasted garlic soup

Pan roasted salmon with aromatic honey and vanilla sauce

Coffee flan with warm chocolate sauce

A Sense-ational Menu

Chinese dumplings

Cracked crabs

Hot and spicy Chinese sauce

Lemon tart

Green tea

Feeding family and loved ones

Prepare special meals for special people. The secret ingredient is the love you add.

A Comforting Menu

Leek and potato soup

Pot pie

Gingerbread cake

Sunday in the South

Fried chicken

Fried green tomatoes

Sliced red tomatoes

Mashed potatoes with gravy

Butter beans

Buttermilk biscuits

Strawberry short cake

Intimate Celebration

Oyster stew

Beef Wellington

Chocolate mousse

Champagne

Valentine Luncheon

Kirs

Individual cheese soufflés

Butter, bibb,
and Boston lettuce salad

Grilled sourdough slices

Almond tart

Truffles

Happy Father's Day

Homemade lasagna

Sausage and peppers

Rolls

A salad with the works

Homemade ice cream sandwiches

A Simple Sunday Dinner

Pot roast

Country bread

Green salad

Apple pie

Inviting the whole crowd

Two may be company, but a crowd is a blast. These menus are for the whole gang.

Large Cocktail Party

Smoked salmon and capers
on toast

Rare roast beef and horseradish
on rolls

Smithfield ham on beaten biscuits

Grilled peppers on focaccia

Marinated mushrooms

Cheese puffs

Buffet for a Crowd

Shrimp Creole

Rice

Caesar sald

Pepper bread sticks

Ginger cheesecake

Chocolate tart

Coconut cake

An Outdoor Candlelight Buffet

Pickled vegetables, olives,
salted nuts

Grilled vegetables

Cold rice salad

Whole roasted fish on banana leaf
or other large leaf

Whole roasted tenderloin on
palm leaf

Small biscuits

Thick slices of country bread

Chewy bread sticks

Dark chocolate tart

White macaroons

Brunch Buffet

Fresh, seasonal fruits

Baked pineapple

Cream scones

Pecan sticky buns

Corned beef hash

Poached eggs

Mimosas, Bloody Marys, and
Double Espressos

A menu for every season

Use these menus to warm up your guests when it's freezing outside, cool them off when it's hot as blazes, or get them in the mood for a change in the weather.

Spring Perfection

Soft shell crabs

Baby lamb chops

Asparagus

Glazed carrots

Raspberries and
fresh whipped cream

Crisp lemon cookies dipped
in chocolate

A Warm Weather Menu

Seviche

Baked red snapper

Corn and diced multi-colored
peppers

Banana mousse

Chocolate wafers

A Family Dinner to Beat the Heat

Club sandwiches with
cold roast chicken, avocado,
and tomatoes

Frozen plum soufflé

Summertime Fruit Party

Crabmeat salad in a honeydew half

Green salad with grapefruit

Roast duck with raspberries

Assorted fruits with
sabayon sauce

Apricot biscotti

Mint tea

Summer Buffet

Beef tenderloin with
béarnaise sauce

Zucchini, squash, and tomatoes

Black-pepper popovers

New potatoes

Nectarine tart

A Fall Feast

Warm lettuce salad with pecans

Poached salmon

Wilted red cabbage

Spinach

Spaghetti squash

Caramel cake

Fall Family Dinner

Cajun meatloaf

Mashed potatoes

Zucchini with lima beans

Buttermilk cake

Homemade applesauce

Mid-Winter Warm-up

Mushroom tarts

Lamb, pork, and beef stew

Endive and walnut salad

Pears poached in cider

Winter Dinner for 21

Oyster stew

Cassoulet

Green salad

Bûche de Nöel

Oyster Roast

Oysters

Chili

Green rice

Butter lettuce with pears,
walnuts, and feta

Irish soda bread

Chocolate chip cookies

A Spicy Menu to Spark Up January

Red chili and lime jicama salad
with oranges, cucumbers, radishes,
and pickled red onions

Roasted goose with
spiced fig gravy

Glazed vegetables

Pecan spice cake with pecan

Chapter 19

Solutions to Ten Common Cooking Disasters

. . . .

In This Chapter

▶ Fixing food that is undercooked, overcooked, or burned

▶ Correcting food that is too bland, salty, or spicy

▶ Saving food that has collapsed or curdled

▶ Rescuing food that turns out mushy or ugly

▶ Getting out stains

. . . .

*W*hat works in a test kitchen and what works in yours may not be exactly the same. People who dream up recipes for cookbooks assume two things: that you will use the right ingredients and equipment, and that you will follow the directions. You try, of course. But when you factor in the phone ringing, the Federal Express courier at the door, the toilet overflowing, your child crying, and the dog barking, your results may be less than picture perfect.

Before you die of embarrassment, remember that you can fix most failures. Failures can even be fun. Depending on your personality and the circumstances, you have a few options: You can

✔ Ignore the failure and make the most of everything else.

✔ Admit the failure and start over.

✔ Forget the failure and order in or go out.

✔ Fix the failure.

In this chapter, we offer some quick fixes for the most common food-related disasters.

Still Kicking

You are carving the roast in front of the guests when suddenly you hear the faint sound of mooing. If undercooked food is your biggest problem, thank your lucky stars. All you have to do is take it back to the kitchen and cook it some more. But don't just leave your guests twiddling their thumbs and thinking about your mistake. Offer them a "quickie course." The following salads take two seconds to throw together and can keep your guests occupied while the dinner finishes cooking:

 ✔ A plate of thickly sliced tomatoes drizzled with olive oil and basil

 ✔ Sliced celery with a little oil and vinegar and crumbled Roquefort cheese

 ✔ Fresh mushrooms with oil and vinegar, herbs, and shaved Parmesan cheese

 ✔ Thinly sliced cucumbers with a little heavy cream, plain yogurt, and curry powder

Heat Exhausted

You got sidetracked and forgot to take the food out of the oven. The fish is tough and dry, and the veggies have turned to mush. After the food is overcooked, you can't go back and uncook it! But in many cases, you can adapt the dish so that it's not only edible but also delicious.

Vegetables: Add to a soup. If soup's not on your menu, add a little cream or butter and serve the vegetable as a puree.

Fish: Flake it up with a fork, add a little binding (egg white or bread crumbs), and make fish cakes.

Meat: Slice it thinly and serve with a sauce or make sandwiches. Chop it and add to a salad or casserole, or sauté with an equal amount of boiled potatoes to make hash.

Blackened (But not on Purpose)

You didn't hear the timer, but your nose knows that it's too late. You take the lid off the pot or open the oven door and see black. The food is worse than overcooked. It's burned to a crisp. Don't panic. You may be able to remove the part of the food that's not stuck to the pot or cut away the charred part. Chili, stew, or a meat sauce are still delicious, even if the

TIP

$10 million question: Is it done?

Two inexpensive gadgets can answer the 10 million dollar question, make your life simpler, and make you a better cook: a meat thermometer and a timer. But even if you don't own these items, you can at least make an educated guess.

To check meat, use the touch test. If your finger leaves a dent, the meat's not done yet. If the meat springs back, it's perfect. If your finger leaves no imprint and the meat is rock solid, you've blown it. (See "Heat Exhausted," in this chapter.)

You can also check beef by poking a metal skewer into the thickest part and waiting 30 seconds. Remove the skewer and touch it to your lip. If the skewer is cold, the meat is underdone; if it's warm, the meat is rare; if it's hot, the meat is well done.

For whole chickens, check the juices. Pierce the thigh with a skewer. If the juices are clear, the chicken is done. If you see red (or pink), keep cooking.

The best way to test vegetables, rice, and pasta is to taste them. (Never cook without tasting.) For the most flavor, vegetables should be between soft and crisp. Pasta and rice are done when they still have a bite *(al dente)*. If the bite hurts your teeth, they need more cooking. If the bite has the consistency of mush, you've already gone too far.

Check your cake by inserting a toothpick in the center. If it comes out clean (nothing sticking to it), the cake is done. You can also use the touch test. If the cake is done, the center springs back when lightly touched. Or, try listening to your cake. Take it out of the oven (use mitts!), and put your ear down close. If you hear air bubbles popping, your cake is whispering, "I'm done."

If you've already unmolded the cake or sweet bread and you realize that it's not done, you can put it back in the pan and continue baking. The cake will be fine (even if you've taken a slice out of it) as long as you do it immediately, before it's had time to cool.

bottom part is burned — just be sure not to scrape up any of the burned part as you salvage your dish. To get rid of any residual burned taste, cover the pot with a damp cloth and let it sit for half an hour. (If time doesn't permit or if the food still tastes burned, throw it away and serve something else.) With the whole pieces of meat or vegetables, be bold. Add some spices or barbecue sauce and rename the dish. Say, "What do you mean you've never heard of *blackened eggplant?*"

Completely Tasteless

You followed all the directions, but the soup tastes like water. A bland, boring, no-taste dish is easy to remedy. A dash of this or a splash of that will bring it to life.

Bread: Toast or grill. Rub with a raw garlic clove and drizzle with olive oil.

Fruit: Add a splash of liqueur, toss with mint, drizzle with lemon or honey, dust with cinnamon, or sprinkle with a little freshly ground black pepper.

Sauce or gravy: Add port, sherry, herbs, mustard, soy sauce, or lemon juice.

Soup: Add cream, sour cream, herbs, croutons.

Stuffing: Add some crunch with chopped nuts, chestnuts, celery, or bacon.

Tomatoes: If the fresh ones have no flavor, substitute whole canned tomatoes in your recipe.

Vegetables: Boil in water with sea salt to bring out flavor. After cooking, toss with toasted sesame seeds, slivered almonds, or your favorite herb.

Too Salty, Too Spicy

Oops! You got a little heavy-handed with the saltshaker. Don't worry. It's not too late to save yourself and your guests from bloat and high blood pressure.

Soup or stew: Slice and add a raw potato. Continue cooking for 15 minutes. (The potato will absorb some of the salt.) Remove the potatoes before serving. For a tomato-based soup or stew, add more tomatoes to dilute the saltiness.

Dialing for help

Whether you are feeling a little insecure about your cooking or in a full-blown state of panic, help is just a phone call or modem connection away. Before you call the suicide hot line, try getting help from one of these toll-free numbers or Internet addresses:

Turkey: Butterball Hot Line 1-800-323-4848 (November 1-December 23 only) Visit the Butterball Web site year-round at www.butterball.com.

Meat and Poultry: USDA Meat and Poultry Hot Line 1-800-535-4555

Baking: General Mills 1-800-328-6787

Land O'Lakes Holiday Baking Hot Line 1-800-782-9606 (November 1–December 24 only)

Bread and Yeast Doughs: Fleischmann's 1-800-777-4959

General Questions: Tele-Chef 1-800-632-4337 ($1.49 per minute, billed only if they can answer your question)

Foodies (online) www.foodies.com/Tips/tips.html. Has advice on selecting, cooking, and storing any and every kind of food — bread, eggs, cheese, olive oil, and so on. You name it, it's there.

For more help online, use your Web browser to enter a search for **cooking advice**. You'll find thousands of informative sites to visit and many valuable links.

Vegetables: Rinse them with hot water, or add a little vinegar or lemon juice.

Meat: Chop the meat coarsely and use it as a filling for omelets, crepes, or fritattas.

Sauce: Make more of the sauce to reduce the saltiness, or try adding a pinch of sugar.

If it's too spicy, add something sweet. Depending on the dish, the sweet ingredient can be balsamic vinegar, honey, fruit juice, or sugar. Some people like spicy food. You may want to let guests adjust the spiciness themselves.

All Pooped Out

Your cake looks like the Grand Canyon, and the mousse could pass for a river. Foods that have fallen and can't get up are usually salvageable, although you may have to use a little creative disguise or give them a quick change of identity.

Cake: A fallen cake still tastes delicious. You can disguise the mistake with frosting or whipped cream. For a completely new identity, cut it in cubes, sprinkle with rum, and serve with fruit or shaved chocolate. You can also fill the crater with fresh fruit such as berries or sliced peaches, and then drizzle the cake with fruit sauce.

Soufflé: Fallen soufflés, either savory or sweet, lose their light, airy quality, but they still taste delicious. Keep your cool. Don't let on that the dish was supposed to be a soufflé. Rename it (fritatta or pudding) and pretend that the rich dense texture was what you intended.

Mousse: If the mousse doesn't set and looks like a runny mess, don't despair. You still have something wonderful to work with. Serve the molten mousse as a sauce over fruit or cake. If you don't tell, no one will know.

Curdled or Lumpy

You tried to rush your sauce by turning up the heat. You didn't stir as constantly as you should have. Suddenly the sauce is curdling or turning into a lumpy mess. Stop the cooking and give it an ice bath. (Set the pan in a larger bowl filled with ice water.) Beat the sauce vigorously with a wire whisk until smooth. Pass the gravy or sauce through a fine strainer and reheat slowly. Or try whirring the sauce in your blender or food processor. Next time, use a double boiler, keep the heat down low, and don't stop stirring.

Mushy

If fruits are too ripe and mushy, use them in breads, cakes, or cobblers. Make smoothies or make a sauce for pancakes, ice cream, or cake. For mushy vegetables, see "Heat Exhausted" in this chapter.

Just Plain Ugly

You followed the directions to a T, but your finished dish doesn't look like the picture in the magazine. Maybe all you need is a little camouflage. Hide a multitude of sins with

- A sauce, a salsa, or a chutney
- Chopped parsley
- Whipped cream
- Powdered sugar
- Extra frosting

Downright Messy

A tomato squirted on the front of your shirt, one of the guests blotted her lipstick on your white linen cocktail napkin, someone spilled red wine on your oriental rug, and there are mounds of candle wax on your buffet table. Spills are one of the hazards of entertaining, but you can prevent permanent stains. You may want to keep these items on hand:

- Club soda
- A sponge
- White paper towels
- Prewash spray product or stain stick
- Laundry detergent
- Hydrogen peroxide
- Chlorine bleach, all-fabric bleach
- Carpet and upholstery cleaner

Before you attempt to treat a stain, know the fabric. If the label reads "Dry Clean Only," get professional help within 48 hours.

If the fabric is washable, blot the stain immediately with club soda and a white towel to prevent it from setting. (Don't rub the stain or you may cause it to spread.) That said and done, get back to the party. After your guests have gone home, you can proceed more vigorously.

> **Beverages (coffee, tea, soft drinks, fruit juices, wine, or liquor):** Soak in cold water. Pretreat with stain remover. Launder with bleach that is safe for the fabric or try bleaching with hydrogen peroxide.

> **Protein stains (egg, milk, cheese, ice cream, blood):** Soak in cold water. (You may want to use an enzyme-based presoak product.) Launder as usual.

> **Chocolate:** Treat with a prewash product containing enzymes. Launder. If the stain remains, try a bleach that is safe for the fabric.

> **Grease (oil, mayonnaise, butter):** Pretreat with spray stain remover or blot with dry-cleaning fluid. Launder in the hottest water safe for the fabric.

> **Lipstick:** Place the stain face-down on paper towels. Sponge the back of the fabric with dry-cleaning solvent or a prewash product. Change the paper towels and repeat the process until the stain lightens. Rub liquid detergent into the stain until the outline is gone. Launder. Repeat if necessary.

> **Candle wax:** Rub the wax with an ice cube to harden, and then scrape it off with a dull knife. Place the stain between two clean paper towels and press with a warm iron. Change the paper towels and repeat until as much of the stain as possible has been transferred to the towels. Treat remaining stain with prewash product or dry-cleaning solvent. Launder. If any stain remains, relaunder with a bleach that is safe for the fabric.

For detailed advice on stain removal, check out Tide Detergent's Web site on the Internet (www.clothesline.com). Enter information about the fabric and the stain and get specific advice for removing it.

Get over it

Nothing replaces a hands-on approach to entertaining and cooking. The only way to improve is to experiment and make mistakes. The key to handling your mistakes is all in your attitude: Think of mistakes as opportunities to learn something new. And while you are busy learning things the hard way, keep your cool. You can always ask a close friend to save face for you by saying, "How clever of you to cook it (or serve it) like this."

Don't worry too much about what the guests think. If you treat a culinary calamity as no big deal, guests won't think much about it either. Most people won't even notice. If they do, they may laugh at the situation, but they will usually try to help you come up with a solution.

Even the most obvious mistake can work to your advantage. Sometimes it's the mistake that gives guests the chance to relax, take a deep breath, loosen up, and have fun.

One of the most intelligent women we know, a distinguished doctor who loves to cook and entertain, decided to experiment with Italian cooking. She prepared a delicious meat filling, stuffed it into pasta shells, and put it in the oven to bake. When she served it to the guests, they almost broke their teeth trying to eat it. She had forgotten to boil the pasta shells before she stuffed them. There was no way she could explain her way out of the mistake, so she made the most of it. She had a good laugh along with her guests while learning something new about Italian cooking.

Chapter 20

Ten (or So) Once-in-a-Lifetime Parties

. . . .

In This Chapter

▶ Entering another world

▶ Going on vacation

▶ Celebrating life's big and important events

▶ Doing something different

. . . .

Desperate for a starting point? Need a hook? Sometimes having a central concept to base your party on can help. Ideas can spring from any variety of sources: movies, unusual menus, holidays, historic events, seasons, eras, and so on. Concepts can be simple or elaborate, conservative or funky. Don't be afraid to try something new or different, no matter how strange or corny the idea seems. A friend of ours in Toronto says that she follows one guiding principle when planning a party: "If my husband thinks that it's a dumb idea, I'm pretty sure it will be fun."

Keep in mind that the creative concept has more to do with a mood than a specific theme. Think of how you want your guests to feel and how you can get them actively involved in the festivities.

Still stumped? Need a little jump start? In this chapter, we offer ten specific party concepts with suggestions for invitations, entertainment, food, and special considerations. (Actually, we lost count again and ended up adding four more. Math is not our strong point.) These plans are only skeletons. You need to flesh out the details and modify or expand them to suit your circumstances, budget, personality, and style.

Taking a Trip to Another World

Try using the themes in this section to get guests out of their lives. Use every trick of the imagination to transport them to another place, another time, another identity, or another world.

Stage a masquerade

The mood: For a few hours, everyone is someone else. Create an atmosphere of magic and make-believe.

Invitations: Suggest one of the great periods of the past or a central theme on which guests should base their costumes. Give plenty of tips so guests don't get stressed out over their costumes or go to enormous amounts of trouble. Invitations can feature an alluring masked beauty adorned with tiny crystals or a tassel glued in place.

Entertainment: The costumes are the main entertainment. Include music and decorations from the period.

Food and drink: Plan the menu around the period or theme.

Things to consider: Think about your guests before you plan this party. Does the theme suit them? Dress codes should never be a burden. Consider the guests' physical conditions as much as their personalities. Young, svelte guests may love dressing as Egyptian pharaohs and royalty, Neanderthals, or mermaids; older, less agile, or overweight guests may be more comfortable in loose flapper dresses or Japanese kimonos. Guests can also dress in regular clothes but wear a wonderfully decorated mask for a costume.

Journey to ancient Egypt

The invitation can say: "Come as Cleopatra, a Persian prince, a Greek water bearer, or an Arabian sheik." Wear scarves and brass jewelry. Serve Moroccan and Turkish food on brass trays.

Black and white masked ball

Recreate Truman Capote's party from 1966. Invite all the fascinating people you know. Women wear white. Men wear black. Everyone wears a mask. Serve black and white foods, such as caviar in peeled new potatoes, black pasta with white scallops, olive bread, coconut macaroons, and dark chocolate truffles.

Go on a gambling junket

The mood: Transport your guests mentally to Monte Carlo. Aim for glamour and glitz. Guests should feel like free-wheeling big spenders.

Invitations: Use symbols that create an immediate image of gambling: dice, cards, poker chips, even Bingo cards or Monopoly money with the invitation on the back. Encourage guests to play the part in Monte Carlo-style dress: black tie, sequins, jewels.

Entertainment: Offer a variety of gambling options. Rent slot machines. Set up poker tables. A true casino party needs professionals. Call an entertainment bureau to organize blackjack, craps, and roulette. Let the planner know how many guests are expected, and she will know what you need. If rentals and party planners are beyond your means, improvise with blackjack, poker, dice games, and Bingo.

Gambling is illegal in many places. For an activity to be defined as gambling, three elements must exist:

- ✔ **Consideration.** The guests pay for their play money or for a chance to win.
- ✔ **Chance.** The guests take chances of winning or losing their play money.
- ✔ **Prize.** The guests can win something of value with their play money.

Avoid a police raid by removing any one of the elements. For example, if guests don't pay for admission or for the play money, they are not risking anything of value. Your party does not include consideration and, therefore, is within the law.

In the case of a charity affair, you could charge admission or sell the play money but eliminate any prize. If guests cannot win anything of value, your gambling party is perfectly legal.

Food and Drinks: Set up a full bar and hire a bartender. Serve heavy hors d'oeuvres: nuts, quesadillas, individual pizzas. (You may want to set small cocktail tables in one room for dining purposes and have the gambling in a separate room.)

Things to consider: Creating the right atmosphere is the key to success. Lighting should be dim. (Use lots of candles.) Use silver, mirrors, and crystal for decorations. Dealers should wear black and white. For a little Las Vegas tackiness, add plastic flamingos on the tables. If you don't mind smoking in your house, hire a cigarette girl (or ask a young, attractive, adventurous friend) to wander around in a sequined leotard offering cigarettes and cigars. Or, you can ask someone to carry a tray of cocktails.

Celebrate the harvest moon — western style

The mood: Festive. Down home.

Invitations: Glue the invitations to sheets of country-western music. Let guests know that it's going to be a foot-stompin' good time. Tell them what to wear: jeans, flared skirts, bandannas, cowboy boots, and cowboy hats.

Entertainment: If you want guests to square dance, spend your money on hiring a good caller and a couple who know how to square dance. The sound of heels clicking adds to the atmosphere if you have the party on a wood or stone floor. Other options include the following:

- ✔ Hire a country or bluegrass band.
- ✔ Hire a clogger to give a demonstration.
- ✔ Hire a line-dance instructor or square dance caller.
- ✔ Organize a hay ride in a horse-drawn wagon. End up with a bonfire and have guests roast marshmallows and/or make s'mores.

If you can't afford to hire anyone, play some good CDs and invite a friend who can teach and/or lead the dancing.

Food and drinks: Steaks on the grill, fried chicken, green bean salad, cornbread, apple pie. Kegs of beer, lemonade, iced tea.

Things to consider: This is a great fall party. You can hold the shindig in a barn or under a tent. If it's an outdoor party, hanging lanterns and throwing hay on the tables adds to the atmosphere. Other items for decoration are leaves, pumpkins and gourds, cornstalks, bales of hay, and farm equipment.

If you don't live anywhere near a farm (and don't have access to a tractor, plow, or bales of hay), improvise with shovels, rakes, and a wheelbarrow.

Attend a Hollywood movie premier

The mood: Very Hollywood, darling. A private showing. A premier experience.

Invitations: Make up a poster or marquee advertising the movie. Roll it up and send it in a tube. Let guests know they will be watching a movie, and enclose complimentary tickets. You can ask guests to dress like the movie theme or come as one of the stars or the director.

Entertainment: Rent a classic movie. (Most people don't mind seeing the classics over and over again.) Or select a foreign or independent film that your guests most likely haven't seen. If you don't have a big-screen TV, rent one. Use posters and props as decorations to envelop guests in the images of the movie. Have an official ticket taker greet guests with cold drinks.

Create an obtuse quiz. Pick out minor details of the movie and make up fun questions. Before showing the movie, let guests know about the quiz. After the movie, you can ask the questions out loud to see who can come up with the answer first. Or you can have guests write down their answers, and you can give prizes to the ones with the most correct responses.

Food and drink: Start with cocktails and hors d'oeuvres. (You may want to relate what you serve to the theme of the movie.) Serve popcorn during the movie, of course. You may want to rent a commercial popcorn machine. After the movie, serve luscious desserts, cappuccinos, and after-dinner drinks.

Things to consider: Intermission. Set up a concession stand.

Relive the big band era

The mood: Reinvent your world with a 1930s/1940s period party. Even if you cannot duplicate the exact style, your party will be memorable.

Invitations: Use a photograph of the glamour puss of the era — Marlene Dietrich, perhaps? Let people know how to dress. Women can wear fabulous dresses, glitzy jewelry, long gloves, fake furs, feather boas, and outrageous corsages. Men can wear hats (yes, they can wear them inside for the party) and broad-shouldered suits and carry flasks.

Entertainment: Hire a combo or pianist with a jazz vocalist. If you don't want live music, use CDs or hire a disc jockey. Present music by such artists as Artie Shaw, Count Basie, Louis Armstrong, Duke Ellington, Ella Fitzgerald, Red Norvo, and Cab Calloway. Tailor the music for cocktails, dinner, or dancing.

Food and drink: Serve a lush buffet including pates, whole roasts and hams, chicken fricassee, aspics, condiments, relishes, rolls, stuffed squashes, baked tomatoes, cakes, and steamed puddings. The cocktails of this era were martinis, gin, and vodka — straight up and on the rocks.

Things to consider: Spin a web with your decorations: Make a tented ceiling in the party room and/or rent and hang a prism glass ball.

Take a trip back in time to the 1970s

The mood: Recreate an era that's so totally square, it's hip. Think: Studio 54. Take guests back to their disco days.

Invitations: Create excitement with psychedelic colors and a disco theme. Suggest ideas for dress: Farrah Fawcett hair, pork chop sideburns, capri pants, bellbottoms, platform shoes, triple knits, and "full Clevelands" (white shoes, white pants, and white belt).

Entertainment: The idea is to constantly assault the senses. Blare disco music — the Bee Gees, Donna Summer, Barry White, Abba — with extra bass so that guests can feel the beat; use moving lights such as strobe lights; show a video of *Saturday Night Fever* and/or episodes of *American Bandstand* in the background to remind guests how to disco.

Food: A retro menu: shrimp cocktails, quiche, marbled steaks, iceberg lettuce salad with Green Goddess dressing, and cheesecake with strawberries. Use your old vinyl records as serving trays.

Drinks: Mr. Pibb, jug wines, and stingers for after the meal.

Things to consider: For decoration, use lava lamps and black lights. If you don't have them stashed in your basement, you can rent them. In fact, you can rent almost anything. How about a hot tub?

Offering Guests a Mini Vacation

Who doesn't need a vacation? Give your guests a chance to relax and forget about phones, faxes, jobs, bills, and children. The themes in this section are a small break from the reality of everyday worries and responsibilities.

Set up your own day spa

The mood: Total relaxation is the order of the day. Set up an atmosphere of calm with soothing music, no phones, and no interruptions. Invite two or three friends. Any more than that can turn into a chatty social event rather than the relaxing experience you intend.

Invitations: Make sure to get across that this party is to be a mini vacation: time to forget your children, your spouse or significant other, your job, and your responsibilities. The invitations can say something like this: "How would you like to rent a house for the weekend, escape to the tropics, or spend a week at a luxurious spa? Come to my party for the next best thing."

Entertainment: Depending upon your budget, choose from the following:

- ✔ Hire a masseuse.
- ✔ Hire a manicurist and/or pedicurist.
- ✔ Rent a yoga video or hire an instructor.
- ✔ Play a meditation tape.
- ✔ Organize a walk or hike.
- ✔ Hire a nutritionist or chef for a low-fat cooking demonstration.

If money is tight, forget hiring anyone. Sit around with masks on your faces and give manicures to yourselves or each other.

Food and drinks: A spa party can easily involve breakfast, lunch, tea, or even cocktails. The food and drinks you choose to serve depend on the meal and the time of day. Suggestions: raw vegetables and salads and other low-fat fare, such as fruit, yogurt, vegetable and fruit juices, and so on. (Yes, wine counts as a fruit, and Bloody Marys count as vegetables.)

Sample Spa Day:

8:00 a.m. Brisk walk

8:45 a.m. Half-hour class in deep breathing techniques to combat stress, lower blood pressure, and deliver maximum oxygen to every body part

9:15 a.m. Breakfast

10:00 a.m. Yoga video

11:00 a.m. Meditation, showers, manicures, pedicures (take turns)

1:00 p.m. Lunch

Things to consider: This can be a good birthday party for the person who has everything. Gifts may be spa-related.

Bring Hawaii to your backyard

The mood: Conjure up the ultimate vacation. Make guests feel as if they just stepped off the plane for an evening in paradise. Aim for informal elegance.

Invitations: If you are the artsy-craftsy type, draw and construct a hula dancer on sturdy cardboard as shown in Figure 20-1. Make a grass skirt out of construction paper. Glue it on at the waist so that you can flip the skirt up and write the invitation on the bikini bottom.

Buy a bolt of discontinued fabric in a wild print. Send one yard per person with each invitation to be used as part of his or her dress. You'll be surprised at all the creative ways people can figure out to wear the fabric.

Entertainment: Hawaiian guitar, ukulele, and /or island music, and calypso or steel drums. Hula dancers, flame throwers. Provide fresh or plastic flowers and string for guests to make their own leis.

Food and drinks: Tropical drinks such as daiquiris, mai tais, and piña coladas with fresh fruit garnishes and tiny umbrellas afloat.

Figure 20-1:
An eye-catching invitation that is sure to transport your guests to Hawaii in their imaginations.

The Invitation

Menu: Conch fritters; suckling pig; Chicken Laulau; grilled mahi mahi decorated with orchids; rice with Maui onions, macadamia nuts, golden raisins, and ginger; salad of pineapple, mango, bananas, kiwi, and lime juice; pineapple ginger crème brulée; chocolate macadamia cookies; tropical fruit sorbets.

Things to consider: Get some help to roast the pig, mix the drinks, and serve the food. Decorate with tiki torches, coconuts, and palm fronds. For centerpieces, use fish bowls with beta fish (beautiful fighting fish with fans) and tropical flowers coming out the top.

If money is tight or you don't have time to fool with elaborate food, decorations, or activities, you can play tropical music, serve tropical drinks, and serve a few hors d'oeuvres, such as shredded chicken salad with ginger kumquat dressing, spring rolls with peanut dip, coconut shrimp, and papaya slices with lime.

Celebrating Life, Love, and New Beginnings

Everyday is worth celebrating, but some occasions call for extra effort. These themes mark new beginnings that deserve a little ballyhoo.

Welcome a new addition to the family (baby showers)

The mood: What can be more exciting than welcoming a brand new person to the world or to your family? Match the mood to the joy of the mother-to-be and to the excitement of the rest of the family.

Invitations: Use your creativity. Invitations can be anything from the baby announcement, a diaper, the mother and father's baby pictures, or a stork.

Entertainment: Guests will be busy oohing and ahhing over the gifts.

Food and drinks: Choices depend on the crowd and the time of day. A luncheon or tea is lovely. Or you can have an evening affair with a light dinner. For dessert, paint diapers on gingerbread cookies with white icing.

Things to consider: When you choose decorations, create an atmosphere that's all baby: cute, sweet, delicate. Think pastels.

Having a shower after the baby arrives is fine. The party can be a combination shower and showing. The father would be proud to be invited, too.

If the guest of honor is married for the second time and has children from the first marriage, it's important to recognize their family position as well. You may want to suggest that guests bring an inexpensive gift for any other children in the family. Or, consider having a party for the children's friends to meet their new brother or sister.

Don't forget to throw a welcome party for foster children or adoptees who are joining a family. Plan your party based on the age and interests of the new family member.

Honor individuals (birthdays)

The mood: Every birthday is a celebration of a unique individual. Plan a party that fits the guest of honor. The theme can be anything from a hunting and fishing expedition to high tea. Match the overall mood to the personality of the birthday person.

Invitations: Enlarge (to life-size) and duplicate a flattering photo of the birthday person. Cut it out like a mask for guests to wear to the party. If the birthday person has a definite style, you can ask guests to come dressed as that person. The party can be a small gathering of the person's very best friends or a mixture of people from all areas of his/her life.

Entertainment: A *quick* (key word) slide show or video highlighting the birthday person's life. The person's favorite music, or music from his teen years. Be prepared to propose a toast.

Food and drink: Whether the celebration is a small dinner or a large buffet, serve the birthday person's favorite foods and drinks. (If the person's favorites are macaroni and cheese and banana splits, that's what you should serve. So what if the party is fancy? Write it in fancy script on menu cards.) Always serve cake with candles, and don't forget the champagne. For a small, distinguished party, choose vintage wines, ports, Madeiras, and champagnes from the decade the person was born.

Things to consider: Hats, balloons, horns, party favors.

Ideas for milestones:

- **30.** Say good-bye to the twenties with a "Roaring Twenties" party. Decorate like a speakeasy. Require a password to get in. Make a forbidden punch. Invite women to wear 1920s-style flapper dresses and dance wildly.

- **40.** An "Over the Hill" hike. Organize a hike over a local hill or mountain or through woods, and wind up on the other side with a picnic.

- **50.** Have a destination party to the birthday person's favorite place or activity. The site can be an hour away (the local golf club) or a world away (Scotland). Invite only the person's very closest friends.

Rejoice in the joining of two lives (engagements and weddings)

The mood: Festive, fun, celebratory. The mood can change dramatically from linens and lace to wild and rambunctious, depending on who's giving the party and whether it's a bridal luncheon or a couples party. (See the following "Things to consider.")

Invitation: For a traditional bridal shower, the invitation should reflect the bride's personality: frilly, elegant, or sporty. An invitation that reflects her personality is a wonderful surprise for the bride. Be sure to give her a copy of the invitation at the shower.

Entertainment: Opening the gifts is the entertainment.

Food and drink: No matter what time of day or night the party takes place, champagne says "celebration." Food choices depend on the time of day and whether it's a women's luncheon, an afternoon tea, or a couples cocktail party.

Things to consider: Inviting the same friends to more than one shower for the same bride is poor taste.

Parties for the bride and her friends are not the only way to celebrate weddings. The following are a few ideas for engagement and wedding parties that include both bride and groom and their friends:

- ✔ **Couples shower.** This form is a good way to bring friends from both sides of the family together so that they can get to know each other and have more fun at the wedding. Put together a short slide show that highlights the bride's and groom's lives from birth to the present. Make up a quiz for the bride and groom to see how well they know each other. The host can administer the quiz out loud. (If all the guests are couples, let them sit back to back and take the same quiz about each other. You can award prizes to those who know each other best.)

- ✔ **Christmas engagement party.** Give the party to the couple for their first Christmas together. Ask guests to bring Christmas items as gifts or to decorate their packages with Christmas ornaments for the couple's first tree.

- ✔ **Round the clock shower.** Each invitation specifies a time of day. The guest is asked to bring a gift appropriate for that time of day. For example: 7:00 a.m. — a subscription to *The Wall Street Journal* or a breakfast tray; 5:00 p.m. — a cocktail shaker or bubble bath; 2:00 a.m. — lingerie or a flashlight.

Commemorate your wedding day (anniversaries)

The mood: Every wedding anniversary is important. For most anniversaries, you want to create an intimate, romantic mood — perhaps just the two of you at a special restaurant. But when your marriage reaches an impressive milestone — say 10, 25, or 50 years — make it a celebration.

Invitations: In addition to all your new friends and your children, remember to invite the people who were there when you started — your wedding attendants. An occasion such as this calls for formal, engraved invitations.

Entertainment: Music and dancing are the best entertainment. Hire gospel singers, a string quartet, a blues band, or a dance band. (See Chapter 11 for more tips on entertainment and Chapter 15 for big party advice.)

Guests can honor the couple with short, clever toasts. Ask guests to prepare toasts ahead of time. Give a copy of the toasts to the couple to keep.

For a tenth anniversary, have the ushers, bridesmaids, and others from the wedding party dress as they did in the year of the wedding. Show a video of the wedding or display photographs so people can see how they looked.

Food and drinks: Cases of champagne. Food depends on your crowd and budget. Anything from an elegant sit-down dinner to a lavish buffet is fine.

Things to consider: If the party is a 25th or 50th anniversary celebration, decorate with silver or gold, respectively. Hire a photographer.

Celebration doesn't mean that you have to invite the whole town. If you've lived in the same place forever and are celebrating your 50th anniversary, you may feel that you must invite everyone. Perhaps you would rather take a trip. The point is to celebrate in a way that makes you both happy.

If you are planning the party in honor of the anniversary of your parents or special friends, consider their personalities and plan the kind of celebration that suits them.

For your own anniversary, consider other out-of-the-ordinary adventures for two or for many:

- Climb Mount Kilimanjaro and eat a candlelight dinner on top.
- Row or drive to a deserted beach to watch the sunrise and eat a breakfast picnic.
- Dine on a rooftop.
- Rent a house, yacht, or houseboat, and have a party.

Doing Something Unexpected

Sometimes you want to have a party just for the sake of getting together with friends. Add an unexpected twist with the themes in this section.

Block party

The mood: The goal of this party is to get to know your neighbors. Create a carnival atmosphere with activities for all ages. You want everyone to get involved and feel like they fit in.

Invitations: Two months in advance, send out a questionnaire to all your neighbors to determine interest and dates available. After you set the date, send invitations. Assign everyone a dish to bring. Encourage neighbors to bring food that reflects their cultural heritage.

Entertainment: Get a few of your neighbors to help plan the activities:

- Kick off the party with a bike, trike, wagon, and stroller parade down the street. (Have participants decorate their vehicles.)
- Organize a volleyball game and/or relay races.
- Rent a dunk tank from a fire hall.
- Prepare secret ballots for neighbors to vote on the best maintained and the most improved home or yard.
- Scout for neighborhood talent and enlist volunteers as street performers.
- Supply chalk for road art and hop scotch.

Food and drink: This is a covered-dish extravaganza. Anything goes. Ask participants to write the name of their dish on a card to set in front of it.

Things to consider: Ask each household for a donation to cover the costs of drinks, paper goods, games, and prizes.

You need to close off the street for your party. In most cities, you need to obtain a block party permit. You may have to submit a petition signed by all the residents. Start working on this two months in advance. Call your city or town hall and ask the following questions:

- Do I need a permit?
- How much does the permit cost? (Figure this cost into the amount you collect from each family.)
- Can the fee be waived?
- Is insurance required? (Most cities do not require it, but a few do.)
- Do I need a petition?
- Can alcohol be consumed in the street?
- Will the city provide road blocks?
- Is there a curfew?

At the party: Use name tags and addresses. Ask neighbors to bring folding lounge chairs so they have places to sit. Think about lighting if the party will last beyond sunset. Consider umbrellas for shade. Providing a comfort and safety kit is a good idea. Include sunscreen, insect repellent, antiseptic, bandages, and pain reliever.

Invite your good-humored friends for a totally tacky good time

The mood: Guests should feel like loosening up, letting their hair down, acting out, doing just the opposite of what is normally expected of them.

Invitations: This is a party for people who know each other well. Dress: outrageous. Write invitations on a collage of coupons, or send the party favor first: a box containing a Hostess Cupcake, Twinkie, small bag of Cheetos, or any common snack food, and the invitation.

Entertainment: Lots of music to get the crowd dancing. Your garage is the tackiest place to have a party. Set up pool tables, table tennis, and pinball machines for entertainment.

No garage? No money to rent equipment? Serve a few drinks out of bottles and cans and snacks right out of the package, and then load the whole crew into a minivan and invade the local pool hall.

Food and drink: Junk food. Hors d'oeuvres: Cheez Whiz, Vienna sausages in the can with tooth picks on the side, saltine crackers. Main meal: Five-can casserole (five cans of any foods you want to combine in a casserole), chicken-asparagus pie, canned-tuna pie, kiss-me-not sandwiches (onions and mustard between two slices of white bread), peanut butter and banana sandwiches, assorted chips and dips. Dessert: Chocolate dump cake, Hostess cupcakes, angel-flake ambrosia with a jar of maraschino cherries, stewed prunes. Wash it all down with a generic brand of beer, sweetened iced tea, root beer, grape soda, and a barrel full of spiked punch.

Things to consider: Decorate with strings of colored lights, plastic flamingos in the yard, velvet Elvis pictures, framed beach towels, and plastic flowers on the tables. Look for props at one of those little shops that are always at interstate interchanges. Have guests assume tacky poses for pictures.

Chapter 21

Ten Frequently Asked Questions about Entertaining

*I*f you are new to entertaining and have a lot of questions, you're not alone. Every year in her seminars, Suzanne speaks to thousands of people about entertaining, and many of the same questions crop up over and over again. This chapter is a quick review of a few important entertaining principles.

Do I need a reason to entertain?

Your friends are not going to question your motives or intentions when you invite them to a party. But if you feel more comfortable having a reason, don't wait until your son is getting married and you have to give the rehearsal dinner. Use these reasons: You want to try a new recipe; you bought a new grill; you have a new boyfriend or girlfriend; you just want to have some fun.

Should I invite tall dark strangers, the new kid on the block, or the letter carrier?

If you are satisfied with the same old, same old, surround yourself with safety: Keep inviting your neighbor, your second cousin, and the girl you met at summer camp 40 years ago. But if you want to burst out of your cocoon — brighten up your parties and your life — invite someone new.

How do I keep the single guest from feeling like the fifth wheel or odd man out?

Give him the seat of honor and plant someone next to him who either is an accomplished flirter or has been married for a million years and craves conversation beyond "Yes, Dear," and "Uh-huh." When you introduce a single person, say something like this: "Meet one of my very favorite friends," so the person feels included and welcomed immediately.

Should I tell my guests what to wear or let them surprise each other?

How would you feel if you showed up in jeans and everyone else was in bow ties and backless gowns? Don't make your guests guess. ("Formal" or "casual" are open to broad interpretation.) You can tell the guests what you and your spouse are wearing, "We're wearing shorts and jeans." Or, "I'm wearing a black cocktail dress. My husband will be wearing a sport coat but not a tie." The more specific you are, the more comfortable your guests will be.

I get confused and frustrated about what to serve. How can I get started?

Start with something you personally love to eat or cook. Keep your menu simple. Two courses are all you need: soup and dessert, main dish and dessert, appetizers and dessert, or two desserts!

Before I plan my menu, should I request medical records and ask guests If they hate spinach?

Absolutely not! You are not a short-order cook at an all-night diner. If for whatever reason a guest cannot or will not eat your food, it is up to her to pick at, move around, or rearrange the food on the plate and act like she enjoyed it immensely or is just too full to eat another bite.

How can I get guests out of the dining room and on to some place more comfortable after dinner?

Offer coffee and drinks in the living room. Entice them with a plate of chocolates. They'll pick up the scent and follow you as if you were the Pied Piper.

How can I stop that crazy guest who insists on doing my dishes?

If it's your mother, let her do it. Otherwise, you can say flippantly, "Oh, we never wash dishes here. We just throw them out and buy new ones." Or you can just say, "Let's sit and talk. I'll take care of the dishes later." Don't ever let on that the mountain of dishes awaiting you is in any way burdensome. Guests should be long gone before you start cleaning up.

What should I do if one of my guests intimidates me?

Do the same thing you always do. Forget about making an impression, and just be yourself.

How can I stop feeling like a nervous wreck when I entertain?

It's just a party. The very worst that can happen is nothing that you can't get over. Delegate tasks that intimidate you to someone else. Don't get uptight if something isn't perfect; more than likely, you're the only one who will notice that some detail isn't just right.

Part VI
Appendixes

The 5th Wave   By Rich Tennant

"Put out the Asian sates, the Russian blinis and the Mexican bean dips, while I whip up something Korean."

In this part . . .

Here we help you evaluate your parties, give you a calendar full of reasons to have more parties, and help you find everything you need.

Appendix A

Evaluating Your Party

- -

*W*hen a guest leaves your house saying, "I never wanted this to end," "I wish this could have been a three-day retreat," or "I can't wait to come to another party of yours," then you know your party was a success. Unfortunately, guests don't always express in words what they are thinking or feeling. Evaluating what went right and wrong with your party is up to you. Appraise the party so that you can repeat the successful parts in the future and improve on anything that may not have worked.

Don't evaluate your party while it's going on, or you will miss the party. This doesn't mean that you can't make little adjustments during the party to make things better. We point out small adjustments throughout the book, such as moving a fascinating guest to a different table, asking shy or uncomfortable people to help you to put them at ease, lingering at the table after dinner if the conversation is too good to be interrupted, or turning down the music or the lights. Being aware of what's happening during the party is essential. Just don't make the mistake of being a critic during the party. Save your real evaluations for the next day when you can assess the party as a whole.

Blast or Bomb?

Was your party a raging success (a blast) or a boring disaster (a bomb)? You probably have a good idea already. Whichever way your party went, evaluating the results is always a good idea.

At a quiet time, relive the party as an observer. First, think of the party's atmosphere. (Was the air electrified or strained?) Next, recall the sounds. (Did you hear merriment, laughter, and animated chatter, or was it quiet and uncomfortable?) Think about the timing. (Did the pace of the party flow, or did it seem to drag on forever?) Then think through the specifics, remembering who connected with whom, what conversations were clicking, what food worked, and so on. Make a mental assessment of how you felt, relaxed or uncomfortable, and why.

The wonder of a great party is that everything seems effortless to the guests. In reality, such a party calls for all the imagination and energy a host can muster. A success is no accident.

One way to tell if your party was a bomb or a blast is by your own level of energy and self-satisfaction. If the guests loved the party and had a great time, the excitement stays with you for days.

Other signs that your party was a blast:

- If guests seemed eager with anticipation when coming through the front door, then your party got started on the right foot.

- If people talked every which way, the people clicked, and your party had a great beat, then the vibrations were terrific.

- If there was a definite buzz and air of excitement, you created heat.

- If the guests cleaned their plates, your food hit the spot.

- If the guests stayed a long time at your party, and crawled out high on a good time, then you either had a hit on your hands or a bunch of drunks. If everyone marched out early or right on time (unless the party was only supposed to be from 6–8 p.m.), your party may have fizzled.

- If people talk about your party anytime in the future, your party sizzled.

What not to worry about

Some things are either totally normal, totally temporary, or totally out of your control. They do not reflect badly on your party. They are things that can happen at any party:

- A guest was late or someone didn't show up.

- Guests were a little anxious for the first 20 minutes.

- A short lull occurred. Conversations all seemed to die down at the same time. It may have seemed like everyone was taking a collective deep breath, but conversations most likely picked right back up.

- The food didn't look exactly as planned (like the photo in the cookbook or magazine). Don't hold yourself to those standards.

- You made a mistake. Most mistakes turn into something that contributes to the party's success by making guests comfortable or entertained. Rarely does a mistake create a bomb.

Why Failures Happen and How to Prevent Them

If your party bombed (which is highly unlikely if you read this book), you may be disappointed, but it's certainly not the end of the world. Think about what didn't work and why and how you can change it for your next party.

Was the problem something obvious?

- ✔ You invited the wrong number of guests.
- ✔ You invited too many similar guests.
- ✔ You tried too many complicated recipes.
- ✔ You weren't well organized.
- ✔ You needed more help.
- ✔ You needed a second buffet table — guests had to wait too long in line.

Or was the problem something not so obvious?

- ✔ The lighting was too harsh.
- ✔ The music was too loud to talk over.
- ✔ The guests were too spread out.
- ✔ Mosquitoes chomped on guests' ankles.
- ✔ The seating arrangement was not effective.
- ✔ The cocktail hour was too long or the guests had to wait too long before eating.

Sometimes determining what exactly went wrong is difficult. The problem could have been a combination of things.

Problem: You set up the perfect party in terms of food, wines, lighting, the setting, and so on, yet still had a flat party. The tedious tone may not have been your fault. You can set the stage, but sometimes the guests aren't in the mood, or the chemistry between them is just not there.

Solution: All you can do is give guests a reason to get excited before your party and hope they come with an open mind and a good attitude. Accept the fact that parties are not going to be perfect.

Problem: You worked so hard and were totally exhausted that you had no energy left to give to your guests.

Solution: One way to avoid this situation is to pace your work over several days. On the day of your party, schedule some time for yourself. Allow time for some fun and/or some rest and relaxation: exercise, a bath, reading, a 20-minute nap — whatever it takes to lower stress levels before your party.

Problem: You lost track of what you were trying to accomplish (which was to have a fun party). Instead, you busied yourself with the small details and spent the whole time in the kitchen.

Solution: People don't notice if you use the wrong plate. They do notice if the host is missing. Next time, stick to a simple plan that you can manage. Get as much done ahead of time as possible, and concentrate on the people instead of the party.

The Final Analysis

Don't be overly critical of your party or too hard on yourself. What you may have thought went wrong, didn't work, didn't taste right, or took too long, probably escaped the guests. Most likely, they thought your party was just perfect.

Remember, you are your own harshest critic. Guests don't usually judge parties by their style or apparent cost, nor do they judge the perfection of the food. The guests are easy. They just want to have a good time.

The number one way to evaluate your party is to ask yourself the following question: Did my party make me comfortable and happy? If the answer is "Yes," chances are, everyone else felt the same way.

Appendix B
Entertaining Calendar

• •

*I*f you read this book, you know how to give a party. You can always throw a party just for the heck of it. But just in case you need an excuse to plan one, we offer a month-by-month list of special dates and events you may want to note on your entertaining calendar. Most of these are U.S. holidays, unless specified otherwise. Some religious holy days are based on lunar phases and calendars other than the Gregorian calendar. They occur on different days, and sometimes in different months. Consult this year's calendar to find out a holy day's exact date.

Other enchanting and alarming events you may want to celebrate include:

✔ Your mother-in-law's birthday

✔ All your friends' and relatives' birthdays

✔ Your child's first day of school

✔ Your child's departure for college

✔ The year you don't have to pay any more tuition

✔ Surviving the seven-year itch (still married)

✔ Your anniversary

✔ Your own birthday

✔ Your pet's birthday

✔ Your first nose job, face lift, tummy tuck, or liposuction

✔ Your high-school reunion

✔ Any major accomplishment

January

National Hot Tea Month (tea for two, ten, or twenty, or just for yourself)

National Soup Month

The Super Bowl

January 1 — New Year's Day (a recovery party: creamed chipped beef, buckwheat pancakes, eggs, Hoppin' John, sausages, biscuits, Bloody Marys)

January 1 — Billionaire Bites the Bullet — Microsoft's Bill Gates married Melinda French in 1994 (a good day to plan a wedding, proposal dinner, or bachelor party)

January 4 — National Trivia Day (Have friends over for a little Trivial Pursuit.)

January 5 — Jeanne Dixon's birthday (Hire a fortune teller.)

January 8 — Elvis Presley's birthday

January 18 — Hot and Spicy Food International Day (Serve up your hottest creations for your coolest friends.)

January 18 — Pooh Day (In honor of A.A. Milne's birthday, creator of Winnie-the-Pooh. Serve honey tea, toast with honey, and honey graham crackers.)

Third Monday in January — Dr. Martin Luther King, Jr.'s birthday

January 21 — Birthday of legendary radio announcer Wolfman Jack (Hire a disc jockey. See Chapter 11 for details.)

January 22 — Saint Vincent's Feast Day (Honor the patron saint of wine growers.)

January 23 — National Pie Day (Bake a homemade pie for a special family dinner.)

January 24 — Anniversary of the first canned beer (Break out a few cases and bring on your best friends.)

January 26 — National Popcorn Day (Rent some movies, invite a few friends, and get poppin'.)

January 26 — Australia Day

February

American Heart Month (a month for healthy meals)

Black History Month

National Cherry Month (*Breakfast:* dried cherry muffins and cherry flavored tea; *lunch:* cold cherry soup, turkey sandwiches with cherry chutney; *dinner:* duck with cherries, cherries jubilee.)

Chinese New Year

February 1 — National Freedom Day (Celebrate one of life's greatest freedoms: the right to have a party!)

February 2 — Groundhog Day

February 4 — Laugh and Grow Rich Day (Hire a comedian.)

Second Week of February — National Kraut and Frankfurter Week (Host a wiener roast with all the fixin's.)

February 9 — World Marriage Day (Invite your favorite couples to celebrate their happy marriages.)

February 11 — Thomas Edison's birthday

February 12 — Abraham Lincoln's birthday

February 14 — Valentine's Day (A sensual menu: oysters, champagne, chocolates.)

February 15 — Lupercalia (An ancient Roman holiday — a fertility/love celebration — honoring the Gods Luperca and Faunus, as well as Remus and Romulus. Why have a boring old Valentine's Day party when you can have a Lupercalia party?!)

Third Monday in February — President's Day

Weekend after Valentines — Second Honeymoon Weekend (Plan one for you and your spouse.)

February 22 — George Washington's birthday

March

National Noodle Month (Use your noodle: Have a pasta party.)

National Peanut Month (Menu: peanut soup, chicken with peanut sauce, peanut brittle.)

National Pizza Month (Invite friends to make their own. See Chapter 13.)

Spring Break — Spring vacation for college students (Time out for beaches and suntans.)

Mardi Gras (Masquerade!)

March 1 — National Pig Day (Barbecue one.)

March 8 — International Women's Day (Cease all housework. Have a party instead!)

March 11 — Commonwealth Day in Canada

March 17 — Saint Patrick's Day (Menu: barley soup, corned beef, cabbage, Irish soda bread.)

Vernal Equinox — First day of spring in northern hemisphere/ fall in the southern hemisphere.

March 21 — Naw Rúz, the Baha'i New Year

March 22 — As Young As You Feel Day (Invite friends to revisit their youth. Plan a party based on your teen years.)

March 24 — Harry Houdini's birthday (Hire a magician.)

March 25 — Independence Day in Greece

March 26 — National Badminton Day (Great entertainment for a picnic.)

Good Friday

Easter

April

The Masters Golf Tournament (Invite golf enthusiasts and serve an assortment of sandwiches: deviled ham, egg salad, and barbecue.)

April 1 — April Fool's Day (Invite half the guest list to come in black tie, invite the other half to dress in jeans. Keep it a secret.)

April 5 (eve) — Chinese Pure Brightness Festival (Honor your ancestors by cleaning up and decorating their graves. Picnic at or near the gravesite.)

First Sunday in April — Daylight Savings Time begins.

Boston Marathon

April 10 — National Siblings Day (Invite your brothers and sisters over for a meal. If you don't have siblings, invite friends who seem like brothers or sisters to you.)

April 13 — Sikh New Year

April 13 — Buddhist New Year

April 14 — Pan American Day (celebrated in all the Americas)

April 19 — Earth Day (U.S. environmental observance — host a picnic or barbecue in honor of the great outdoors. Sow packets of wildflower seeds or plant a tree. Leave the site as clean or cleaner than you found it.)

Passover

Fourth Wednesday — Secretaries Day (Give secretaries or assistants flowers, chocolates, or a bonus.)

April 23 — William Shakespeare's birthday

Monday after Easter — Egg Salad Week begins (Use up all those Easter eggs.)

April 23 — Anniversary of Maxim's opening (the legendary restaurant) — 1893, Paris, France (Plan a gourmet French meal with fine wines and champagnes.)

April 25 — Liberation Day in Italy

April 25 — Liberty Day in Portugal

April 30 — Dia del Niño in Mexico (Everyone is a kid again on this day.)

May

Asian History Month

National Barbecue Month (Fire up the grill.)

National Hamburger Month (Buy *The Burger Meister,* by Marcell Desaulniers, Simon and Schuster, 1993 — America's best chefs give their recipes for America's best burgers plus the fixin's.)

National Egg Month (Plan a "Who's Counting Cholesterol?" brunch. Serve Eggs Benedict, quiche, egg salad, deviled eggs, custards.)

Older Americans Month (Honor your elders by including them in your entertaining.)

Kentucky Derby (Serve mint juleps and derby pie while watching the races.)

May 1 — May Day

May 5 — Cinco de Mayo

May 5 — May Day in the United Kingdom

May 5 — Kodomo No Hi in Japan (Children's Day)

May 6 — Anniversary of Babe Ruth's first Major League home run (Invite friends to play baseball or whiffleball. If you are stuck indoors, play baseball trivia. Serve ballpark food.)

May 8 — Happy Birthday, Coca-Cola! (Celebrate with a cookout and lots of Coke. Decorate with old Coke crates, old Coke bottles, and the Coca-Cola polar bear. Give away Coca-Cola T-shirts and caps as party favors.)

May 11 — Eat What You Want Day (Your own special day to treat yourself.)

Monday – Sunday ending on Mother's Day — International Herb Week (Cook with your favorite fresh herbs. Decorate with branches of herbs and make herbal sachets for gifts.)

Second Sunday in May — Mother's Day (Treat your mom to breakfast in bed; host a party honoring all the motherly influences in your life, including aunts, grandmothers, older sisters, and friends.)

May 12 — Limerick Day

May 19 — Victoria Day in Canada

May 24 — International Jazz Day (A great reason to give a cocktail party.)

Last Monday in May — Memorial Day (Croquet anyone?)

Memorial Day weekend — Indy 500

May 30 — Peter the Great's Birthday, 1672, Moscow (Menu: iced vodka, blini with caviar, borscht, coulibiac of salmon, pashka.)

June

Dairy Month (Menu: Vichyssoise, pork loin braised in milk, potatoes Anna, crème brûlée.)

National Beef Steak Month

Turkey Lovers Month (Now that you've gotten over Thanksgiving, surprise your guests with a summer version of turkey: turkey burgers, turkey salad, turkey scallopini.)

National Fresh Fruit and Vegetable Month (Try some new ones.)

National Iced Tea Month

National Frozen Yogurt Month

Professional Bowling Association Championships (Rent the video *King Pin*. Continue your party at the bowling center.)

First Friday and Saturday in June — Donut Days (Donuts and coffee for breakfast. Donuts and ice cream for late-night snacks.)

Wimbledon Tennis Championship (Host a brunch for the finals. Be sure to include traditional strawberries and cream. If watching is less exciting to you than playing, book some courts and organize your own mini-tournament. Award prizes to the winners and serve the strawberries and cream afterward.)

National Basketball Association (NBA) Championships

June 6 — Queen's Day in Australia

June 9 — Dragon Boat Festival in China

June 14 — Flag Day

June 17 — Unity Day in Germany

June 18 — National Splurge Day (Ultimate decadence: Château d'Yquem [Sauterne] with roast beef.)

June 21 — Summer solstice (First day of summer in the northern hemisphere/ winter in the southern hemisphere.)

Third Sunday in June — Father's Day (Dad deserves to eat his all-time favorite foods.)

July

National Baked Bean Month (Forget the canned versions. Make the real thing: Use pea beans, Jacob's Cattle, Yellow eye, Soldier's bean, navy or Great Northern. Serve with warm smoked loin of pork and/or Boston brown bread.)

National Ice Cream Month

British Open Golf Championship

World Cup Soccer competition

July 1 — Canada Day

July 4 — Independence Day (Invite friends to participate in a traditional picnic. Organize a bike and trike parade for the kids. Serve all-American food — anything from hot dogs to lobsters, ice cream to apple pie, black and white sodas to American champagne.)

July 9 — Independence Day in Argentina

July 14 — Bastille Day in France

July 18 — Oscar Mayer Weinermobile Birthday (Hot dog!)

July 20 — Anniversary of man's first landing on the moon (If the moon is full, have a moonlight dinner.)

August

National Catfish Month

August 2 — National Mustard Day (Cook the best hot dogs and taste-test dozens of mustards.)

August 3 — Friendship Day

August 3 — Sisters Day

August 16 — Watermelon Day (Watermelons galore and a seed-spitting contest.)

August 17 — José de San Martin Day in Argentina, Chile, and Peru

August 22 — Be An Angel Day (Be an angel and entertain your friends who need a little tender loving care.)

August 26 — Women's Equality Day (Celebrate by switching roles with your mate: Whoever does the cooking lets the member of the opposite sex take charge of the day's meals. The other can trade off for one of the mate's usual chores.)

September

National Honey Month

National Organic Harvest Month

National Rice Month (Base menus on sushi, risotto, paella, gumbo, étouffée, and jambalaya.)

Pleasure Your Mate Month

Self-Improvement Month

First Monday — Labor Day

First Sunday following Labor Day — Grandparents' Day

September 9 — Chung Yeung in China (a festival honoring ancestors)

September 9 — Kiku No Sekku in Japan (a flower festival)

September 16 — Independence Day in Mexico

September 22 — Autumnal equinox for the northern hemisphere (Think wild mushrooms, duck, cabbage, apples.)

September 22 — Birthday of the ice cream cone (Make homemade waffle cones, plain and chocolate dipped. Fill with the best ice creams.)

September 22 — Proposal Day (Ask someone to marry you over a romantic meal.)

September 28 — Confucius's birthday (Have a Chinese meal.)

October

Do-It-Yourself Month

Family History Month (Host a meal for all generations of your family. Everyone can share stories.)

National Dessert Month (Who can resist an all-dessert party? See Chapter 8 for help with your plans.)

World Chocolate Awareness Month (Menu: Mole of chicken and chocolate chili sauce, chocolate flan, hot chocolate.)

National Pizza Month (It was so much fun in March, somebody decided to declare another whole month to do it again.)

National Pork Month (Have a pig-out party with plenty of pork loin, ribs, sausages, and ham.)

National Seafood Month (This is the month to give an oyster roast, cook a bouillabaisse, fry catfish, and learn to butterfly shrimp.)

National Toilet Tank Repair Month (If it takes a party to get you to tune up your toilets, then go for it.)

Oktoberfest (Menu: variety of German beers, sauerbraten, weinerschnitzel, sauerkraut, veal sausages, knockwurst, red cabbage, spaetzel, apple strudel.)

World Series — U.S. baseball championship series (Set up the big screen and serve roasted peanuts, hot dogs, Cracker Jack, and beer.)

October 1 — World Vegetarian Day

October 2 — Charlie Brown's (from the cartoon strip *Peanuts*) birthday (a good day for a children's party)

Rosh Hashanah

October 3 – 12 — National Pickled Pepper Week

Yom Kippur

Second Monday in October — Thanksgiving Day in Canada

Second Monday in October — Columbus Day

October 12 — National Children's Day

October 12 — National Day in Spain

October 15 — National Grouch Day (Take a grouch to dinner.)

October 16 — National Dessert Day (Invite guests for a meal. Serve dessert first. Or see Chapter 8 for help planning an all dessert party.)

October 16 — National Boss Day (Schmooze with the boss. Invite the head honcho to lunch or dinner. See Chapter 17 for advice and a few warnings.)

Third Saturday in October — Sweetest Day

October 25 — Make a Difference Day

Fourth Sunday in October — Mother-in-law Day

October 28 — George-Auguste Escoffier's birthday — 1846 (Learn how to cook from a master. Buy the *Escoffier Cookbook: A Guide to the Fine Art of Cookery,* Crown Publishers, Inc. — in print for over a quarter of a century with nearly 3,000 recipes.)

October 29 — Anniversary of the 1929 Stock Market Crash (Plan a gambling party. See Chapter 20 for a few ideas.)

October 31 — Halloween

November

National Peanut Butter Lovers Month (What goes with peanut butter? Jelly, jelly beans, bread, crackers, bananas, celery, cheese, onions, chocolate. . . .)

National Pecan Harvest Month (Start making pecan pies for Thanksgiving.)

Grey Cup (Football championship in Canada)

November 1 – 7 National Fig Week

November 1 — El Dia de los Muertos in Mexico (a day to honor ancestors)

November 2 – 8 National Split Pea Soup Week (Make a remarkable and easy pea soup: peas, ham, marjoram, water, salt. Simmer until peas are tender.)

November 3 — Sandwich Day (Honor the birthday of John Montague, inventor of the sandwich.)

First Tuesday — U.S. Election Day

November 6 (eve) — Guy Fawkes Night in England

November 8 — Cook Something Bold and Pungent Day (Serve Thai food.)

November 11 — Veteran's Day/Armistice Day

First Saturday after November 11 — Sadie Hawkins' Day (Plan a dance. Invite all women and ask each one to bring a male escort. During the party, women have their pick of dance partners. Men must wait to be asked.)

Fourth Thursday in November — Thanksgiving (See Chapter 15 for help.)

December

Bingo's Birthday Month

December 6 — Saint Nicholas' Eve

December 9 — Clarence Birdseye's birthday (Honor the frozen-food king with a meal from your freezer.)

December 13 — Saint Lucia Day in Sweden (Traditionally, the eldest daughter serves her family an early morning breakfast in bed — coffee and cookies on a tray.)

December 16 — Anniversary of the Boston Tea Party (Well, what else? A tea party!)

December 17 — Wright Brothers' Day

December 22 — Winter solstice in the northern hemisphere — summer in the southern hemisphere (Trick guests' palates with foods not normally associated with the season. See Chapter 7 for details.)

December 24 – 31 Hanukkah

December 25 — Christmas (See Chapter 14 for menu ideas and survival tactics.)

December 26 — Boxing Day, Canada and United Kingdom (Eat leftovers.)

Kwanzaa — African-American festival (See Chapter 14 for a delicious menu.)

December 31 — New Year's Eve (Invite the whole crowd, or steal away with someone special.)

Appendix C

Resource List

· ·

*I*f you have a credit card and/or checking account, you can have the world at your door overnight. You can actually plan and shop for an entire party without lifting a finger except to dial the telephone and answer the doorbell.

The following are some of our favorite mail-order sources for specialty foods, cookware, tableware, and party props. Most sources can ship their merchandise anywhere within the United States and Canada. Some can ship internationally. Call for catalogs and more information or check out convenient Web sites for online information and ordering.

Meats

Beef

Denver Buffalo Company, Denver, Colorado, 800-289-2833. **Buffalo steak, burgers, sausages, hot dogs.**

Stock Yards Packing Company, Chicago, Illinois, 800-621-3687 or www.sypco.com. **Filet mignon, prime strip steaks, Porterhouse steaks, surf and turf, gift packages.**

Pork

Aidells Sausage Company, San Francisco, California, 800-546-5795. **Sausages — variety.**

Comeaux, Lafayette, Louisiana, 800-323-2492. **Andouille and boudin.**

Deitrich's Meats, Krumsville, Pennsylvania, 610-756-6344. **Pennsylvania Dutch ham.**

New Braunfels Smokehouse, New Braunfels, Texas, 800-537-6932 or www.nbsmokehouse.com. **Texas barbecue.**

New World Provisions, Monticello, New York, 800-741-3871. **Suckling pig (12-20 lbs.).**

Nueske's Hillcrest Farm, Wittenberg, Wisconsin, 800-382-2266. **Bacon and sausage.**

Smithfield-Gwaltney of Smithfield, Smithfield, Virginia, 800-678-0770. **Smithfield ham — cured 6 months.**

S. Wallace Edwards and Son, Surry, Virginia, 800-222-4267. **Edwards' Virginia hams — cured 3 months.**

Poultry and game

D'Artagnan, Jersey City, New Jersey, 800-327-8246 or (201) 792-0748. **Quail, squab, poussin, pheasant, grouse, red leg partridge, wood pigeons, venison, duck.**

Greenbury Smoked Turkeys, Tyler, Texas, 903-595-0725. **Smoked turkey.**

Summerfield Farm Products, Culpepper, Virginia, 703-547-9600. **Free-range veal, lamb, poultry, venison.**

Wild Game, Inc., Chicago, Illinois, 773-278-1661. **Fresh game and goose.**

Seafood

Balducci's, Long Island City, New York, 800-225-3822 or www.balduccis.com. **Soft shell crabs.**

Bayou Land Seafood, Breaux Bridge, Louisiana, 800-737-6868. **Crawfish.**

Celebrate Maryland, Ellicott City, Maryland, 800-999-8330. **Soft shell crabs, crab cakes, and stuffed crabs.**

Dean and DeLuca, New York, New York, 800-221-7714 or www.dean-deluca.com. **Smoked salmon.**

Joe's Stone Crab Restaurant, Miami, Florida, 800-780-2722. **Stone crab claws** (October-May only).

Maine Lobsters Direct, Portland, Maine, 800-556-2783 or www.maine.com/ lobsters. **Lobster and complete lobster feasts.**

SeaBear, Anacortes, Washington, 800-645-FISH or www.amsquare.com/ seabear. **Smoked salmon and party combinations.**

Shetland Smokehouse, UK, www.zetnet.co.uk/smoke/. **Smoked and marinated salmon and all the best Scottish seafoods.**

Pastas and Grains

Hoppin' John, Charleston, South Carolina, 803-577-6404. **Stone-ground grits.**

Oak Manor Farms, Ontario, Canada, 519-662-2385 or www.imagitek.com/ oakmanor/. **Organic grains, rice, and pasta.**

The Flying Noodle, Duxbury, Massachusetts, 800-566-0599, or 617-934-1527, or www.flyingnoodle.com. **Pastas, sauces, and oils shipped anywhere.**

Cheeses

Allevva Dairy, Inc., New York, New York, 800-425-5382 or 212-226-7990. **Buffalo mozzarella.**

Dean and DeLuca, New York, New York, 800-221-7714 or www.dean-deluca.com. **Assorted.**

Vella Cheese Company, Sonoma, California, 800-848-0505 or 707-938-3232. **Dry Monterey.**

Westfield Farm, Hubbardston, Massachusetts, 508-928-5110. **Hubbardston Blue — a surface-ripened, blue goat cheese. White Buck — a surface-ripened, white, slightly aged goat cheese log.**

Wieninger's Goat Cheese, Hunter, New York, 518-263-4772. **Low-sodium, aged, raw milk cheese.**

Desserts

Balducci's, Long Island City, New York, 800-225-3822 or www.balduccis.com. **Fancy cakes.**

Godiva, 800-9-Godiva or www.godiva.com. **Chocolates and truffles.**

Joe's Stone Crab Restaurant, Miami, Florida, 800-780-2722. **Key lime pie (October-May only).**

Kathleen's Bake Shop, Southhampton, New York, 516-283-7153. **Chocolate chip cookies.**

Mousetrap Cheese, Salem, Indiana, 800-238-5003. **Derby pie.**

Old Kentucky Chocolates, Lexington, Kentucky, 800-786-0579. **Bourbon chocolates.**

Richart, New York, New York, 212-371-9369. **Chocolates, beautiful designs.**

The Chocolate Tree, Beaufort, South Carolina, 800-524-7980. **Handmade English toffee and tiger paws.**

The Village Bakery, Melmerby, UK, www.village-bakery.com/home.htm. **Hand-made organic bread and cakes (including Christmas plum pudding) baked in a wood-fired brick oven.**

Coffee and Tea

Silk Road Teas, Lagunitas, California, 415-488-9017. **Chinese teas — more than 200 varieties.**

The Greenbriar, White Sulphur Springs, West Virginia, 304-536-1110. Ask for gourmet shop. **Peach iced tea.**

Lion's Coffee, Hawaii, 800-338-8353.

Urth Coffee, Los Angeles, California, 310-657-9001. **Organic coffees.**

Miscellaneous

Balducci's, Long Island City, New York, 800-225-3822 or www.balduccis.com. **Balsamic vinegar.**

Byrd Cookie Company, Savannah, Georgia, 800-291-2973 or 912-355-1716. **Benne wafers.**

Chili Willie's Spices by Post, UK, dwsmith.demon.co.uk/cw/index.htm. **Whole and ground spices, Indian foods.**

Food in Italy, www.imkt.com/foodinitaly/. **Complete source for Italian food, wine, and cooking products. Information in English or Italian.**

Frieda's, Inc., Los Alamitos, California, 800-421-9477. **Unusual fruits and vegetables, and Asian products.**

Gibson Farms, Hollister, California, 408-637-4183. **Dried fruits, chocolate-dipped apricots.**

Jack Cooper's Celebrity Deli, Edison, New Jersey, 800-525-3354 or 908-549-4580, or www.celebritydeli.com. **Authentic Jewish deli food.**

Jessica's Biscuit® Cookbook Store, www.jessicas.com/index.html. **Enormous index of cookbooks.**

Peanut Shop of Williamsburg, Williamsburg, Virginia, 800-637-3268. **Peanuts.**

Pepe's Tamales, El Paso, Texas, 888-826-2539 or www.pepestamales.com. **Tamales.**

Pure Hawaii, Kailu-Kona, Hawaii, 800-704-8406 or 808-322-1737, or aloha.net/~den/dtcm.htm. **Macadamia nuts, pure Kona coffee.**

The Bertrand Gourmet Store, www.bertrand.com. **French foods, including cassoulet, foie gras, meats, poultry, and cheeses.**

The Maine Wild Blueberry Co., Machias, Maine, 800-243-4005. **Blueberries.**

Variety

Dean and Deluca, New York, New York, 800-221-7714 or www.dean-deluca.com. **In addition to the specialties listed in this chapter, this company also offers meats, cheeses, vinegars, pastas, international ingredients, fruits, nuts, teas, coffees, cookware, and gift baskets.**

Elizabeth Botham & Sons Ltd., UK, +44(0) 1947 602823, or www.botham.co.uk/index.htm. **Cheese, plum bread, toffee, preserves, marmalades, chutneys, biscuits (cookies), specialty cakes.**

Mimi's CyberKitchen, www.cyber-kitchen.com. **Find everything you need for cooking at home. Links to mail-order food merchants, recipes, kitchen accessories — you name it.**

The Food Stores, 888-EAT-FOOD (888-328-3663) or thefoodstores.com/index.htm. **A listing of every kind of food product imaginable from the best mail-order companies in the world.**

Cookware and Equipment

Williams-Sonoma, San Francisco, California, 800-541-2233 or www.dreamshop.com.

Zabar's, New York, New York, 800-697-6301 or 212-787-2000.

Tableware

Crate and Barrel, 800-323-5461 or 212-305-0011.

Dean and DeLuca, 800-221-7714 or www.dean-deluca.com.

Pottery Barn, 800-922-5507.

Tiffany and Co., New York, New York, 800-526-0649.

Wolfman Gold and Good Company, 212-431-1888.

Party Props

Oriental Trading Company, Omaha, Nebraska, 800-228-2269. **Favors, balloons, costumes, crafts, and so on.**

Paradise Treasures, Hawaii, www.ilhawaii.net/pt/index.html. **Fresh orchid leis, tropical floral arrangements.**

Superior Studio Specialties, Los Angeles, California, 800-354-3049; Toronto, 416-787-1813; Montreal, 514-932-6111. **Four thousand different items for any theme imaginable.**

Index

IDG BOOKS WORLDWIDE REGISTRATION CARD

Visit our
Web site at
http://www.idgbooks.com

ISBN Number: 0-7645-5027-6

Title of this book: Entertaining For Dummies™

My overall rating of this book: ❏ Very good [1] ❏ Good [2] ❏ Satisfactory [3] ❏ Fair [4] ❏ Poor [5]

How I first heard about this book:

❏ Found in bookstore; name: [6] _____ ❏ Book review: [7] _____

❏ Advertisement: [8] _____ ❏ Catalog: [9] _____

❏ Word of mouth; heard about book from friend, co-worker, etc.: [10] _____ ❏ Other: [11] _____

What I liked most about this book:

_____

_____

What I would change, add, delete, etc., in future editions of this book:

_____

_____

Other comments:

_____

Number of computer books I purchase in a year: ❏ 1 [12] ❏ 2-5 [13] ❏ 6-10 [14] ❏ More than 10 [15]

I would characterize my computer skills as: ❏ Beginner [16] ❏ Intermediate [17] ❏ Advanced [18] ❏ Professional [19]

I use ❏ DOS [20] ❏ Windows [21] ❏ OS/2 [22] ❏ Unix [23] ❏ Macintosh [24] ❏ Other: [25]_____

(please specify)

I would be interested in new books on the following subjects:

(please check all that apply, and use the spaces provided to identify specific software)

❏ Word processing: [26] _____ ❏ Spreadsheets: [27] _____

❏ Data bases: [28] _____ ❏ Desktop publishing: [29] _____

❏ File Utilities: [30] _____ ❏ Money management: [31] _____

❏ Networking: [32] _____ ❏ Programming languages: [33] _____

❏ Other: [34] _____

I use a PC at (please check all that apply): ❏ home [35] ❏ work [36] ❏ school [37] ❏ other: [38] _____

The disks I prefer to use are ❏ 5.25 [39] ❏ 3.5 [40] ❏ other: [41]_____

I have a CD ROM: ❏ yes [42] ❏ no [43]

I plan to buy or upgrade computer hardware this year: ❏ yes [44] ❏ no [45]

I plan to buy or upgrade computer software this year: ❏ yes [46] ❏ no [47]

Name: _____ Business title: [48] _____ Type of Business: [49] _____

Address (❏ home [50] ❏ work [51]/Company name: _____)

Street/Suite# _____

City [52]/State [53]/Zip code [54]: _____ Country [55] _____

❏ **I liked this book!** You may quote me by name in future
IDG Books Worldwide promotional materials.

My daytime phone number is _____

IDG BOOKS ™
WORLDWIDE
THE WORLD OF
COMPUTER
KNOWLEDGE®

❏ YES!

Please keep me informed about IDG Books Worldwide's World of Computer Knowledge. Send me your latest catalog.